Global Justice, Markets and Domination

Global Justice, Markets and Domination

A Cosmopolitan Theory

Fausto Corvino

*Postdoctoral Research Fellow in Theoretical Philosophy,
Department of Philosophy and Educational Sciences,
University of Turin, Italy*

Edward Elgar
PUBLISHING

Cheltenham, UK • Northampton, MA, USA

Published by
Edward Elgar Publishing Limited
The Lypiatts
15 Lansdown Road
Cheltenham
Glos GL50 2JA
UK

Edward Elgar Publishing, Inc.
William Pratt House
9 Dewey Court
Northampton
Massachusetts 01060
USA

A catalogue record for this book
is available from the British Library

Library of Congress Control Number: 2020944676

This book is available electronically in the **Elgar**online
Social and Political Science subject collection
http://dx.doi.org/10.4337/9781839102561

ISBN 978 1 83910 255 4 (cased)
ISBN 978 1 83910 256 1 (eBook)

Printed and bound by CPI Group (UK) Ltd, Croydon, CR0 4YY

Contents

Acknowledgements

This book was conceived and written for the most part during the years spent at Scuola Superiore Sant'Anna, in Pisa. I am therefore grateful to Barbara Henry for having always encouraged me to write this text and for her useful advice in all phases of writing. I would also like to thank Alberto Pirni and Anna Loretoni for the various occasions of meaningful exchange.

The book was then refined and completed at the Università degli Studi di Torino. I would therefore like to thank the members of Labont (Center for Ontology) for inviting me to present some of the theories featured in this book and for their helpful insights.

Parts of the second and third chapters of this book have appeared in previous versions as: 'Labour Commodification and Global Justice', *Kriterion: Journal of Philosophy*, **33** (1), 53–88 and 'Republican Freedom in the Labour Market: Exploitation Without Interpersonal Domination', *Theoria: A Journal of Social and Political Theory*, **66** (158), 103–31. I am extremely grateful to the publishers and the editors of the two journals for allowing me to develop and rework the content of the two articles.

Harry Fabian and Alex Pettifer from Edward Elgar Publishing and three anonymous reviewers played a key role in helping me modify and improve my initial proposal.

Finally, my most important thanks go to my mother, father and grandmother, for their unconditional and steadfast support, beyond any work that I may publish.

General introduction to global justice in a market society

The main argument of this book is that although the capitalist mode of production represents the source of an unprecedented accumulation of well-being, and has contributed so far to an increasing extension of human capabilities, it has posed a substantial obstacle to the exercise of individual autonomy, because for most people it has meant the subjection of the individual possibility of obtaining well-being to participation in a market relation – most commonly, a job contract. From this premise, I shall maintain that capitalism exercises a form of structural domination over all those individuals who are excluded from the control of productive assets. Capitalist structural domination, which does not necessarily materialise either in realised coercion or in destitution, consists in the fact that those who can only hire out their labour performance are deprived of any acceptable alternative to seeking sustenance in the market and hence they lack social freedom in the exercise of their basic capabilities. More specifically, I shall neither engage in arguments such as those declaring that at least some people are worse off in terms of income or capabilities than they would be in a pre-capitalist or a hypothetically alternative mode of production, nor shall I seek to demonstrate that people are less secure in the exercise of their basic capabilities than they were before – when they were vulnerable to health, atmospheric and similar risks. Instead, I shall maintain that capitalist structural domination prevents most individuals from exercising their basic capabilities without someone else being willing to rent out their labour performance. This latter fact creates two normative problems. The first one is that this peculiar form of domination can pave the way to economic exploitation, even in highly obnoxious forms. The second one is that capitalist structural domination is a normative concern in itself, because it curtails freedom, regardless of its secondary consequences.

In this book I shall mainly focus on the second problem. With capitalism I refer to an economic system, and more generally a social system, in which the majority of the means of production have been privatised, labour performance has been transformed into a commodity, and the production and the allocation of goods – including the same labour commodity – is entrusted to the market mechanism, that is to say to the logic of supply and demand (Van Parijs 1984; Crouch and Streeck 1997, pp. 1–18; Milanovic 2019, pp. 1–11). This system consists of both institutions and norms that safeguard and implement the private property regime and allow for a more or less unhindered functioning of the market mechanism, according to the political interpretation of the role that the public sector should have in regulating the interactions between private agents in the marketplace and in making up for resulting unbalances and loopholes.

The difficulty with the argument I aim to defend, that is to say, that capitalism intrinsically curtails a specific freedom of a specific but large group of individuals – the freedom of those who are excluded from the ownership of private property, from seeking survival in social interactions that are not market-based – is that I also recognise that capitalism promotes freedom overall, at least in a diachronic sense, meaning in comparison with previous social systems. Accordingly, the right 'anti-power' (Pettit 1996) to capitalist structural domination does not consist in the elimination of the source of domination, but rather in the neutralisation of its negative effects through rendering dominated individuals minimally resilient to economic shocks, be they of micro or macro origin. In brief, I shall propose what I have named 'a minimum de-commodification of labour power' (MDL) as a normative principle of justice, stemming from the negative duty not to pose avoidable constraints on the individual autonomy of others. The latter would consist in decoupling a basic set of capabilities from the market nexus.

Moreover, I shall maintain that some characteristics of the global market render MDL a global principle of justice. More precisely, the responsibility for contributing to MDL lies, primarily, with all those individuals who obtain, more or less directly, marginal increases of wealth through commodified workers, that is to say people who are compelled to accept a contract for lack of admissible alternatives. On the other hand, the scope of MDL cannot be delimited by political borders, but rather overlaps the broader extension of capitalist interactions.

In a few words, the common thread of this book is the normative global proviso of a minimum de-commodification of labour power as the 'anti-power' against a form of structural domination that is inherent in the capitalist social system. The corollary is that MDL would contribute to maximising freedom, given that it would render everyone freer within the social system that best promotes freedom overall. More in practice, MDL could be obtained either through granting market-free income or by strengthening welfare provisions. The only prerequisite for a policy measure to effectively promote MDL is that it should be unconditional, meaning that the allocation of its benefits should not be subject to the willingness of the recipient to accept a given job offer, perhaps after having dropped a certain number of other offers, or to take part in work training programmes.

The logic behind MDL is to safeguard a basic sphere of individual autonomy that is immune from the influence of the market mechanism. We might
also say that MDL would grant anyone the right to withdraw from the market
– either voluntarily or involuntarily – without suffering a loss of well-being
that would jeopardise the very possibility of surviving in a minimally decent
manner. Despite being dictated by a normative concern with freedom from
systemic domination, which in turn stems from unequal access to the means of
production, the implementation of MDL would also have a positive impact on
the interactional forms of exploitation that occur in the labour market. Namely,
it would set a limit on the asymmetries of power that in most cases characterise the bargaining between those who are selling their labour performance
and those others who are interested in buying it. The former would never be
obliged to trade their survival for the worst job conditions that a common
individual would accept when her basic sustenance is at risk.

There are two main original arguments in this book. The first one is the normative treatment I am proposing of labour commodification, which should be
understood along two different levels: in relation to classic theories of global
justice and to the way critical theory has commonly analysed, and criticised,
'reification' and alienation. The second one is what I have named the account
of 'exploitation without interpersonal domination', according to which capitalist structural domination materialises only in exploitation at the workplace,
hence the whole issue of proletarian unfreedom should be properly framed at
the systemic level, while the unfair conditions that a given employer imposes
on a dominated employee simply reflect the opportunity that the former has to
exploit the vulnerability of the latter – but cannot be considered in itself as the
source of the same vulnerability and thus of domination.

The text is structured in the following way. In Chapter 1, I propose an
analytical definition of labour commodification and seek to explore its philosophical roots. In Chapter 2, I maintain that highly commodified individuals
are subject to a form of systemic domination, and I develop the account
of 'exploitation without interpersonal domination'. In Chapter 3, I present
a theory of global justice based on a minimum de-commodification of labour
power, also explaining why I consider it as something new in the cosmopolitan
debate. In Chapter 4, I deal with four strong objections usually levelled against
cosmopolitan justice: the compatriot priority principle, the coercion view, the
allegations of uselessness, and infeasibility.

However, before getting to the heart of the theory I would like to present,
I think it is necessary to clarify the nature of the underlying normative argument. Accordingly, in the remaining part of this introduction I shall firstly
explain why by adopting as my critical objective the unequal access to the
means of production I am advancing a normative claim that is different from
the one targeted by positive and negative theories of global justice. Secondly,

I shall stress that MDL is not intended as an ethical criticism that addresses capitalism 'as a form of life' (Jaeggi 2015, 2018), but rather as a moral argument underpinned by the inviolability of individual autonomy.

RELATIONAL THEORIES OF GLOBAL JUSTICE

When approaching theories of global justice, the first distinction to be made is the one between practice-dependent and practice-independent accounts (see James 2005; Abizadeh 2007; Sangiovanni 2007, 2008, 2016; Ronzoni 2009; Armstrong 2012, pp. 25–34). The former maintain that global duties of justice are owed in virtue of shared social practices, while the latter assert that duties of justice hold among individuals living in different countries regardless of the existence and of the extent of their interactions. The classic thought experiment for understanding the difference between the two different approaches consists in imagining two communities that are separate and without any possibility of communicating – they can be two islands or two different planets. One is very well off, while the other is very poor. Do you think there exist normative reasons for redistributing wealth from the first towards the second community so as to make the two communities more equal? If you think so, here you have a practice-independent conception of justice; conversely, if you do not think so, this would imply that you embrace a practice-dependent conception of justice.

The typical example of a practice-dependent account of global justice is the global egalitarianism that flourished in the wake of Rawlsian contractualism, which holds that the globalisation of national social systems has reached such a level of interconnection that the normative need emerges to find rules for dividing benefits and burdens of the global economy fairly. More specifically, there are two main contractualist justifications for global justice. One is based on cooperation and draws attention to the fact that there exists a sort of cooperative surplus, meaning that there is more aggregate wealth in – and thanks to – a world in which economic agents who are located in different countries interact continuously, than in a hypothetical or historically antecedent scenario of self-contained local societies. This empirical evidence poses the demand to agree on global principles for splitting the cooperative surplus so as to neutralise the arbitrary advantage or disadvantage of being born in a more or less advantaged country (Pogge 1989; Beitz 1999; Moellendorf 2002; Brock 2009; James 2012), precisely as John Rawls (1999a) sought to propose principles of socio-economic justice, for national societies, that could level out the advantages stemming from those individual factors that he deems morally arbitrary, that is to say, both natural and social assets.

The second justification is based on coercion, and paradoxically it was built on a critique that philosophers such as Thomas Nagel (2005) and Michael

Blake (2001) moved against global theories of justice. We might also concede, their argument goes, that geographically displaced individuals contribute to making the world better off, at least in aggregative terms. Yet, these individuals are not subjected to the same coercive practices that, for example, exist at the national level and are embodied in both civil and criminal laws. Coercion is one of the preconditions of socio-economic justice, in the sense that a redistribution of resources is the only way through which coercive practices can become acceptable to the worse off, as, for example, to those who are in poverty and are prevented from appropriating someone else's property. Further, rendering coercive practices justifiable is the only way to rid them of the aura of arbitrariness, which in turn could make coercion acceptable from a liberal perspective. Some other philosophers have taken on this theory and have counter-argued that coercion also exists at the global level, either in the form of state border control (Abizadeh 2007, pp. 345–57), or in the practices in use within international organisations that are entrusted with financial stability or trade rules – the latter are apparently non-coercive, since in theory no one obliges a given country to take part in the structure of global trade, for example, but are coercive in practice, because in many cases opting out from the global economy is not a viable option (Valentini 2011).

Global egalitarians usually stick to an empirical premise. Given that they seek to develop their theories as an extension, or more correctly an amendment, of Rawls's contractualism, they maintain that Rawls was correct in the theoretical passages of his moral constructivism, that is to say in the way he sketches the circumstances of justice, the original bargaining situation, and the same rationales guiding the representatives of the bargaining, but he was wrong in interpreting the basic structure of society as overlapping the political borders of states. More precisely, Rawls (1999a, pp. 6–10; 2001, pp. 11–22; 2005, pp. 257–88) describes the basic structure of society as the set of institutions that, in a liberal society, determine the allocation of benefits and burdens of cooperation (e.g. the constitution, the legal and the economic systems, the family and so on). Furthermore, he maintains that the basic structure is the primary site of justice, meaning that the task of the representative taking part in the hypothetical bargaining of the social contract consists in finding the right principles for regulating the institutions that make up the basic structure, rather than the single interactions that take place among the individuals who are subject to these institutions (see also Murphy 1998). In this sense, it would be correct for the social contract to hold that access to public health care should be more or less inclusive, or that income taxes should be more or less progressive, but it would not make sense for the social contract to establish which moral principles should guide two private individuals engaged in a market transaction, or to hold that billionaires should donate a given percentage of their income to one charity rather than another.

Since the majority of global egalitarians are Rawlsian, they cannot deny the equation between the site of justice and the basic structure of society; hence they can pursue two main paths to defend global principles of justice. The first one consists in arguing that globalisation has extended what Rawls meant with the basic structure beyond national borders, so as to encompass the whole world, and a series of empirical arguments can be deployed in this direction (Scanlon 1973; Pogge 1989; Beitz 1999; Moellendorf 2002; James 2012). It might be argued, for example, that the way capital gets continuously reinvested in different national economies lays the foundations for global circumstances of justice, given that marginal increases of profits are allowed by international passages of semi-laboured products throughout the whole chain of production. It might be added that global trade creates both winners and losers, hence it is morally wrong to allow arbitrary factors, as, for example, the strength of single countries in bargaining trade rules, in determining the extent of gains and losses. Usually, anti-cosmopolitan theorists (at least those contemplating the scope of justice) object that even though global trade, and more generally global flows of capital and products, are obviously a reality, the absence of state-like institutions makes any attempt to extend the scope of justice futile (Blake 2001; Nagel 2005; R. Miller 2005). To this, global egalitarians might either reply that the set of rules administered by financial and trade international organisations has the same urgency of constitutional rules (Beitz 1999, pp. 148–9; see also Valentini 2011), or they might bite the bullet and argue that the basic structure of society is nowadays global because of economic reasons, even though state-like institutions do not exist at the global level (Moellendorf 2002; James 2012).

The second path in defence of global justice consists in conceding even more to anti-cosmopolitans, thus recognising that a global basic structure does not exist, but holding that the basic structure of society is an instrumental condition of justice rather than one of existence (Abizadeh 2007; Ronzoni 2009). More specifically, it might be maintained, as Arash Abizadeh (2007, pp. 325–41) does, that global economic interactions do not reflect the cooperative ideal Rawls had in mind, that is to say interactions that are fair, because we lack those global institutions that might allow mere economic interactions to evolve into cooperative practices. However, it is exactly this lack of global regulations that poses the normative demand for creating global institutions that could render global interactions fair. From this perspective, the site and the scope of justice do not coincide. The former consists of the basic structure of society, which is still local, while the latter refers to all those individuals who take part in interactions that might become fair, and they are not necessarily living within the same country. In sum, Abizadeh concludes, the misalignment between the scope and the site of justice creates a diffuse responsibility for a realignment through building up global institutions that allocate the global cooperative surplus fairly.

From these different ways of defending a global scope of justice, which may accompany either a national or a global conception of the site of justice, more or less encompassing principles of justice can be derived (see also Corvino 2019a). Philosophers and theorists such as T.M. Scanlon (1973, pp. 1066–7), Thomas Pogge (1989, pp. 246–59), Charles Beitz (1999, pp. 150–53) and Darrel Moellendorf (2002, pp. 80–86) have argued that if we correct the wrong empirical conception Rawls had of the world, as made of independent states that have reached a lower level of interconnection than the real one, or at least lower than the one we have today, with the theory of justice as fairness, it automatically follows that Rawls's second principle of justice should be global in scope ('social and economic inequalities should be arranged so that they are both (a) to the greatest benefit of the least advantaged persons, and (b) attached to offices and positions open to all under conditions of equality of opportunity' (Rawls 1999a, p. 53)). In particular, they have focused their normative attention on the first part of Rawls's second principle ('social and economic inequalities should be arranged so that they are [. . .] (a) to the greatest benefit of the least advantaged persons), the so-called 'difference principle', that in their view should become a 'global difference principle'. The latter would imply a global mechanism for redistributing wealth so as to contain global inequalities within the limit in which they are to the advantage of those who are worst off in the world. In other words, in a hypothetical scenario of perfect global equality of wealth, a global difference principle would allow those individuals who live in the most advantaged countries to create inequality of wealth only if this is expected to have a positive impact on the well-being of those other individuals who would be least advantaged. In more practical terms, given that we already live in an unequal world, the global difference principle would require developed economies to make large investments in the development of poorer countries. This can occur either through global institutions, as postulated by Abizadeh, or through international mechanisms that are more voluntary and infringe less on national autonomy.

Some other theorists, in particular Simon Caney (2001; see also Barry 1973, pp. 128–33), have focused instead on the principle of global equality of opportunity, which is enshrined in the second part of Rawls's second principle of justice ('social and economic inequalities should be arranged so that they are [. . .] (b) attached to offices and positions open to all under conditions of equality of opportunity'). A globalised version of (b) would entail that two individuals living in two different countries that are unequally developed should have the same chances of succeeding in life, net of differences in individual abilities.[1] In other words, the principle of global equality of opportunity would regard as unacceptable that a child born in Gambia and who has excellent educational achievements has much less chance of occupying a prominent position in either multinational companies, or international organisations, or international law firms than a child born in Vienna with just above-average educational achievements (see also Moellendorf 2002, p. 79).

It is important to note that the principle of equality of opportunity and the difference principle, which Rawls combines at the national level posing the former as lexicographically superordinate with respect to the latter, are not necessarily in a chain of mutual realisability. As an example, consider the case in which the child born in Vienna, grown up, retains a consistent margin of life opportunities over the other individual born in Gambia, but he takes part in a global mechanism of wealth distribution that fuels resources to his Gambian counterparts as long as he makes career progressions. In this situation, a global difference principle might be met, while the principle of global equality of opportunity would not. Accordingly, many theorists insist on the difference principle, while reasoning on global justice, because it is much easier to be implemented, through global funds and development agencies that allocate the resources on local territories, for example.

At the same time, this distribution of resources would also contribute to reducing global inequality of opportunities, because it would grant the worst off more resources to compete with the best off. Yet, a comprehensive implementation of global equality of opportunity would require a much more complicated programme of reform and homologation of both schooling and recruiting practices that, admittedly, risks sounding utopian, at least for the moment. Much more realistic, in its chances of implementation, is the interpretation of the global original position given by Gillian Brock (2009), according to whom the output of the global social contract would not be a sort of global egalitarianism, as postulated by her cosmopolitan colleagues, but rather a set of principles that look at absolutes, instead of relativities. Thus, Brock defends a global floor as a demand of global justice, that is to say, an agreement on a capability threshold below which no one should be allowed to fall.

NON-RELATIONAL THEORIES OF GLOBAL JUSTICE

Non-relational theories of justice ground distributive duties on factors that are intrinsically human and pertain neither to interactions nor to the creation of

---

[1]   A global difference principle would, in contrast, equalise the distribution of outcomes stemming from unequal individual abilities.

a cooperative surplus; this is why they can be defined as practice-independent. This makes it almost obvious that these theories should be applied globally. The only thing required is to recognise a kind of anthropological and biological equality between human beings. There are two main strands of non-relational theories of justice. The first one takes the individual as an agent of value maximisation, where value can be either understood as realised well-being, as preference satisfaction, or as happiness, and it can be either taken in its absolute value or pondered over factors that are inversely proportional to well-being or subject to one or more thresholds. In sum, I am referring to utilitarianism, prioritarianism and sufficientarianism – at least in its classic formulations (Mulgan 2007; Holtug 2007, 2015; Shields 2016; Corvino 2019b). The second strand is centred on human needs, and more generally on an Aristotelian-like belief that humans depend on society to lead 'flourishing' lives; hence society as a whole bears a responsibility towards its single components to provide them with the opportunity to achieve the things they might want to be or to have. Here the reference goes obviously to the capability approach (Nussbaum 2006, 2011; see also Robeyns 2016), but also to the more recent formulations of capabilitarian sufficiency (Nielsen and Axelsen 2017), which somehow oscillate between the first and the second strands of practice-independent theories.

The basic tenet of utilitarianism is that every human being can experience gains and losses of utility and the moral imperative, to which both individuals and institutions should adhere, is to ensure that general utility is increased as much as possible. Then, utilitarian philosophers disagree about what utility consists of and whether the imperative of utility maximisation applies to single actions or to a set of rules. For some, utility is realised happiness or satisfaction, for others it is the realisation of either preferences or desires, for still others it consists in the fulfilment of an objective list of human needs, or more specifically in perfecting human nature (Mulgan 2007, pp. 61–92; Crisp 2017).

Moreover, some people believe that it would be right to take an action which violates some rules that overall maximise utility, on condition that this action brings about a positive balance of lost and gained utility regarding its direct consequences. Imagine, for example, that you are late for an important appointment, you are driving, and you come up to a red light. A so-called 'act utilitarian' might say that if you are sufficiently sure that no one is passing by, no one is watching you, and the person waiting for you is suffering a loss of well-being for every minute he is kept waiting, you might be justified in proceeding without waiting for the green light. Conversely, even under such circumstances, a 'rule utilitarian' might object that the right action to take is not the one that maximises utility in itself, but rather the one that conforms to the rule increasing overall utility, in this case respecting red lights (see also Emmons 1973).

Nevertheless, even though utilitarians are usually criticised by egalitarians because they look at aggregate utility while considering the equality in distribution only of derivative importance,[2] it is important to recognise that there is a sort of 'hidden egalitariansm' in the utility function, meaning that a given unit of utility matters the same, from a moral point of view, regardless of the person who produces it and of her social position (Sen 1992, p. 13). Paradoxically, it is exactly this egalitarianism of utility functions that paves the way to outweighing mechanisms between the best off and the worst off, and more generally to adaptive preferences. Accordingly, a middle-class person living in a developed country could have very limited distribution duties towards an individual living in a poorer country if the former experiences strong frustrations and the latter has adapted to live in her situation of deprivation, or maybe she has not had the opportunity to imagine a different life. This is why prioritarian philosophers have postulated that the absolute value of each unit of utility should be pondered over a number that reflects the welfare level of the person that realises utility – the higher the welfare level, the lower the pondering factor. In this way, trade-offs between the top and the bottom of societies, due to the discomfort of those who are in the former group and/or the adaptive preferences of those who are in the latter group, are severely restricted (see also Corvino 2019b, pp. 525–36).

Again, another possibility for correcting for the unequal drifts ignited by the egalitarianism of utility functions, in addition to and/or in the place of the prioritarian amendment, consists in holding that well-being matters, in the moral calculus about justice, only above a given sufficiency threshold. Accordingly, justice would require leading any individual above the sufficiency threshold and any inequality that occurs above the threshold is irrelevant from the point of view of justice in distribution. The clear advantage of sufficientarianism with respect to both utilitarianism and prioritarianism, from the perspective of the worst off, is that it resolutely excludes any trade-off between the top and the bottom, while the limit is that it gives up on every aspect of redistributive leverage among those who are sufficiently well off (Casal 2007).

Not every sufficientarian thinker is a repentant utilitarian. Instead, many sufficientarians have developed their theories as an alternative to telic egalitarianism, arguing that what is intrinsically valuable is not equality but everyone having enough of something, or even adding that equality per se is a dangerous

---

[2]   In many cases, rendering a distribution of goods more equal increases overall utility because of the law of decreasing marginal utility, so in this sense we might say that equality can be instrumental for utilitarians to implement their moral imperative. Just think how a global redistribution of wealth might move resources from people who get a low utility from them – because they are rich – to other people who might get much higher levels of utility – because they are poorer (see Singer 1972).

normative objective because it leads to 'moral disorientation and shallowness' and deflects attention from 'considerations of greater moral importance' (Frankfurt 1987, p. 23). It is difficult to generalise on the nature of sufficientarianism, given that some thinkers limit their attention to the importance of the sufficiency thresholds (Shields 2012; Axelsen and Nielsen 2015), while others combine it with forms of either prioritarianism or utilitarianism both above and beyond sufficiency (Crisp 2003; Huseby 2010). Rather, what it is important to stress here is that the simple idea at the basis of sufficientarianism is either based on the revised conception of the individual as a subject who can experience gains and losses of utility and be an engine of its maximisation in the world, or as an alternative view to the one that equality is important per se and hence we should strive, normatively, for a more equal distribution of resources. In both cases, as also for utilitarianism and prioritarianism, the normative provisos are disentangled from the social relations that subsist among the members of the distributive scheme. Looking at the issue from another perspective, we may say that it does not really matter for utilitarians, prioritarians or sufficientarians how far off the individual who could best serve the normative objective is – be it to maximise utility, to maximise the value of pondered utilities, or to minimise the number of people who live below sufficiency – if she is assigned the right resources.

The second main strand of non-relational theories of justice is the capability approach, in the normative formulation initially given by Martha Nussbaum (2000, 2006, 2011), and in parallel with the treatment of capabilities as measures of well-being that Amartya Sen (1992, 1999) made in the course of the last decades. Nussbaum's basic intuition, from where her whole theory unravels, is that some specific human abilities 'exert a moral claim that they should be developed' (Nussbaum 2000, p. 83). This is a moral idea that stems from the very empirical fact that human beings have special needs that require special 'nourishment' (see also Nussbaum 1995). When the latter is denied, and these needs remain unfulfilled, human beings lose the ability to flourish. The main difference between humans and animals, then, lies in the percentage of external intervention that they respectively need to flourish. An animal, in general, only needs life and some assistance during the first years of life. A human being needs much more, from education to health care, recognition, freedom of expression, and so on.

There are three kinds of human capabilities. Firstly, 'basic capabilities', those that do not need particular external intervention to start functioning. For example, the capability for speech is developed by the child almost automatically when she is raised in a normal context, with other human beings. In this respect, speech differs from writing skills. Secondly, there are 'internal capabilities' that require the individual to reach a mature condition of readiness before she can start making them function. The capability for sexual pleasure, for example, is developed without any support once the individual reaches a given age. Lastly, there are 'combined capabilities', that is to say internal capabilities that need to be combined with 'external conditions for the exercise of the function'. Nussbaum offers the example of a woman who automatically develops the capability for sexual pleasure at a given point of her life, and for her to enjoy this capability she only needs that other people abstain from odious practices such as genital mutilation. At the same time, for the 'internal' capability for sexual pleasure to evolve into the 'combined' capability for sexual expression, it also takes social circumstances to be arranged in a way to guarantee this capability – e.g. widows should be allowed to marry again and girls should not be discriminated against or penalised for engaging in relations before marriage (Nussbaum 2000, pp. 84–5).

Therefore, combined capabilities are those that an individual can realise when two conditions hold. First, the social organisation does not interfere with the development of the internal capability. Second, the social organisation 'prepar[es] the environment' for the internal capability to evolve into a combined capability (Nussbaum 2000, p. 85). Here we get to the basis of the moral argument put forward by Nussbaum. Since we cannot expect human beings to develop combined capabilities on their own, and the enjoyment of a basic set of 'combined capabilities' is a fundamental prerequisite for a flourishing life lived with dignity, every human being exerts a moral claim to be provided with the necessary means to develop this basic set, and the correlative duty falls upon humanity as a whole.

As we can immediately see, Nussbaum's approach to justice is non-relational.[3] Human needs do not presuppose interactions to arise, rather they pose the demand of creating social interconnections when they are lacking and are needed to allow a certain group of individuals realising a basic set of combined capabilities. This is why the capability approach is in itself a cosmopolitan theory, which, differently from classic forms of contractualism, manages to take into account ex ante the interests of those individuals who are prevented by bodily or cognitive obstacles to relate as equals to the rest of society. Conversely, the drawback of a non-relational account of justice that moves from needs, in comparison, for example, with contractualism, is that it takes much more in terms of ethical justifications to explain why individual limits, intrinsic to human beings, command contribution by other members of society even in the absence of a cooperative surplus. And obviously, it is much more

---

[3]   At least as far as the minimum for conducting a decent life is concerned, given that Nussbaum does not exclude that her theory can be complemented with more encompassing theories of justice. See Nussbaum 2006, pp. 22–5.

complex to explain how the responsibility of society towards the individual unfolds between its individual members.

THE INJUSTICE THAT BOTH RELATIONAL AND NON-RELATIONAL THEORIES FAIL TO CAPTURE

Theories of global justice, be they relational or non-relational, are founded on the premise that the current global distribution of resources should be changed because of the consequences it triggers rather than because of the way it originated. So, global egalitarians criticise global inequality because it falls short of the optimal arrangement that free individuals would agree upon in a hypothetical session of the global contract. Utilitarians recommend that the rich should give a considerable part of their wealth to the poor because the latter would yield greater utility from it. Prioritarians propose a similar argument, although they are interested in 'compound states of affairs' (Holtug 2007, p. 132), that is to say pondered value, rather than simple utility. Sufficientarians insist on the axiological argument that a world in which $n+1$ people have enough is better than an alternative world in which only n people have enough. The capability approach maintains that every human being exerts a moral claim to live a life with dignity, and that a global redistribution of resources could accomplish this goal.

All these theories fail to sanction the forms of injustice that are inherent to the capitalist mode of production, which is the common social system through which individuals yield the wealth that global justice theories consider as 'unjustly' allocated throughout the world. The main one is that the vast majority of people taking part in jointly productive practices are compelled to do so for the lack of viable alternatives. Accordingly, there are two normative problems with the unequal distribution of resources in the world. The first one is that wealth is produced in a condition of systemic unfreedom. The second one is that after it has been produced, wealth is distributed in a way that is normatively unsatisfactory, be it because the distribution is unfair, or falls short of maximising utility or value, or because it prevents some individuals from fulfilling a basic set of combined capabilities, and so on. Obviously, the two problems are intertwined, because the more unequal – or also the less performing in maximising utility or value – a given distributional scheme is, the greater the barriers that keep people stuck in a market relation. And vice versa, the more access people have to the means of production, the more possibilities there are to arrive at a fair distribution of the wealth produced. Yet, the two problems remain distinct and should be addressed in a different way (see also Forst 2001, pp. 167–70; Laborde 2010, pp. 49–53; Buckinx et al. 2015).

Both relational and non-relational theories of justice are well fitted to deal with the second problem concerning wealth distribution, but they lack the necessary theoretical tools to properly address the first problem. For an individual who has an improvement in well-being from time *t* to time *t1* could experience in the same time period *t–t1* a greater commodification of her work. In other words, she may find herself with more resources at her disposal but less freedom than before. The reason why this trade-off between well-being and freedom is usually overlooked in the discourse on socio-economic justice is that the trade-off only takes place as long as the welfare gains start from a low level and are contained. If in the transition from *t* to *t2* (subsequent to *t1*) the increase in well-being resulting from wage work is substantial, then the individual could set aside a sufficient amount of resources to guarantee for herself a level of independence from market relations equal to or greater than she had at the time t. Conversely, when we consider the situation of a person who experiences a slight increase in well-being, shifting, for example, from relative poverty to just above the line of relative poverty, it might be the case that this improvement in well-being has occurred at the price of labour com- modification – and an example might be a person who is contracted to work the land that she used to cultivate for free before, and, thanks to the productive investments of the land grabber, she is paid a wage that is higher than the income she managed to get before as a self-producer (see Cotula et al. 2009). This poses a double problem, as already hinted at earlier. A loss in individual autonomy raises a normative issue per se, meaning that either it is justifiable or it is arbitrary and hence unjust. Moreover, as a result of the trade-off between well-being and freedom, at time *t1* the individual may be better off in terms of income but more exploitable than at time *t*, meaning that the loss of the opportunity to obtain a minimum income from self-employment reduces the individual's margin of discretion over the offers of those who control the means of production.

NEITHER FUNCTIONAL, NOR ETHICAL, BUT A MORAL CRITICISM OF CAPITALISM

Assuming that I have provided sufficient reasons to justify the difference between classic approaches to global justice and the one based on capitalist structural domination, at least enough to convince the reader that it can be worth going through the following pages and to test the soundness of the general argument, there are two other preliminary points that I should address. I have to demonstrate that mine is neither an attempt to re-present in a new guise the classic arguments against capitalistic society, on which 'critical theorists' have written so much, nor a nostalgic exaltation of an Arcadian pre-capitalist society.

I start with the first issue. In a quite recent but already seminal article, Rahel Jaeggi (2016) tackles the question whether we can say there is something intrinsically wrong in capitalism, which was famously posed in these terms some years before by Philippe Van Parijs (1984) in another article. When we speak of something 'intrinsically' wrong with capitalism we refer to something wrong that we could not have under different social arrangements (Van Parijs 1984, pp. 85–6). So, for example, neither by saying that the spread of smart-phones is regrettable because it puts social relations at risk, nor by complaining that human beings are led to put their own gain before everything else, nor by denouncing that metalworking industries are an imminent danger because of their contribution to climate change, would we be making an argument against capitalism in itself. In fact, beyond the question of whether they are more or less true, the first and third points pertain to the contemporary condition, and they might hold true as well under different modes of production. A socialist society, just to mention one possible alternative, would not necessarily under-take a green transition, and nothing excludes that even if private property were nationalised, public industries would keep on producing and commercialising smartphones, which in turn are connected via public Wi-Fi. The second point, concerning human egoism, is a descriptive assertion on human beings in general, and could not even be considered as a proper criticism against an intrinsic feature of capitalism, because the origins of the problem substantially transcend its boundaries.

Accordingly, Jaeggi (2016, p. 47) maintains that there are three possible levels on which to criticise elements intrinsic to capitalism. The first level is functional and pertains to the capacity of the capitalist system to fulfil its purpose. Here, everything depends on what we mean by the purpose of capitalism. If we stick to a morally neutral view, we would have to say that capitalism can at a certain point become dysfunctional if it ceases to create marginal increase in wealth, thus making society progressively worse off in aggregate terms, or if it undertakes a self-destructive process (Jaeggi 2016, pp. 47–53). Both criticisms are misplaced at the moment, given that in spite of recurrent crises, global gross domestic product (GDP) keeps on growing every year, capitalism has proved to be quite resilient, and because there are no implementable alternatives in sight, at least for now. It might be said that capi-talism is dysfunctional because climate change poses serious threats to humans and non-human animals (Hannah 2019; McDuff 2019). But some people would reply to this by saying that within capitalism we could obtain a win–win solution, in terms of both sustainability and economic growth, through a sort of Green New Deal aimed at financing the green transition (Klein 2019; A. Turner 2019). If this were true, phenomena such as life-threatening CO_2 accu-mulation could not be taken as intrinsic features of capitalism – since we can conceive the latter without the former.

A seemingly functional argument against capitalism, which is both empiri-cally grounded and which targets its intrinsic features, could be that capitalism is bad because it leads to global inequality and/or to massive poverty. Let us assume that that empirical causality is sound, even though recent economic trends might show something different (Milanovic 2016), but I will come back to this in a while. The problem with this kind of objection, as rightly noted by Jaeggi (2016, pp. 49–53), is that it cannot prescind from some moral premises, or in other words from value-laden functions that we assign to capitalism. By saying that capitalism is falling short of a normatively desirable distribution, we automatically assume that this distribution is part of capitalism's functions, which is something we cannot infer from a morally neutral interpretation of the purpose of capitalism – that is to say, as a mode of producing wealth. Consider the example of the knife made by Jaeggi (2016, pp. 48–9), whose function, she says, is clearly to cut. We might elaborate a little further on the knife and hold that it can either be used to harm someone just for the sake of causing him pain, or to go to the aid of other people, as when it is held against a terrorist in the attempt to stop him.

We might speculate on whether in each of the two cases the knife has been used to determine good or bad results, or even on whether its same use can be justified, but these kinds of speculations, which pertain specifically to its use, have nothing to do with its function, which remains, simply, to cut. In the same way, we can propose different normative evaluations concerning the use people make of the wealth yielded by capitalism, and of the way they distribute it, but these would not reach the function of capitalism, which is to guarantee a more or less constant rate of growth. More specifically, these normative evaluations are the ones that lie at the core of theories of global justice (or justice in general) which are doomed, because of the value judgements that precede them, to stop before the functional level, at the moral one. Moreover, as already noted, classic theories of distributive justice are very good for proposing a normative critique of the process of wealth distribution but not as much for criticising the human condition in the process of wealth production – even when coupling positive with negative duties of justice, but I will focus on this in the next section.

A moral critique that focuses on wealth production instead of distribution is the one which holds that there is something wrong in the way those who control capital relate to their employees; namely, the former exploit the latter (Jaeggi 2016, pp. 53–60). The idea of exploitation, together with that of dom-ination, will be at the centre of Chapter 2. However, here we might say, quite generally, that an individual A exploits an individual B when the former gives the latter less than the fair amount of something, and usually in job contracts we focus on wages. The theoretical challenge consists in explaining what a fair remuneration is all about (see also Arneson 1981; Roemer 1985; Vrousalis 2013). As we shall see in Chapter 1, a first articulate response to this question was given by Karl Marx (2013 [1867]). In a nutshell, his theory of exploitation proceeds in two stages. First, a group of individuals deprives another group of individuals of access to the means of production, with an active role played by modern states in promulgating laws that enclose common property. Second, newly formed capitalists extract so-called 'surplus value' from workers by paying them less than the value they convey to the objects they work on. Both steps of Marx's theory have been criticised over the years, and more specifically what is called into question is the relevance, nowadays, of the concepts of 'primitive accumulation' and 'surplus value'. We shall have time to deal with both issues later on, but merely to defend the relevance, at least under specific circumstances, of Marx's theory today, I shall point to four well-known facts. Firstly, thousands of people living in developing countries keep on losing their means of subsistence because of land grabbing, that is to say because the land on which they rely for sustenance is sold by their countries to foreign investors. Secondly, millions of people, especially young people, throughout the world are paid a wage that is barely sufficient to put a roof over their heads and perform minimum social and biological functions – namely, eating, being decently dressed and if they are lucky having dinner or a couple of drinks with friends during the week – while offering their employers, be they private or public, a work performance that allows the raising of much higher profits than the welfare they enjoy. In many other cases, young workers are even asked and encouraged to work for free, to enrich their CV, that is to say to obtain the minimum requirements necessary to enter, as passive subjects, into the circuit of surplus–value extraction. Thirdly, thousands of people living in developing countries work for a few dollars per hour on semi-laboured products which are then sold on the global market at astronomic prices. Fourthly, even those workers who manage to get good wages in sectors where technologies progressively increase labour productivity are, in fact, only getting back a small part of the value they produce, while the largest part of this value turns into profits.

The third level of intrinsic criticism of capitalism is instead ethical. This critique contends that the problem about capitalism is that it negatively impacts on the human condition in a way that other forms of production would not do. As an example, it might be held that capitalism erodes cultural differences by promoting a kind of fast-food and cheap-garment homologation – and, obviously, a hypothetical proponent of this argument would have to explain why fast foods and the fact that millions of people wear the same cheap clothes are ethically bad. Or it might be said, as did the young Marx (1988 [1844], pp. 69–84), that wage work, which is a defining feature of capitalism, alienates individuals from the object they produce, within the productive process, in relation to other individuals and with respect to their existential purpose. Jaeggi (2015, 2018) further develops this line of argument and maintains that we could (and should) criticise capitalism as 'a form of life', that is to say as 'a bundle of social practices' that subvert the true ethical significance of human life. And the main ethical problem on which she focuses her critique is alienation, the social phenomenon through which human beings lose control of their actions and consequently suffer a loss of meaning in relation to the world around them. All this poses a relevant ethical problem because it distances the human being from her own social existence, while the two entities are ontologically intertwined (Jaeggi 2014). In short, we could summarise Jaeggi's normative argument as an ethical complaint about the 'detachment or separation from something that in fact belongs together, the loss of a connection between two things that nevertheless stand in relation to one another' (Jaeggi 2014, p. 25).

My argument in this book is neither functional, nor ethical. It is a moral one, yet differently from classic moral critiques of capitalism, it maintains that the normative problem does not reside in interactional relations on the market place – e.g. exploitation by employers over employees – but is rather systemic and pertains to the distribution of the means of production and to the extreme levels of labour commodification that it brings about. More specifically, my critique is not functional insofar as I assume that for the purpose of creating well-being and enlarging individual capabilities, capitalism is the best mode of production with which humans have ever experimented. I recognise, obviously, that huge distributive problems have existed throughout the history of capitalism and continue to exist today, although in a different form, but I hold that these problems are not intrinsic to capitalism, given that they can be reverted through regulations, and the fact that globalisation makes global cooperation for redistributive purposes very difficult is not a direct consequence of capitalism. I hold the same about environmental problems related to climate change. More specifically, I embrace the view that it is possible – and even desirable – to disentangle economic growth from unsustainable emissions, through right investments and more public control of the economy. Another viable position that I can accept without upsetting the structure of my argument is that the only possible way to save our planet is to renounce economic growth, which does not necessarily account to a rejection of capitalism in itself, given that it could also be possible to imagine a capitalist society that voluntarily chooses to renounce the increase of growth rates. Here we are moving on speculative grounds; hence what I can do from a normative point of view is to accept the economic forecast that seems to me more reasonable in the light of the literature I have gone through in the last years. Yet, should my position be empirically wrong, because in the future we may find out that capitalism is structurally incompatible with human preservation, there are two possible ways to accommodate this new empirical evidence in my critique of capitalism. If capitalism continues to exist, in spite of the fact the humans will be sure that it is functionally detrimental, the moral argument I shall propose in the next pages can be read in parallel with the functional critiques that I am sure future theorists will provide in a refined way. If, instead, capitalism is superseded, the arguments that lie behind the minimum de-commodification of labour power can be read in a historical perspective as a normative critique of the social system that has characterised an important stage of human civilisation.

Moreover, when dealing with labour commodification I shall leave aside ethical considerations of a cultural character, and consider the phenomenon of alienation as of normative derivative importance with respect to the distribution of the means of production. If I have to be more accurate, I remain agnostic about the critiques that revolve around the way we live and the consumer choice we make within capitalism, not because I disagree with many of these claims, but because I consider them as less stringent, from a normative point of view, than a moral and political argument based on individual freedom. Moreover, cultural criticisms of capitalism are subject to trade-off counter-objections of this kind: would you prefer to eat cheeseburgers in a fast-food restaurant that contaminates the artistic beauty of Piazza del Duomo in Milan or to starve in the middle of a medieval famine? I would opt for the former. My position with regard to alienation is more complex, however. I recognise the urgency of the issue, which I shall also discuss later, yet a purely ethical treatment of alienation makes sense, in my view, only if the moral level of critique is not practicable. This is the position taken, for example, by Jaeggi. She provides many arguments as to why both the functional and the moral levels of critique could be inconclusive and falls back on an elegant ethical theory. I agree that alienation is a huge ethical problem, yet I also believe that there is room for a moral and political critique of capitalism. Hence, I shall argue that alienation is a problem, first of all, as a consequence of the fact that a large group of human beings can only seek basic sustenance in wage income, which in turn accounts for structural domination.

In sum, this book is positioned on the moral level of critique of capitalism, with important political corollaries stemming from the moral premise based on the preservation of individual autonomy. I maintain that some intrinsic features of capitalism, namely the privatisation of the means of production and the consequent commodification of labour, cause many individuals to lose their freedom. Yet, I shall contend that within capitalism freedom is lost neither in the marketplace, at the moment when capitalists meet commodified wage-workers and impose obnoxious conditions, nor at the workplace, where capitalists can force the limits of what has been agreed during the bargaining phase of the contract. I shall hold, instead, that within the capitalist social system many individuals lose their freedom, for systemic reasons related to the privatisation and the distribution of the means of production, long before they enter the market. Usually it is a condition that accompanies the individual from her birth. Accordingly, I argue that what then occurs on the market is a matter of exploitation, which is of course morally reproachable, but does not account for capitalist domination. The latter is only systemic.

There are several advantages in adopting a structural approach to capitalist domination. First, the scope of responsibility for domination is substantially extended, in comparison with a purely interactional approach, to those who more or less directly support the current division of the means of production. Second, despite the fact that responsibility for domination of wage-workers is politically dispersed, the employers who profit from the asymmetries of power with employees (created by structural domination) to exploit them, remain morally blameworthy of exploitation. In this sense, exploitative employers carry a double responsibility: a political responsibility for domination of wage-workers (shared with a large group of people) and moral responsibility for their exploitation. Third, from the political perspective that I am outlining, the concept of exploitation is reduced to the minimal moral premise: human beings shall be free from domination. In other words, I will not hold that individual A exploits individual B because A offers B less than it would be fair to give her in return for her work performance, where 'fair' may refer either to a wage that includes the value that the worker transfers to the object of production in terms of work effort, or to a wage that is not disproportionately lower than the marginal increases of profits that the employer obtains thanks to the work performance she hires – two parameters that would require the previous acceptance of thicker moral premises, that is to say, either that wages should somehow embody work hours, or that profits should be distributed more or less equally among all the individuals that contribute to yield them. I shall contend, instead, that A exploits B insofar as A offers B a remuneration that is lower than B would have accepted had she not been in a condition of systemic domination, that is to say, had she had other valid alternatives to seeking sustenance in a market relation.

NEGATIVE DUTIES OF JUSTICE

Theories of justice normally include both a positive and a negative component. The positive component of a theory of justice is that for which a given individual (or group of individuals) has a series of duties to do determined things for the benefit of another individual (or group of individuals). So we may say, for example, that among all the members of a social group who receive an income there exists a positive duty to pay taxes, according to schemes that can be more or less progressive. And as we have seen before, this positive duty can be either practice-dependent (e.g. for contractualists) or practice-independent (e.g. for utilitarians, prioritarians or sufficientarians). Usually, every theory of justice that prescribes certain positive duties recognises the existence of parallel negative duties. The most uncontested of the latter is that you should not cause avoidable harm to others; and if you do so, you need to provide compensation. Some theorists have adopted a negative approach to global justice. They have postulated that wealthy individuals owe a redistribution of wealth to poor foreigners as a matter of redress for having caused them harm, or more generally for having violated one or more of their rights. There are two main theoretical reasons for taking this stand. The first one consists in globalising a theory of justice that is merely focused on property rights; the second one is to bite the bullet of statist thinkers concerning the domestic scope of positive duties of justice while arguing that, even if their counter-objection were true, the unquestionable duty not to cause avoidable harm to others would justify the provision of compensation to the world's poor.

The first is the case of left-libertarians, who argue that wealthy individuals owe a redistribution to the world's poor for having appropriated more than their equal share of the world's natural resources. More generally, left-libertarians share with right-libertarians – whose most famous contemporary exponent is Robert Nozick (1974) – the belief that all individual rights, including property rights, stem from individual full self-ownership. Every individual owns herself, as she might hold an external object, insofar as she retains 'full control rights' over her intellectual faculties and her body, 'full rights to transfer' the control rights – e.g. by signing a job contract or offering the performance of a service to a friend – and 'full payment immunities' for the possession of control rights (Vallentyne 2000, pp. 2–5). The latter point is the trickiest and marks the difference between libertarianism (both left and right) and the various forms of egalitariansim, because it implies that those who manage to accumulate great wealth through just transactions, that is to say, transactions that do not violate justice in acquisition, cannot be asked to renounce even a small share of this wealth by virtue of what Robert Nozick (1974, p. 156) defined as 'patterned' principles of justice. Then, left- and right-libertarians disagree on how human beings come to own external objects, and in particular natural resources. Right-libertarians follow John Locke in contending that natural resources are originally unowned and human beings acquire property rights over them by applying their own work on them (Nozick 1974, pp. 174–82; see also Otsuka 1998). Conversely, left-libertarians postulate that natural resources are equally owned at the origin. Thus, from this normative premise they rightly infer that the extreme forms of poverty and inequality are unjust, because they violate the original just distribution of natural resources; hence compensation is owed by over-appropriators to under-appropriators (Steiner 1994, pp. 266–82; 2009).

I think it is useful to enter into even more detail at this point, because the libertarian theory of just acquisition of natural resources will become central in outlining the contours of MDL. Right-libertarians usually recognise the validity of the so-called Lockean proviso, according to which a given individual can appropriate a natural resource as long as she leaves 'enough, and as good left' (Locke 2003 [1689], ch. 5, para. 33, p. 114). As Nozick (1974, pp. 175–8) has rightly stressed, there is both a 'stringent' and a 'weaker' interpretation of the basic idea of the proviso, namely that any individual appropriation should make others worse off. The 'stringent' interpretation would be extremely challenging for right-libertarianism, because it would oblige it to a subsistent restorative redistribution. In fact, the 'stringent' interpretation would imply that one individual makes another worse off either by preventing her from being better off *tout court* or by subtracting from her what she was previously free to use. Conversely, the weaker interpretation implies that one individual can make another worse off through an appropriation only in the first sense of the stringent interpretation.

The normative consequences of the two interpretations are fundamental. The stringent interpretation would imply that there can be no trade-off between access to natural resources, on the one hand, and the widespread advantages of modern economic growth sparked off by capitalism, on the other. Accordingly, even if we assume that everyone is better off within capitalism, the denied access to natural resources makes a large group of individuals *in some respects* worse off than if there had been no private appropriation of natural resources. Thus, those who control nature-based means of production, such as land, would owe compensation to commodified individuals, regardless of how good the latter are *all things considered*. Nonetheless, right-libertarians, including Nozick, usually avoid this radical conclusion by inclining towards a weaker interpretation of the Lockean proviso. They maintain that even though the private appropriation of natural resources has prevented many individuals from using some specific objects, this has not prevented them from improving their conditions, for example getting hired by those who control the means of production. In other words, right-libertarians appeal to trade-offs between wage-money and direct access to natural resources, holding that within capitalism the former can tremendously counterbalance the latter. Moreover, libertarians might even go further and contend that the establishment of private property has made even those who do not receive job offers better off, because it is implied – in a fairly questionable way, honestly speaking – that the means of production will end up in the hands of those who can use them in the most efficient way, so as to take entrepreneurial risks and increase social well-being (see Nozick 1974, p. 177). Hence, it might be postulated that a currently unemployed and subsidised person is better off than she would have been in a pre-capitalist society in which she had access to a small share of natural resources. And as we can see, these possible declinations of the weaker interpretation of the Lockean proviso minimise the space for wealth distribution.

On the other hand, left-libertarians are able to move a more imposing redistributive lever because, unlike right-libertarians, they do not postulate that natural resources are originally up for grabs – although conditioned to a more or less stringent interpretation of a Lockean proviso – but are equally owned by all human beings. Then, left-libertarians are divided over what an equal ownership of natural resources entails. A first view is that natural resources can be privatised upon collective consent, and obviously here the challenge consists in explaining how this consent can be given without incurring unsustainable administrative costs. The second view is that natural resources should remain equally owned; hence individuals can only use them temporarily – as when you go for a picnic in a public park – but clearly it is extremely difficult to imagine how this scheme might work in a society that has reached the current level of technological development. Lastly, the most implementable view of equal ownership is that natural resources can be unilaterally seized, on condition that the 'competitive value' of the natural resources taken from the common pool is paid for. This is the view adopted by Georgist libertarians, who owe their name to the nineteenth-century American political economist Henry George and who have among the most important contemporary representatives Hillel Steiner and Nicolaus Tideman (see Vallentyne 2000, pp. 5–10; see also Vallentyne and Steiner 2000).

More specifically, the competitive value of natural resources is best understood as a rent rather than a full appropriation, given that we should never lose sight of the fact that future generations will advance legitimate claims on initial joint ownership. The payment of the competitive value should not be confused with what Peter Vallentyne (2000, p. 9) calls 'full-benefit taxation'. Let us imagine that both individuals A and B seize 100 sq. m of land each; the competitive value of 100 sq. m of land is 40 coins and the initial egalitarian ownership of natural resources entitles every person to control resources only up to the value of 10 coins. Let us also add that A is more talented and industrious than B, so she manages to get 80 coins per year from her land, while B only gets 60 coins. According to Georgist libertarians, both A and B have to give away the same amount of coins, namely 30 coins per year (40 minus 10), while according to purely egalitarian accounts – that embody a more or less encompassing conception of full-benefit taxation – A and B should be charged differently, for they should also be taxed on the coins that they yield net of the competitive rent of their land, respectively 40 coins (80 minus 40) and 20 coins (60 minus 40).

As we can see, Georgist libertarians are in a certain sense 'more egalitarian' than right-libertarians, but as their right-colleagues, they fall short of justifying a taxation of income differentials stemming from individual efforts and also to compensate for cases of brute luck, that is to say, for either market or individual failures that cannot be avoided. Yet, a theoretical attempt to make left-libertarianism converge on more egalitarian policies, while not renouncing self-ownership and the assumption that distributive justice is limited to restoring justice in acquisition, is the normative treatment that Hillel Steiner

(1994, pp. 274–80; 2002; 2009) makes of genetic endowments. He postulates that any achievement an individual obtains in life is the result of three different elements (in addition, obviously, to social and natural contingencies that limit individual agency): genetic endowments, individual efforts in developing personal talents and the social output by parents in raising their children. From a libertarian perspective, it would be unjust to tax the individual for the share of her achievements that are imputable to the last two factors, which are in turn attributable to individual self-ownership (either of the individual herself or of her parents). Yet, genetic endowments are a sort of natural resource that parents mix in conceiving their children and that pre-exist them; hence they are excluded from self-ownership. Cutting a long story short, Steiner maintains that those parents who 'use' a genetic heritage of above-average quality have to pay a tax to a global fund, exactly as those over-appropriators of other natural resources are expected to do.

Keeping aside the way Hillel Steiner seeks to level out the social advantages stemming from different individual talents without recurring to 'patterned' principles of justice, and focusing exclusively on property rights, left-libertarians tackle the problem of the unequal division of the means of production, at least of its natural component, and like the MDL proposal I shall advance in this book, they do not claim that the initial equal ownership should be restored; rather, they accept that private property has made society substantially better off in a diachronic sense – and on this they agree with right-libertarians. Nonetheless, there are two important differences between left-libertariansim and MDL that I hope will become clearer in the next chapters, but which can – and should – be briefly summed up here. First, left-libertarians are bound to a very thick normative premise, namely that natural resources are initially jointly owned; whereas MDL only postulates that individual autonomy is inviolable. Many philosophers, and in general many people, would resist the former claim, but very few would oppose the latter. Second, nothing rules out the possibility that a person who has been compensated for the violation of her property rights over natural resources ends up back in a condition of extreme labour commodification, that is to say, she can exhaust her compensation and be compelled to enter into a market relation, and this could happen either because she has mismanaged the resources she received from the left-libertarian fund or because of contingencies that were out of her control. If that occurs, left-libertarianism would be unable to justify any social intervention aimed at guaranteeing her a decent life outside the market. In this sense, we may say that left-libertarianism is simply concerned with property rights while MDL takes as its point of reference the human condition per se, in respect to which property rights may be instrumental in ensuring autonomy – a basic precondition for the human condition to be decent – but they do not represent the necessary point of departure.

Another, different use of the concept of negative duties of justice, in a global context, is the one shown more recently by Thomas Pogge (2008). Instead of taking as a cue the duty to not violate the property of others – which, as we have seen, requires a previous assumption about what a just distribution of property originally is – he focuses on the much less questionable concept that it is wrong to cause harm to someone else when this can be avoided without incurring unsustainable costs. Accordingly, he justifies a global distribution of wealth on the grounds that people living in developing countries are giving their democratic support to governments that in turn keep a global order in place which causes avoidable human rights deficits to the world's poor (Pogge 2008, pp. 18–32). Hence, the former owe compensation to the latter, which can take the form both of efforts to reform the global order and transfer of resources to the victims of injustice (Pogge 2008, pp. 202–21). It is important to point out, as indeed it is pressing to do to the same Pogge, that the notion of harm he employs for the global realm is quite restrictive, in the sense that A harms B as long as A – more or less directly – causes a violation of B's human rights, but A does not harm B for the sole reason of providing B with a treatment that is less than optimal. Let us consider, as an example, the case in which A and B are respectively the governments of a developed and a developing country bargaining over the terms of bilateral trade agreements. Let us also assume that A leverages its greater economic power to reap an agreement that disproportionately benefits its farmers to the detriment of B's farmers. From Pogge's perspective, we might say that the government of country A – and indirectly those citizens who have elected it or have not taken a clear stance against it – are harming the farmers of country B only on condition that human rights deficits – such as cases of extreme poverty, denied access to natural resources that are necessary for basic sustenance, and so on – can be directly ascribable to the agreement. Moreover, to qualify as such in the sense indicated by Pogge, the alleged 'harm' should be avoidable, meaning that A can renounce at least some of the benefits it gets through the worst agreement that B is willing to sign, without incurring human rights deficits itself. And the negative consequences of the agreement for B should be foreseeable by A. Conversely, if one of the aforementioned conditions fails to apply, A cannot be said to violate a negative duty of justice to B, no matter how unfair the agreement.

However, the scope of Pogge's theory is not limited to single interactions between global actors, but it is systemic. He maintains that the global order as a whole is harming the global poor, where by global order he refers to the set of institutional and economic rules, both formal and informal, that have been shaped by the most powerful economic agents, both states and non-state agents, in their own interest. Pogge provides several empirical arguments for justifying his normative claim. Developed countries have opened up their markets to foreign products much less than they forced developing countries to do, in particular in those sectors in which they are more competitive, namely agriculture and manufacturing (Pogge 2008, pp. 20–21). Corrupted and authoritarian elites of developing countries have been acknowledged by the international community as having the right to issue public debt and dispose of national resources on behalf of the people that they rule undemocratically (Pogge 2008, pp. 118–22). The wealthy people of the world – be they in poor or rich countries – are using a disproportionately large share of natural resources, thus obtaining consistent profits from them, without compensating those other people that have been excluded from the use of these resources, namely the world's poor (Pogge 2008, pp. 207–9). Lastly, world history, in particular in the last couple of centuries, has been marked by forms of exploitation and violent colonialism that have unjustly contributed to creating global inequality (Pogge 2008, pp. 209–10).

All these elements combine to determine a systemic violation of the negative duty of the world's poor not to be avoidably harmed. However, when it comes to devising global policies for realising compensation, Pogge drastically reduces the range of his analysis by focusing exclusively on the over-appropriation of natural resources. Thus, he advocates what he calls the Global Resources Dividend (GRD), a measure that I shall discuss in more detail at the end of Chapter 3 in relation to MDL, and that consists in those individuals yielding profits out of natural resources paying a small tax to a global fund, which in turn is supposed to cover human rights deficits due to poverty worldwide. As an example, he talks about a GRD tax amounting to 3 dollars per barrel of extracted oil and he estimates that world poverty could be reverted through an annual investment of 300 billion dollars, which amounts to only 0.67 per cent of global GDP in 2005 (Pogge 2008, pp. 210–14).

Pogge's theory will recur in several places in the course of this book, but what I can say for now is the following. Although both Pogge's theory and MDL appeal to negative duties of justice to advocate a global redistribution of wealth, and as we shall see in a while both do so on subjunctive rather than diachronic grounds, the former proposes a poverty-based criticism of inequality in the distribution of natural resources, holding that inequality is bad because it causes the world's poor to be poor, while MDL launches a freedom-based criticism of inequality, according to which inequality is bad because it renders those lacking resources unfree, regardless of their welfare level. Moreover, while Pogge deploys many convincing empirical arguments for justifying the violation of the specific negative duty he has in mind – not to cause harm – paradoxically his compensatory policy is based on the weakest of his theoretical justifications, namely the over-appropriation of natural resources. This argument is inextricably linked to a normative theory of justice in acquisition, which Pogge interprets in Lockean terms, and this risks watering down the stringency to which he aspires by recurring to negative instead of positive rights. In other words, if it is quite uncontested in every political and moral phi-losophy that it is bad to do harm to someone else when this can be avoided and causes a net loss of global welfare, it is not so commonplace that the current distribution of resources should be evaluated, from a normative point of view, in relation to the hypothetical distribution we would have if something like the Lockean proviso had be respected from the start.

All in all, I feel in line with the critical approach that Pogge was the first to adopt with respect to world poverty, arguing that before wondering what we could do to benefit the world's poor, we should ask what we could do to stop harming them. As I said, and as I will stress later on, Pogge's theory and MDL look at two different kinds of harm, and nothing entails that the two approaches are mutually exclusive. Quite the opposite, I believe they can be complemen-tary in providing a comprehensive analysis of the forms of injustice that those individuals who monopolise the means of production perpetrate over those others who, to put it in Marxian terms, only own their labour performance and enjoy the freedom of disposing of it. This gives me the chance to clarify another important issue. The theory based on MDL comes before the theories of justice based on positive duties but does not replace them. Accordingly, I argue that before discussing how we should split social wealth, we should ensure that all those people who take part in the production process do so as a truly voluntary choice – that is to say, not simply free from interactional domination but also from capitalist structural domination. Yet, I do not deny that after (and/or in parallel to) guaranteeing freedom from domination, we should also devise positive principles of distributive justice. I simply remain neutral with regard to the latter, at least in this book, because I do not want to disperse the argumentative focus.

GLOBAL INEQUALITY AND CONVERGENT GLOBALISATION

Both positive and negative theories of justice are usually welfare-sensitive. They look at the current distribution of world resources and opportunities and argue that it is more or less just, depending on how close it comes to or how far it deviates from a normative ideal, and the correspondence between the actual distribution and the ideal one varies with the variation of individual welfare. In plain words, if we take as an example a society in which there are only three persons, A, B and C, and assume that A and B are very well off, while C is poor, I believe that every theory of justice would hold that any change that makes C better off goes in the direction of the underlying normative ideal – be it sufficiency, equality, the maximisation of utility, a compensation for injus-tice, and so on.

Welfare-sensitiveness is apparently reasonable, and I have no intention to criticise it. My point is that we should not just be content with it, because it is insensitive to some forms of domination that are essential for assessing the justice of a particular social order. Let us assume that C is poor and gets her small income from some assets she controls –cattle, a field, the renting of a small business premises. Let us assume now that A and B subtract from C the few assets at her disposal and offer her the possibility to work for them, and through this change in conditions C becomes richer than she was before. If C is made better off than she was before, I guess that very few people would complain. Yet, it should also be noted that as a wage-worker C is no longer able to unilaterally control the minimum income she was able to obtain before; rather, her entire income – although being now higher – becomes dependent on the willingness of both A and B to hire out her labour performance. From this it follows that A and B are now in a position to obtain from C things that they could not obtain before, because they can exert on C the leverage of the hunger risk that was inaccessible to them in the antecedent scenario. In short, C is now better off but at the same she is more dominated in comparison with her previous situation.

We are speculating here on a closed society with only three individuals, in which C cannot look for other employers and there are no public subsidies. Yet, someone might object that even in this hypothetical situation she would prefer to rent out her labour performance to others rather than be free but poorer. This is a legitimate claim, and I guess that the majority of people who can get an acceptable income through waged work are quite happy about their condition, or at least would not trade it for a lower but self-sufficient income. Indeed, my criticism is not diachronic but subjunctive. It does not consist in regretting a past situation, or in imagining a more or less realistic Arcadian history; rather, it aims at correcting for forms of injustice that arise in the transition from one state of affairs to another, even though the transition is *all things considered* favourable.[4] Thus, when considering our previous example, I am not contending that C should go back to the initial situation, where she was poorer. I am arguing, instead, that in her new and *all things considered* better situation, C should be freed from domination, when this is achievable without others incurring insurmountable costs. The normative reason is that individual autonomy is a free-standing normative ideal that lays down widespread negative duties of justice. To be more precise, the normative strength of the claim that C should be now free from domination does not depend on the fact that she was free before. When I look at capitalist domination in historical

---

[4]   On the difference between a diachronic and a subjunctive treatment of harm I am indebted to Pogge (2008, pp. 23–6) and Meyer (2003).

terms, in the course of this book, I shall simply do so to understand how the phenomenon has arisen and how it has evolved during the years, but I will never engage in normative arguments based on historical injustice.

The problem with the welfare-sensitiveness of classic theories of justice is that once C passes to the new condition, and more generally, the wealthier C gets, the more it becomes difficult for anyone to hold that there is something morally wrong in C's condition. Let us imagine that after a few years of paid work, C gets the same monthly income as A and B. More precisely, we could assume that the three individuals make the following agreement. A and B will keep on controlling the only means of production available in our hypothetical closed society, and they are willing to hire them out because they would like to minimise physical work, while C is ready to provide her labour performance. The agreement is initialled and the overall output that the society yields in this way is equally distributed. Any theory of justice that focuses on the fairness of the distribution – be it of resources, opportunities or capabilities – or on the maximisation of a value – be it utility, priority-amended utility, and so on – or on compensating for injustice in appropriation, would look positively at this egalitarian scheme. Yet, what they would not be able to give the right normative weight to is that A and B can do without C, but C cannot do without A and B. The latter can lay off C, return to work and not suffer income loss, while C would literally starve in the medium run.

We are here arbitrarily assuming that in this closed society wage-income cannot be turned into productive assets. This could happen, for example, if on a desert island A and B controlled the only available fields and cattle, let C work on them and paid her in vegetable and dairy products – so that at the end of the month A, B and C all have exactly the same quantity of food. Thus, if we move from the envisaged experiment to real life, we should relax the assumption of closeness and accept that a high wage income can be turned into productive assets, and hence move in the direction of labour de-commodification and limit capitalist domination – e.g. wage income can be invested in financial products or used to buy means of production. Accordingly, the shortcoming of welfare-sensitive approaches to justice would be apparent only in social schemes that remain inegalitarian and in which proletarians like C are simply paid what they need to 'reproduce themselves', that is to say, to rent a small house, buy food and make some modest weekly outings. Nonetheless, I considered it important to give the example of this envisaged experiment to show that even within a society in which income is equally allocated there can be capitalist domination.[5] Moreover, we should also note that the envisaged

---

[5]   It might be objected that the society I have described is not fully egalitarian because even though income is shared equally, A and B have private property, while C

experiment does not even describe the whole dire situation of real-life proletarians, for C is the only individual A and B can rely upon to avoid engaging
directly in full-time work, and this creates some bargaining margins for C. If
we want to make this situation more similar to the real one, we should introduce some other individuals (D, E, F and so on) who are extremely poor and
have no access to the means of production, and who would be glad to take C's
place were she to give up or be laid off.

In saying that welfare-sensitiveness is not enough for assessing the justice
of a given distribution of resources, my purpose is to not get lost in mental
speculations. Rather, I want to underline that its critical leverage can happen to
be drastically reduced in a situation where economic flows reverse an existing
inegalitarian trend. This is exactly what is occurring with globalisation, which
has been divergent for almost two centuries and from the 1980s has become
convergent (Baldwin 2016; Milanovic 2016). From the Industrial Revolution
onwards, that is to say from the first half of the nineteenth century, modern
economic growth has determined the first inequalities between countries,
namely between those who achieved industrialisation and entered the global
market and those who did not, at least not immediately. To be more precise,
before the Industrial Revolution there was negligible growth in the course of
human history. We could say that living conditions never changed substantially from one century to the next, the only exceptions being some technological innovations such as sailing boats, the plough, the press, and so forth,
whereas from the introduction of the steam engine onwards, new technologies
have progressively increased labour productivity, thus maintaining constant
economic growth rates never seen before (Maddison 2005).

Obviously, inequality has always existed in human history, and if we look
at both ancient and modern history we would not have many difficulties in
bringing to mind cases of enormous injustices in the allocation of resources
and opportunities of life. But inequality was mostly a domestic issue, meaning
that despite the income gap between the rich and the poor in a given society
being surely high, there was not so much difference – at least from an income
level – in being poor in one country rather than in another one. From the
Industrial Revolution onwards, inequality became also a global problem.
Global inequalities became even more pronounced after the Second World
War, when the Western bloc boomed, the Soviet Union could not keep up the
rate of economic growth and both Africa and South Asia lagged far behind
(Milanovic 2016).

---

has not. However, my conclusions regarding the imperviousness of capitalist domination would remain unchanged, even if we imagined that C was given more income than
both A and B, so rebalancing the gap in private property.

It is exactly in these historical contingencies that the normative problem of global justice flourished, in both its practice-dependent and practice-independent versions (see Abizadeh 2007; Sangiovanni 2008; Ronzoni 2009). From the first perspective, the basic argument of global justice was quite linear, as we have already seen. Global markets allow the maximisation of industrial-led growth and it is unfair that this cooperative surplus should be unequally distributed. Obviously, the normative strength of this argument does not depend solely on the fact that some countries industrialised while others did not; rather, it rests also on the contingency that people from poor countries and people from rich ones were enmeshed in a common web of production and trade, and that this web is so extensive and its effects are so pervasive that it can be compared to a domestic scheme of social cooperation (Beitz 1999, pp. 125–76; Moellendorf 2002, pp. 30–67; James 2012). Conversely, the practice-independent version moved from the less controversial empirical claim that some areas of the world are extremely wealthy, while some others are wretched with dire poverty. Therefore, any transfer of resources from the former to the latter would meet a normative criterion, be it to guarantee every human being a set of basic capabilities (Nussbaum 2006), to maximise global utility (Singer 1972), and so on.

From the 1980s onwards, the global economic trend has reversed. Developing countries have continued growing faster than developed ones, and global poverty has progressively diminished. This occurred mainly because new information technologies have allowed for the delocalisation of investments from developed to developing countries, with a consequent transfer of job opportunities. From this moment on, even though domestic inequalities have continued to increase, inequality between countries has progressively decreased, as has world poverty (Baldwin 2016, pp. 79–110). Some few data can convey the idea. In the period from 1950 to the mid-1970s, US GDP per capita was twenty times higher than Chinese GDP: 20 to 1. Towards the end of the first decade of the twenty-first century, the ratio was reduced to 4 to 1 (again in favour of the United States), exactly the same ratio that existed between the GDP per capita of the two countries in 1870, at the beginning of capitalist globalisation (Milanovic 2016, p. 130).

Practice-dependent theories of global justice work well, intuitively, as long as the worse off get in proportion a smaller share of the global cooperative surplus than the better off – as is the case in the first phase of globalisation, when the better off were becoming wealthier at a much faster pace than the worse off, or, to put it in other terms, as long as the worse off are the losers of globalisation and the better off are the winners. Yet, convergent globalisation has made everything much more complex. Middle classes in developing countries, in particular in Asia, are winning in comparison with middle classes of developed countries, since the former have had much higher income growth rates than the latter. The richest individuals in developed countries have been winning over all the others, given that the transfer of job opportunities from the middle classes of developed countries to the middle classes of developing countries has allowed them to cut labour costs. To this we should also add that plutocrats are also the ones who can mostly invest in automation, to the detriment of human workers in general. Aside from all of this, there is also a group of individuals living in countries where there has never been real and propitious economic growth.

I am not maintaining that convergent globalisation undermines practice-dependent justice as such, but surely it renders it harder to read it in a global perspective, because winners and losers of the global market can no longer be classified on the basis of their geographical location. It is no coincidence that the 'new discontent' of globalisation is now the middle and the lower classes of developed countries (Stiglitz 2017). Paradoxically, the practice-dependent argument can also become hostage to reactionary anti-global rhetoric by those who have turned from winners into losers in the switch from divergent to convergent globalisation. This is usually a sign of misplaced grievance, given that globalisation has never given signs of being dysfunctional, in the sense of being unable to yield enough wealth for all, and the real problem is rather that an extremely samll percentage of human beings is taking almost half the available wealth (Oxfam 2020). In a few words, against the welfare sensitiveness of practice-dependent accounts of justice, it might be objected that if the worse off are catching up, in terms of welfare, with the better off, globalisation is already moving in the right direction, and the real social challenge does not consist in a global redistribution of resources, but rather in a class struggle between lower and middle classes on the one hand and plutocrats on the other, that is, internal to developed countries (Corvino 2019c).

The same discourse holds true for practice-independent accounts. Extreme poverty has been declining in the world since the 1980s, both in absolute and in relative terms. In 1980 there were more than 1.9 billion people in extreme poverty in the world. In 2015 the figure was less than 800 million (Our World in Data 2019). If we look at the issue from a broader historical perspective, we may note that at the outset of the Industrial Revolution, in 1820, 80 per cent of the world's population was in absolute poverty, while nowadays the number has fallen to 10 per cent (Roser 2017). Some people object that the history of poverty decline cannot be generalised to include the whole world because it is mostly related to the astounding economic growth in China. As a matter of fact, at the beginning of the 1980s almost 88 per cent of Chinese people were in conditions of extreme poverty, while today only 2 per cent remain below this poverty threshold (Roser 2017). Accordingly, given that the Chinese population accounts for slightly less than 20 per cent of the global total, it is obvious that such a blatant decline of poverty in China has had a decisive impact on the decline of poverty in the world. However, it suffices to look at a chart on the evolution of world poverty, both with and without China, to realise that from the 1980s world poverty has been declining independently from China. Moreover, as rightly noted by the World Bank, after 2005 world poverty has been higher in percentage terms if we include China than if we exclude it – meaning that extreme poverty has been so limited in China over the last 15 years, that the Chinese impact on the constant decline of world poverty has been almost negligible (Roser 2017).

Owing to this empirical evidence, it gets very complicated for practice-independent theorists to play a critical role with regard to globalised capitalism. More concretely, they may express well-grounded moral concerns regarding the fact that a consistent number of people continue to live in dire conditions and well-off people could avoid this at a very low price – considering for example how little money the poor would need to substantially improve their welfare and increase their life chances, and how much money the rich spend on unnecessary things (Singer 2010). Yet they fall short of elaborating a political critique of the global order, that is to say in assigning causal responsibility to the well off for the fact that some people are still very badly off. The same discourse holds true for negative theorists of global justice, as long as the latter rely on the empirical premise that global norms and rules are somehow harming the world's poor (Pogge 2008).

Apparently, one theoretical possibility for preserving the normative strength of classic theories of global justice at a time of convergent globalisation might consist in holding that world poverty is declining despite the current global order, rather than because of it (Pogge 2008, pp. 19–23). The argument could be elaborated, for example, in the sense that industrialisation and openness to world trade are beneficial per se, yet powerful state and non-state actors have shaped the global order so as to collect a relatively disproportionate amount of the collective benefits. Thus, it might be said, world poverty is surely declining, but it could decline even faster if it were not for the injustice perpetrated by the well off. However, also this discourse risks being over-moralised, because it would entail that the global order, that is to say the way in which global capitalism is administered, is *all things considered* beneficial for the world's poor, but not sufficiently beneficial with respect to a normative ideal of fair cooperation – e.g. the world's poor are getting less benefits than they would get if global economic rules were decided behind a global veil of ignorance (Moellendorf 2002, pp. 70–72; Caney 2005, pp. 125–31).

The normative critique I shall develop, instead, is not limited to the global order but targets the same global capitalism, and it can do this because it is not based on a welfare-sensitive setting. Consequently, its scope is not curtailed by convergent globalisation, at least as long as the latter does not yield diffuse wealth – in addition to relieving extreme poverty. Global capitalism undermines individual freedom even when both world inequality and poverty drop. The two phenomena are not necessarily antithetical; on the contrary, the opposite usually occurs. The people who are pulled out of extreme poverty are normally taken away from rural, semi-rural or slum contexts and given a wage contract in the industrial or service sectors. As a consequence, their margins for bargaining are very narrow and their dependence on wage income is extreme. In sum, the economic fluxes that render globalisation convergent are probably *all things considered* favourable – meaning that it is perhaps preferable to be above the threshold of extreme poverty and more dominated in a capitalistic fashion than being below the threshold and slightly less dominated – but this does not necessarily render people less commodified; in actual fact, quite the opposite is true.

1. Labour commodification

The United Nations Development Programme's *Human Development Report 2014* was the first of a long series of annual documents to emphasise the role of 'human vulnerability' in assessing individual well-being, where human vulnerability corresponds to the probability that the exercising of certain capabilities will be hindered in the future. More generally, the report opened with the overall observation that 'Globalization has on balance produced major human development gains, especially in many countries of the South. But there is also a widespread sense of precariousness in the world today – in livelihoods, in personal security, in the environment and in global politics' (UNDP 2014, p. 1). Moreover, it drew the conclusion that the challenge of development does not simply consist in withdrawing people from conditions of poverty, but also in making sure that they do not become poor again in the future (UNDP 2014, p. 4). The concept of human vulnerability is strictly related to the one of 'human security', which was at the core of a previous *Human Development Report 1994*. Basically, the idea at that time was that after the end of the Cold War, the notion of security, which had been interpreted so far at the national level as the security of one given country (or group of countries) vis-à-vis the possible aggression by another country (or group of countries), had to be seen in an individual perspective. Accordingly, human security as opposed to national security means security in everyday life, from diseases, oppression, unemployment, and so on. As the report stated: 'In the final analysis, human security is a child who did not die, a disease that did not spread, a job that was not cut, an ethnic tension that did not explode in violence, a dissident who was not silenced. Human security is not a concern with weapons – it is a concern with human life and dignity' (UNDP 1994, p. 22).

Human vulnerability and human resilience are two faces of the same coin. Human beings are vulnerable to a series of natural and social threats, while human resilience is the ability to cope with the sources of vulnerability. The milder the negative effects these shocks can have on a person, the higher the human resilience of this specific person, and vice versa (UNDP 2014, pp. 15–16). Accordingly, the balance between someone's vulnerability and her resilience gives the measure of her security. Interpreted in this way, we might say that the notion of human security represents the fourth step of a long theoretical evolution in the discourse on well-being assessment, and more generally on development, that goes from utility to resources first, then from resources to capabilities (and hence to human development), and lastly from the mere exercising of capabilities to a secure exercising of them. The prevailing philosophical and economic view, until the first half of the twentieth century, was that the purpose of development was to yield aggregate increases of well-being, the latter interpreted either as the balance between positive and negative states of mind or as the satisfaction of preferences and desires, regardless of how they were distributed. From John Rawls onwards, the discourse on justice has shifted to a fair distribution of resources, independently of the well-being that individuals can get from the resources they control (Rawls 1999a, pp. 47–101; see also Dworkin 1981a, 1981b). The human development paradigm, which was initially elaborated in the first *Human Development Report 1990* (UNDP 1990) coordinated by Mahbub ul Haq, and which subsequently ran rampant in the works of Amartya Sen (who also worked on the report) and Martha Nussbaum, contested *resourcism* for the first time from a different perspective than the utilitarian one. It maintained that well-being is not so much about how many resources people control, but rather about how many things they are free to do with these resources, no matter whether they do them or not (Sen 1992, 1999).

The main advantage of 'capabilitarianism'[1] over utilitarianism is that it does not fall prey to adaptive preferences, insofar as the fact that a given individual is not excessively displeased with having some capabilities curtailed (e.g. freedom of speech, relating on a gender-equal basis with his/her partner, having a decent income guaranteed) because she was born in that situation or has progressively adapted to her conditions, does not count in assessing her well-being. The latter depends exclusively on how large her set of capabilities is, regardless of the happiness or satisfaction she gets from it. Conversely, the advantage of capabilitarianism over Rawlsian resourcism is that it can give proper weight to the fact the individuals might control two equal sets of resources and yet have very unequal options in life, because either natural or social contingencies affect their individual pattern of conversion of resources into well-being (Sen 1999, pp. 58–65; Nussbaum 2000, pp. 111–66). An example of the former case is two poor homeless persons, one living in a cold city in Northern Europe and the other in a seaside town in South America, both having the same small income (adjusted for the different cost of living), but leading two different lives, because the one living in the north needs to buy

---

[1]   I follow Ingrid Robeyns (2016) in using the term 'capabilitariansim' instead of 'capability approach' to take into account all the 'clusters of scholarships' that during the years have used the notion of 'capabilities' and that cannot be reduced to the two clusters that Martha Nussbaum usually identifies with the capability approach: her normative theory of justice and the economic work on capabilities as the metric of well-being.

winter clothes and cannot think of sleeping outside; hence, although having the same income as his South American counterpart, his peculiar needs, dictated by natural circumstances, make him poorer. On the other hand, an example of social contingencies causing an unequal conversion into well-being of two equal sets of resources is the one of two children who receive exactly the same modest monthly amount of money. One attends a common school in the suburbs, where everyone dresses very casually – hence the child encounters no relational obstacles; the other one attends a fancy school in the city centre, where wearing designer clothes is a fundamental requirement to be included in extra-curricular social activities – hence the child feels discomfort and/ or suffers discrimination. Accordingly, even though both children can buy exactly the same things, they experience two different levels of well-being. From the capabilitarian perspective, human development consists in enlarging human capabilities rather than simply increasing income, be it individual or aggregate. This is not because the two objectives are antithetical – quite the opposite. Income growth is usually instrumental in enlarging capabilities, yet the former without the latter cannot be taken as a measure of well-being and hence as an indicator of development.

The paradigm of human security takes on the path marked by human development but goes further. Development cannot simply consist in enlarging capabilities – it also requires the creation of social conditions that can guarantee the enjoyment of these capabilities over time. If we go back to our first example, we might suppose that if in the seaside town there is widespread street crime, the homeless person living there will be less secure in the exercise of his capabilities, although these capabilities are larger than the ones of the homeless person living in Northern Europe. The same holds true for the two children. Consider, for example, the case that the father of the child going to school in the suburbs is a staunch poker player. Despite being better off, from a capabilitarian perspective, than the other child, the first child is much more exposed to the risk of abruptly losing his higher level of well-being. We might say that the synthesis of the theoretical evolution of the Human Development Reports is that the proper units of measurement of well-being are capabilities, rather than either utilities or resources, and that development cannot simply consist in ensuring the widest possible number of capabilities for as many people as possible, but also in securing these capabilities by rendering vulnerable people resilient to natural and social risks.

The relation between risks, vulnerability, resilience and well-being is apparently simple. Risks and vulnerability are threats to well-being, while resilience is assumed to promote it. In mathematical terms we could say that well-being is, among other things, a function of risks, vulnerability and resilience (UNDP 2014, p. 17). In the middle of a civil war, for example, you can defend vulnerable people – i.e. children, women, civilians – by disarming the fighting parties or proposing a reasonable peace agreement. Likewise, in an epidemic crisis, you can safeguard the vulnerable – i.e. the elderly, the sick – by distributing (or identifying) the vaccine that can halt the virus. In both cases, you would promote the well-being of vulnerable people without intervening in the variables of vulnerability and resilience, but simply by addressing the origin of the risk. This is not only one of the options, but it is also the preferable one, where viable, because it would make no sense, for example, to try to make vulnerable people more resilient by offering them military training, in the first case, or by merely distributing health masks, in the second case.

There are other cases, in turn, in which it is impossible to intervene in the origin of the risk, because the solution, even if desirable, is out of reach of the agents directly involved. A typical case concerns measures of adaptation to climate change, where measures of mitigation fail to achieve satisfactory results. In Rotterdam, for example, people are vulnerable to floods caused by global warming, because 90 per cent of the city lies below sea level. Since it is very difficult for the inhabitants of Rotterdam to intervene unilaterally in the origins of a problem such as climate change, which is both global and inter-temporal (today we suffer the negative consequences of past emissions), they have decided to protect themselves by investing in a huge storm surge barrier, *Maeslantkering*, that in case of necessity can close off the waterway that connects the city to the North Sea (Miner and Wilks 2020). They have also planned the urban architecture in such a way that it is able to absorb any flooding without causing damage to people and buildings (Kimmelman 2017).

The case of socio-economic risks linked to globalised capitalism falls within a third category. The most rational strategy to protect those most vulnerable to these risks is to make them more resilient, but not simply because it is impossible to intervene unilaterally in the origin of these risks, but also because this would be undesirable from a normative point of view. In a diachronic perspective, capitalism has the potential to create sufficient resources and technical means, in absolute terms, to enlarge the set of individual capabilities for everyone – and as was argued in the Introduction, this continues to be so also in the phase of convergent globalisation. Accordingly, capitalism has, at least so far, led to continued economic growth, which has had positive effects, not least on the living standards of the world's most vulnerable people, and the data on world poverty reduction speak for themselves (World Economic Forum 2019). Yet, the problem is that within a market society the potential enlargement of individual capabilities goes hand in hand with the precarisation of even basic capabilities for those who are excluded from the control of the means of production. This is accompanied by the globalisation of socio-economic risks, which exacerbates the economic and existential precariousness of the proletariat, because it makes economic shocks less predictable and less controllable. Quoting an expression used some years ago by David Held (2010, pp. 36–9), we might say that we live in 'a world of overlapping communities of fate', where the distinction between domestic and foreign affairs is becoming increasingly blurred. Or, following Ulrich Beck (2009 [2007], p. 8), we might say that we are becoming members of 'a global community of threats'.

1.1 A DEFINITION OF LABOUR COMMODIFICATION

In all the cases in which it is not possible – either in a technical and/or normative sense – to reduce the exposure to risks, at least in the short run, the only way to protect vulnerable individuals is to increase resilience. With regard to socio-economic risks, such as those determined by capitalism, the crucial element in building socio-economic resilience is in assets (see Crouch 2013, pp. 66–72). The notion of assets is admittedly quite general, but following the useful taxonomy given by Adolfo Morrone et al. (2011) we might nail it down in terms of economic capital, human capital, social capital and public/collective assets. Economic capital consists of material goods and financial assets. Human capital is both knowledge and competences. Social capital, as Robert Putnam (2000) has brilliantly explained, arises from both 'norms of reciprocity' and 'networks of civic engagement'. In Putnam's view, social capital has a positive and visible effect on the economic system by lowering the costs of cooperation and, more generally, by creating a social environment of mutual trust.[2] The main difference between social capital and purely economic capital is that the former is a public good, meaning that a context of mutual trust benefits the economic system in its entirety, with obvious issues of free-riding arising as for any other public good, whereas more private forms of social capital pertain to individual networks of aid and reciprocity that can help the individual to recover from economic shocks. Finally, collective assets refer to all the welfare services provided by the public sector. I would also add that when we discuss resilience in a global context it is useful to include in the category of collective/public assets common goods, like unfenced fields held in common property or water basins.

Labour commodification is, namely, the process through which human labour gets transformed into a commodity, that is to say into a good that is traded on the market according to the law of supply and demand, and with more or less pronounced market imperfections that may favour either the selling or the buying counterpart – asymmetries of information, monopolies, and so on. This process advances through dispossessing the individual of the

---

[2] For a critical view of the effects of social capital on growth, see Florida 2005, pp. 30–31.

control of assets (economic capital, human capital, social capital and public/ collective assets), with the only exception being her labour power, thus rendering her more vulnerable to socio-economic shocks – be they more or less systemic. Part of the labour power would seem to be a function of human capital, yet it would be more correct to say that human capital is antithetical to labour commodification insofar as refined working skills allow the individual to obtain a relatively high salary in the absence of other assets, which in turn can allow the accumulation of economic assets, and vice versa finding oneself without other assets makes it difficult to invest in the enrichment of human capital. Obviously, human labour existed long before it became a commodity. From the prehistoric human beings who went hunting to the feudal vassal who worked the land in exchange for the protection of his lord, passing through the medieval slaves, human beings have always carried out both intellectual and physical activities, more or less coercively, to obtain the resources necessary for satisfying their needs. Two facts render commodified labour different from pre-capitalist labour. The first is that commodified labour is entirely regulated by the market mechanism, while previous forms of labour were (mainly) guided by social rationales of power that were external to the economic sphere – e.g. the relation between plebs and aristocracy, free women and men vs. slaves, and so on (see Esping-Andersen 1990, pp. 38–41; Bourdieu 2000; Polanyi 2001 [1944], pp. 45–58; Crouch 2013, pp. 63–6). The second fact, as we shall see in more detail in Section 1.2, is that the commodification of labour goes hand in hand with what Marx called 'the primitive accumulation', that is to say the concentration of the means of production in the hands of a restricted social group and the consequent creation of the proletariat (see also Hudis 2010).

As the British economist Guy Standing (2007, p. 69) has rightly pointed out, 'commodification is always a matter of degree'. When someone sells her labour performance for 'instrumental reasons' in a situation of 'economic insecurity', her labour is commodified. The more relevant the instrumental reasons in her decision to enter the labour market, the higher the degree of commodification of her labour. Even if they often appear together, the degree of labour commodification, on the one hand, and the harshness and the length of the job, on the other, are not structurally interconnected. The commodification of labour power is a function of the reasons that induce its owner to sell it on the market. The intrinsic characteristics of the job that finalises the transaction in which the worker offers her performance, and the employer buys it by providing a wage, have nothing to do with the degree of commodification. Honestly, it is unlikely to happen in real life, but from a purely theoretical point of view a person's labour may have a high degree of commodification while the job she performs is enjoyable and takes her very few hours per day. Let us consider the following case.

A company operating in a developing country is forced to reduce the supply of its products because of global economic slowdown. As a consequence, Sylvia, who works for this company, loses her job (UNICEF 2019, pp. 23–37; see also UNCTAD 2019). She has lived her life on the edge of moderate poverty. She lacks economic assets, and she does not possess any natural asset from which she might produce food. She has no access to any productive common good. She lives in a developing country that denies her welfare provisions. She simply has at her disposal her limited human capital. The only way for her to react to this sudden loss of income is to offer again her labour performance on the market, hoping that someone will be willing to buy it. In the unfortunate event in which she might fail in this market operation, the continuation of her life will be at risk. In a few words, her labour power is highly commodified, because her living standard is completely dependent on her capacity to sell her labour power and on someone else's willingness to hire it. In the case outlined above this dependence is so strong that her own survival comes to depend on the destiny of her labour commodity on the market. If she does not manage to obtain a new source of income from her human capital, she will inevitably fall below the extreme poverty line.

Imagine that after many weeks of intense research, Sylvia has not managed to find any employer who is willing to hire her. She has almost lost all hope, when unexpectedly she finds out that she has a talent for painting. Sylvia buys canvases and starts pouring acrylic colours on them. After she completes the first few paintings, she realises that she can make a living from selling her canvases to some wealthy persons living in her district. After some practice, Sylvia estimates that if she paints two hours per day, every day, she can produce enough paintings to live a decent life. Art is not her greatest passion, yet the two hours she daily spends painting are enjoyable, and for the remaining 22 hours of the day she is entirely free to do whatever she wishes.

Sylvia's new job is surely not harsh, not unsafe and not much alienating. We might easily say that her new painting activity is the job many people dream of. Her living standard is much better than when she had the previous job. She has plenty of free time, she is not stressed, she is free to read novels, write poetry, watch movies, and so forth. Nonetheless, her labour continues to be highly commodified. Rather, we might say that it is even more commodified than before. The reason is that she has no choice but to paint canvases. She has explored the labour market and she has found nothing. If she stops painting, she will inevitably fall into severe poverty. Given her situation of asset poverty (presented above) her survival is completely dependent on the production of a minimum number of canvases per month. In order to yield this result, she needs to work a minimum number of hours per day. If she does not, and if she does not manage to find another asset to rely upon, she will get into deep trouble. It might be counter-argued that having discovered her new talent, Sylvia could spend the first year painting day and night, selling in a short time the amount of paintings that she could instead sell over decades, thus accumulating enough capital to invest in a different productive activity and escape the proletarian condition. Accordingly, to dispel this objection in advance and refine our thought experiment, we can assume, objectively or more realistically, that the buyers Sylvia has identified will like to buy a canvas at more or less regular intervals of time, instead of concentrating everything in a few cumulative purchases.

I hold that now that Sylvia has a wonderful job she is more commodified than before, for two reasons. The first one is that when she had the first job, she was not sure that she would not have been able to get a new one. In fact she had a second option, a sort of safety net, for even if she would have never expected it, after she lost the job in the company, she had the painting career waiting for her. On the contrary, now she has explored the labour market for weeks without finding anyone willing to hire her. This means that now she has the empirical evidence that in the event of another imminent job loss she will not be able (or we can say that it is unlikely that she will be able) to find a new source of income. In the end, she is now more bound to the necessity of painting canvases than she was before to working hard in the company. The second reason is that her first source of income, even though much more unpleasant, was more reliable than the second one. When she worked for the company, her job security hinged upon the world demand of product P. Resorting to an oversimplified economic analysis, we might say that as long as the price and the demand of P were constant, Sylvia could have remained somewhat secure in her job, whereas now, her income depends on the willingness of a tiny group of art collectors to hang her paintings on their walls.

Sylvia's new job is great. All she has to do every day is sit for two hours on the beach painting canvases. Despite this, her level of labour commodification is substantial. The labour, on the other hand, of a miner working hard for eight hours per day underground might be much less commodified if this miner happens to live in a country where the state guarantees free education, free health, and a minimum unemployment subsidy. This miner is not working for survival, as Sylvia is doing (she is painting for survival). The reason why he goes every morning to the mine is to guarantee a slightly more than decent standard of living for his family. He knows that if he decides to opt out of the labour market, or is involuntarily excluded from it, his family would not fall below a minimum capability threshold that is determined by the level of welfare provision. His children would be able to attend school. He would still be free to go to the ophthalmologist. The unemployment benefits would be enough to prevent starvation. While nonetheless conducting a much more tiring and harsh life than Sylvia started doing after she discovered her artistic talent, the miner is more resilient than she is to an income loss, for he can react to a sudden economic shock by relying upon public assets.

The same thing holds true for a worker who loses her job, as in the case of Sylvia (we can also assume that they were colleagues working for the same company and were fired on the same day, for the same reason), but who owns a small field (a few square metres) and two cows. This second worker can build her resilience upon a few natural goods. She can cultivate the field and herd the cows. She will barely manage to keep her family from falling into starvation through the few natural products she manages to yield, or to barter or to sell. Sylvia's colleague is surely more commodified than the miner – neither of them are working for survival, but Sylvia's colleague would lose many more capabilities than he would because of dismissal. Her children have food, home-grown, but they cannot attend school. In case of illness, the members of the family cannot pay a doctor for a visit. On the other hand, she is less commodified than Sylvia because the possibility of home-growing food detaches her survival from participation in the labour market. Sylvia's colleague has a minimal source of resilience stemming from natural assets.

We have seen so far that if we want to measure the degree of commodification of someone's labour, we should not look at the way the transaction gets finalised on the market – namely, the job contract and the job tasks that stem from it. Instead, we should focus on the reasons that prompt the person to supply his labour power on the labour market. The more substantial the price (in terms of loss of capabilities) that the worker would pay for opting out of the labour market, the higher the degree of commodification of his labour. The economic resilience of an individual to an income shock determines the degree of commodification of his labour power. Resilience is a function of asset availability; thus, in a final analysis we can say that the degree of labour commodification depends on the level of asset availability.

Total commodification and total de-commodification of labour are extreme theoretical cases that are very unlikely to appear in concrete forms. They represent the start and end points of a spectrum on which every individual has occupied a specific position throughout the history of humankind. This position expresses a degree of commodification (or de-commodification, depending on which perspective we adopt) and is determined by the individual composition of social income at any given time. The latter can be easily read through an elementary equation presented by Guy Standing:

$$SI = SP + W + CB + EB + SB + PB$$

SI is the social income of the person we are referring to. It is the result of all the following elements. *SP* is self-production, everything that the individual can produce on his own, relying on his physical and intellectual abilities, and on the natural and artificial assets he happens to possess. *W* is the wage, the income the individual gets by selling his labour power. *CB* is the community benefits, coming from the family and the local community (e.g. a grandmother who watches her grandchild while the parents are at work is providing a community benefit; the neighbour who invites me to share his barbeque and his burgers is doing the same). *EB* is the enterprise benefits, those offered by the private enterprise to its employees (e.g. a private company that pays the monthly contribution to the retirement fund of its employee is providing an enterprise benefit). *SB* is the social benefits, meaning all the services (in terms of social services, insurance and other transfers) that the state offers to its citizens (e.g. school, health care, police, libraries, military defence, streets, public transportations, soup kitchens and so on, as well as unemployment benefits, basic income, and similar direct money transfers). Lastly, *PB* is private benefits, meaning all the private sources of income, such as investment gains or private health insurance (Standing 2007, p. 69).[3]

The composition of *SI* indicates 'the degree to which a person is subject to market forces' (Standing 2007, p. 69). Every social and political transformation involves a change in the elements that constitute *SI*. The historical and continuous struggle over its composition reflects the confrontation between economic forces and the needs of a society to survive and reproduce. The central element to look at while measuring the degree of labour power commodification is *W*. When *W* grows in comparison with the other factors that make up *SI*, we are moving towards labour commodification. When *W* decreases in proportion to other factors, we are heading towards de-commodification of labour power (Standing 2007, pp. 69–70).

1.2   KARL MARX ON THE HISTORICAL ORIGINS OF LABOUR COMMODIFICATION

We have seen so far that the level of labour commodification is given by the reasons that lead the individual to enter the labour market. The more instrumental these reasons are, that is to say, the more the individual works just for the purpose of earning a living, the higher her level of labour commodification. At the same time, we can get quite a precise measure of the incidence of the need to secure basic economic capabilities on the individual's decision to perform a job by looking at the composition of her social income. For the more wage-income is predominant over other sources of income, the more

---

[3]   While Morrone and colleagues (2011) talk about assets in relation to vulnerability and resilience to market shocks, Standing is interested in describing the variables of individual well-being (assuming that we equate income with well-being). Accordingly, Standing's equation is a good proxy not simply for understanding the reasons behind labour commodification but also for measuring it.

the individual is compelled by contingencies to commercialise her labour performance. In other words, the fewer assets a person controls, the more she will rely on wage-income for securing her survival. When this happens, the individual is not resilient to social risks and hence she is bound to the job contract as a matter of guaranteeing her basic well-being.

There remains to understand when the job contract became so central for subsistence. Intuitively, we can already say that wage became the dominant variable in determining social income when all the other variables went down. This would imply that at some point a radical social transformation occurred, such that it had evident repercussions on human life. Moreover, it would not be surprising, because as Guy Standing maintains, any social transformation that involves a conflict between economic power and society, interpreted as a community of individuals with the primary need of surviving and reproducing, is mostly a matter of an internal struggle over the composition of social income (Standing 2007, pp. 69–70). Just as intuitively, it is also possible to realise that, from a historical point of view, the commercialisation of most existing labour should be traced back to the advent of the capitalist form of production. But is labour commodification a precondition or a consequence of capitalism? And did the social transformation that determined the mobilisation of labour on the market occur as a spontaneous phenomenon, or was it rather a radical change imposed from on high?

In *Capital*, Karl Marx offers us a first systematic response to these questions. He indicates the commodification of labour power as one of the two fundamental historical elements that are necessary for the capitalist form of production to appear, the second one being the pre-existence of considerable masses of capital concentrated in the hands of a limited class of individuals. This is so because labour power is a sort of magic element in Marx's economic theory. It is the only commodity that at the moment of consumption can generate surplus value, that is, the source of capitalist accumulation, the sap that feeds the modern system of economic production:

> In order to be able to extract value from the consumption of a commodity, our friend, Moneybags, must be so lucky as to find, within the sphere of circulation, in the market, a commodity, whose use-value possesses the peculiar property of being a source of value, whose actual consumption, therefore, is itself an embodiment of labour, and, consequently, a creation of value. (Marx 2013 [1867], p. 113)

If we want to understand why labour possesses this 'peculiar property of being a source of value' we ought to go back to the possible elementary forms of circulation of commodities: the cycle 'commodity–money–commodity' (C–M–C) and the cycle 'money–commodity–money' (M–C–M). In the cycle C–M–C, person A sells the commodity C1 on the market and she receives in exchange from person B the amount of money M, that indicates the value of the commodity. Then person A uses the amount M to buy a new commodity, C2. In this case there is no capital accumulation. The value of C1 is the same as C2. The reason behind this exchange is mere consumption. Therefore, Marx says that those who want to explore the laboratory of capital should keep their eyes on the cycle M–C–M. Here person A uses a given amount of money M1 to buy a commodity C1 from person B. Then she sells C1 to person D and she earns a new amount of money, M2. At first sight, this cycle may seem tautological, or even senseless, because person A enters the cycle with money and comes out of it with the same thing, money. In order to make the cycle worthy, person A should obtain at the end something different from what she put in it at the beginning. M1 and M2 cannot be qualitatively different, but they should differ from the quantitative point of view.

The cycle M–C–M can make sense only if M2 is bigger than M1. This can happen as long as person A uses M1 to buy a commodity that at the moment of consumption is able to generate surplus value (Δ). The equation $M2 = M1 + \Delta$ is the base of capitalism. But what is this commodity that when consumed creates surplus value (Δ)? Marx says that this commodity is labour power (Marx 2013 [1867], pp. 98–113). The latter is bought and sold at its value. Like every other commodity, the value of labour power is given by the working-time necessary for its production. If the labourer has to work six hours in order to produce her daily means of subsistence, six hours of work are the value of her daily labour power. There are two different ways in which the capitalist can get surplus value. The first is by extending the working day beyond the hours that are necessary for the worker to obtain the means for her subsistence, and which coincides with the value of her salary – the surplus value obtained in this way is defined by Marx as 'absolute'. The second is through a reduction in the amount of work required to produce a given commodity, normally obtained through an increase in labour productivity, for example through the use of new technologies – Marx refers in this case to 'relative' surplus value.

The absolute surplus value is determined by the difference between the total number of hours worked by the labourer during a day and the number of working hours she needs to support herself to return to work the next day (which corresponds to her salary, i.e. the number of hours actually paid). To put it simply, if a labourer has a working day of nine hours and she needs to work six hours to get her daily means of subsistence, the absolute surplus value that is extracted from her is three hours. Labour power is a magic commodity, because those who buy it, investing M1, will create a value M2, where M2 > M1 (the higher the rate of surplus value, the wider the difference between M2 and M1) (Marx 2013 [1867], pp. 127–37). The money that the capitalist invests in the labour commodity is what Marx considers as the variable capital (V) and consists, more simply, in the wage he pays. Accordingly, the production of any commodity involves constant capital (C) *plus* variable capital (V), and the latter yields surplus value (Δ) for free. Hence we may say that among the factors of production V + C, the vital element is V, because differently from C it is capable of creating Δ, and Δ is what renders M2 > M1, that is to say, what allows revenues to be higher than costs. Obviously, even without recurring to the labour commodity V, a person might accumulate an indefinite amount of C, so as to greatly exceed the M2 we are considering here, but the point is that without V, C would remain 'dead wealth', in the sense that when placed in the M1–C–M2 cycle, it is unable to create a margin of difference between M1 and M2, no matter how big M1 is (see Marx 1994 [1864], pp. 384–466).

However, the accumulation of capital obtained through the lengthening of the working day has clear limits, and the most insurmountable of all is that after 24 hours the day ends. Therefore, this is where the second strategy pursued by the capitalist comes into play, which is to extract relative surplus value. While keeping the total working hours of the labourer constant and also her pay, the capitalist can reduce the hours that are necessary for the worker to produce each single unit of product by providing her with new technologies that increase her productivity. If the capitalist is the first, or in any case one of the first to dispose of a given new technology, he can continue to sell the product at the same price as his competitors, and in doing so he obtains greater profits than them. However, this is only a temporary advantage, because as the technology spreads, competition between capitalists leads to lower prices. While this makes it impossible for a single capitalist to obtain relative surplus value over the others ad infinitum, it also leads to a general lowering of the prices of those goods that labourers buy through their wages. This means that the labourer needs to work fewer hours in order to be able to buy the goods necessary for her subsistence – which have become cheaper – and therefore the capitalists regain the margin to lower wages, or even to keep them constant in the face of continuous marginal increases in their profits (Harvey 2010, pp. 163–88; Marx 2013 [1867], pp. 215–22). Either in its short-term or in its more structural form, the capitalist's obtaining of relative surplus value implies, in Marx's view, the exploitation of salaried workers (exactly as in the case of the extraction of absolute surplus value), as these latter get less than the value they produce.

The ratio Δ/V gives us the rate of Marxist exploitation, for it indicates how much surplus value (either absolute or relative) the capitalist obtains for each hour paid to the worker, and the more value the employer obtains vis-à-vis paid hours, the more the employee will be exploited (see Zwolinski and Wertheimer 2017). As rightly emphasised by David Harvey (2010, p. 131), the rate of exploitation should not be confused with the rate of profit, which is given by $\Delta/(C + V)$ and indicates how much the employer receives in return for all the forms of capital invested. Three points are important to highlight. The first one is that the rate of exploitation is always higher than the rate of profit, but it is in the former that we find the real measure of individual unfreedom. Notwithstanding that, as stressed by Harvey (2010, pp. 131–4), capitalists usually prefer to point to the rate of profit to demonstrate that if we also take into consideration constant capital, the marginal value they obtain from the production of any single commodity (or the provision of any single service) is not so high, while in reality it is the rate of exploitation that we should consider for assessing the benefits they obtain to the detriment of employees, in virtue of the unequal distribution of the means of production.

The second point is that the rate of exploitation is not directly proportional to the rate of profit; hence, it may happen that an employer subjects an employee to heavy exploitation, in a Marxist sense, while earning little money (Harvey 2010, p. 131). Let us simply consider a case in which an employer uses, in proportion, large quantities of constant capital and obtains a high rate of surplus value from the small variable capital he buys. Let us also imagine that the market price of the final product he commercialises slightly exceeds the total costs of production (C + V). In this situation, there is a very high rate of exploitation leading to a modest rate of profit. Yet, also the opposite may occur, namely that an employer earns enormous profits while imposing a low rate of exploitation of his employees. This is not an atypical case in the contemporary economy; suffice it to think of some of the giants of the techno-logical sectors, which remunerate more than adequately their staff and record high rates of satisfaction on their part. Some might say that these companies profit from the existence of market distortions, as for example operating in monopolistic or semi-monopolistic sectors, or commercialising private data collected from their users without paying for the appropriation of what is in effect a means of production, but these contingencies are not directly related to the exploitation of the labour force. Obviously, any sort of generalisation would be misleading, because there are other companies that combine the use of sophisticated technologies with an almost nineteenth-century exploitation of workers.

The third point is one that Marx does not deal with directly, but that David Harvey (2010, p. 170) has the merit to underline. Within Marx's theory of surplus value, cases can occur in which the increase of the exploitation perpe-trated through the obtaining of relative surplus value goes hand in hand with an improvement in the living conditions of workers. This happens, for example, when technology lowers the price of certain consumer goods to such an extent that labourers may find themselves in the condition of being able to do things that were previously inaccessible, because they were too expensive, without this being accompanied by an increase in their wages (think, for example, of air travel, computers, sophisticated mobile phones).

Both Marx's labour theory of value and the theory of exploitation have been criticised throughout the last two centuries. More specifically, some authors have pointed to the fact that given the empirical unprovenness of the former, we cannot defend the theoretical arguments of the latter. The problems with the labour theory of value can be divided, as correctly emphasised by Jonathan Wolff (2002, pp. 113–18), into two main categories. The first one pertains to those cases in which the value of an object is obtained without labour, or to be more precise, when its value is enormously higher than the labour it incorporates. Some examples can be found in contemporary art, which in many instances directs barbs at the market mechanism and tends to emphasise the logic of determining value creation. One recent example is '*Comedian*', the artwork created by Maurizio Cattelan at Art Basel Miami Beach 2019. Cattelan bought a banana at the Miami fruit market for 30 cents, taped it to a museum wall with grey adhesive tape and immediately after the opening it was valued at $120,000 (Farago 2019). It is obviously very problematic to explain, in terms of working hours, the value acquisition that this banana underwent. Similar examples can be found in those commodities that are simply found and picked up in nature, such as truffles, or in the world of collecting, in vintage wines, and so forth. It might be objected that these are borderline cases that cannot be taken to counterfeit an entire theory, so here we come to the second category of problems encountered by the labour theory of value, namely production with a high rate of technological components. Consider, for example, the great profits that can be generated today by creating a simple software program and marketing it in the form of 'apps'. Honestly speaking, it is very difficult to analyse this instance of value creation by looking at labour embodied in the software or in its advertising or its selling – at least exclusively. And the same discourse holds true for economically gigantic enterprises such as Facebook, Google or WhatsApp.

This does not necessarily entail that the labour theory of value is always wrong, but rather that we cannot take labour to be the only productive factor from which employers can extract surplus value and hence determine capital accumulation. Accordingly, even in the advanced stage of capitalism we are experiencing today, for many people surplus value is extracted from their labour performance, not only in developing but also in developed countries. It suffices to consider the world of precarious work, of the gig economy and even more emblematically of the interns who are asked to work for free in order to strengthen their CVs. In short, many workers, especially young workers, are paid less than the value they give back to their employers (or are requested to work undeclared more hours than is required by the employment contract), and this surplus value extracted by labour contributes in a substantial way to the accumulation of capital by employers. Therefore, a more realistic way of looking at labour is as one of the commodities that if inserted in the cycle

M1–C–M2 can determine a difference in value between M2 and M1, such that M2 > M1. John Roemer (1985, pp. 36–8) gives the example of oil. It takes less than a barrel of oil to produce another barrel of oil; hence, if we replace a labour theory of value with something like an oil theory of value, we may say that those who control capital and have access to oil, or to commodities that have been realised – at least in part – through oil, we can explain the process of capital accumulation in terms of the difference between the oil that is introduced into the production process and the percentage of value that can be traced back to the oil that is contained in the final product.

Some authors have defended, somehow reformulating, Marx's theory of exploitation, seeking to disentangle it from the labour theory of value. In particular, G.A. Cohen (1988, pp. 209–38; see also Vrousalis 2014) has argued that an employer can be said to exploit an employee, from a Marxist perspective, as long as the employer appropriates a percentage of the value enshrined in the products that have been realised by workers, regardless of whether it was labour or any other thing to transfer value into these products – hence the employee is paid less than what he produces. Yet, the normative problem encountered by Cohen consists in explaining what is wrong about the fact that the employer appropriates part of the value of the final product, given that he provides the means of production, bears the investment risks and pays a wage to the employee. Cohen has no other choice but to challenge 'the private ownership of the means of production' as 'morally illegitimate' (Cohen 1988, p. 235). Further, in order to do so, he has to rely on some moral premises concerning justice in distribution, which end up being free-standing – or, in other words, Cohen seems to propose a moral condemnation of exploitation that is based on the prior adoption of distributive principles, thus turning away from Marx, for whom the exploitation of workers is the direct consequence of an incontrovertible (at least in his view) empirical fact, namely their violent expulsion from common goods and the accumulation of small properties in the hands of a few capitalists. Another notable attempt to rescue the notion of Marxist exploitation from the quicksand of the empirical validity of the labour theory of value is that of Roemer (1982, 1985, 2017). He has maintained that the problem with Marxist exploitation is not a matter of asymmetrical interactions between employers and employees at the point of production, but rather it is an issue that is resolved in the exclusion of employees from the means of production. I shall deal in more detail with Roemer's theory in Chapter 2, where I explain how the account of exploitation without interactional domination differs from the one proposed by Roemer. What I can say here is that the limit of Roemer's argument is the same as for Cohen, that is to say, he explains the injustice inherent in the unequal distribution of the means of production in terms of a positive account of justice.[4] This explains why in his recent works he has maintained that his 'task has been to propose a revision of socialism's ethical goal, away from the elimination of (Marxian) exploitation, toward the achievement of distributive justice conceived as comprehensive equality of opportunity, plus cooperation achieved through an ethos of solidarity' (Roemer 2017, p. 309).

In any case, what is important for me to stress at this point is that the normative argument that I want to construct and that will lead me to defend a minimum de-commodification of labour power is independent from both Marx's labour theory of value and theory of exploitation. In Marx's view, the commodification of labour is a necessary condition for the establishment of the capitalist mode of production, for capitalism presupposes capitalist accumulation, which presupposes surplus value, which presupposes labour to be sold as a commodity, which presupposes the capitalist division of the means of production. Accordingly, Marx's chain of causality moves the other way around, and it might be summarised as follows:

1. The unequal distribution of the means of production leads to labour commodification;
2. Labour commodification allows for the extraction of surplus value;
3. Surplus value is the architrave of capitalist accumulation;
4. Capitalist accumulation keeps in place the capitalist mode of production.

Marx's normative concern, in which he glimpses the origin of exploitation and oppression of workers, lies in the shift from step 1 to step 2. On the other hand, steps 3 and 4 are necessary for Marx to present his normative argument as an intrinsic criticism of capitalism, because if capitalists could do without extracting surplus value, at least theoretically, then it would be possible to think of an alternative and just form of capitalism, without any need to recourse to the socialist revolution. The complexity of Marx's argument is also the reason for its fragility, or more precisely it is the reason why many over the years have questioned its validity. As we have seen above, Cohen has sought to disengage Marx's criticism of capitalism from the difficult empirical premise of the labour theory of value, by replacing the concept of surplus value with the one of appropriating part of someone's else labour. Conversely, Roemer sought to construct a Marxist criticism of capitalism out of step 1 only, but in doing this

---

[4]   The difference between Cohen and Roemer is that, although both reject the idea that the normative problem of exploitation consists – solely – in the appropriation of surplus value and both seek to rescue Marxism by appealing to a positive account of distributive justice, Cohen still insists on a normative critique of the interactions that occur at the point of production, while Roemer relegates the latter to secondary issues.

he had to commit his argument to distributive normative premises that cannot be self-justified.

My argument is that we can – and should – elaborate a convincing critique of capitalism by focusing on step 1 only, and independently from any distributive normative premise, relying on the normative ideal of freedom from domination – in other words, we may say through a negative rather than positive treatment of step 1. This can be done by integrating step 1 with step 2.2 (below), instead of steps 2, 3 and 4.

1.   The unequal distribution of the means of production leads to labour commodification;

2.2   Labour commodification amounts to structural domination.

Accordingly, I shall maintain, in the course of this book, that it is exactly in the process of labour commodification that we can and should find the source of proletarian unfreedom, while everything legal that goes on between a free individual and a non-free individual (in a capitalist sense) is only an interactional derivation of the systemic problem. The advantage of this approach is that it represents a credible method for criticising capitalism even in those situations where there is no extraction of surplus value and regardless of which commodity adds value to the production process. Moreover, as we shall see in more detail later on, by maintaining that the unequal distribution of the means of production is a normative problem per se, for reasons pertaining to individual autonomy, I shall seek to provide a solid explanation (or at least so I hope) as to why asymmetries of power at the point of production, leading to unequal exchanges between employers and employees, are a normative problem from a non-moralised perspective, that is to say independently of any prior acceptance of the equal distribution of resources as the right starting point. More precisely, I shall argue that inequality is bad because it leads to unfreedom, not because people have a natural right to a given share of natural resources, or because the current distribution of private property deviates from what would be chosen in a moralised session of the social contract, or because sufficiency is good in itself, and so forth.

Therefore, I shall now concentrate my brief analysis on the two components of step 1, namely how workers came to be commodified and how capitalists came to control enough wealth to invest in the labour commodity. As we shall see, the two phenomena are strictly interrelated and call into question the concept of 'primitive accumulation' for explaining why workers shifted from pre-capitalist to capitalist forms of subordination – in other words, why capitalists managed to take the place of feudal lords. Lastly, I shall explain how my critique relates to another Marxist argument that it is possible to raise about labour commodification and that we might summarise in a sort of step 2.3:

1. The unequal distribution of the means of production leads to labour commodification;
2.2 Labour commodification amounts to structural domination;
2.3 Labour commodification leads to alienation – and hence it is bad.[5]

For Marx (2013 [1867], p. 114) the precondition to the transformation of human activities into commodities (hence, to the triggering of the capitalist form of production) is the worker being 'free in the double sense'. First, he ought to exercise full self-ownership over his body, his intellectual abilities and the activities he can perform through them (see also Christman 1991). Second, he ought not to possess any other commodity for sale, except his labour power. The first freedom is granted to everyone – usually at attainment of the age of majority – in almost every contemporary society, with the exclusion of some residues of old forms of slavery. Generally speaking, we might say that before the individual limits his ownership of his own labour power through job contracts that demand some form of exclusivity,[6] he has an unencumbered title over it. On the other hand, the second freedom is complete only when the aggregate value of social income is given by wage-money alone – in other words, when the value of any of the other components (self-production, community benefits, enterprise benefits, social benefits and private benefits) is higher than zero, the second liberty of the worker is less than complete. And this explains why complete commodification and complete de-commodification are the extreme poles of a large spectrum that encompasses infinite intermediate positions.

Sylvia, for example, the worker of the hypothetical case we were considering before, is free to dispose of her labour performance and she is also free from the possession of productive assets and of other market-independent sources of income. Paradoxically, the first freedom, which defines the difference of status with a slave, is also the one that determines her extreme

---

[5]   The three versions of step 2 are not necessarily mutually exclusive, but each of them leads to a different critique of capitalism. Step 2 leads to the Marxian critique based on the labour theory of value and the theory of exploitation (and, as we have seen, it can also be adjusted in the way suggested by Cohen 1988). Step 2.2 leads to the domination-based critique that I focus on in this book. Step 2.3 leads to an ethical critique of capitalism that is centred on alienation.

[6]   For example, a person employed in the public sector may be obliged by contract to refrain from the provision of any other work activities in favour of private companies. Or a professional football player may be prevented from selling his image for the advertisement of a company that is a competitor of his own sponsor.

subjection to the market. While the slave is also a proletarian, his bond with the master does also tie him to the means of production of the latter. With this I do not mean that the situation of the slave is less tragic than the one of Sylvia, nor that the slave is less exploited – quite the opposite, for the master can do violence to the slave, dismiss him at any time and also put an end to his life. Yet as long as the master is interested in profiting from his services, the slave is able to conduct a market-independent existence. He is not constantly forced to look for someone who will hire his labour performance, because he can rely on the productive assets of his master. Obviously, the life of the slave is no less precarious than Sylvia's, but while the former is dependent on the will of another individual, because of an asymmetry of power legitimised by existing social norms, the latter is dependent – also – on market interactions. Moreover, in pre-capitalist societies individuals could usually count on social securities that did not depend on the market, as for example family or other social bonds (even the master/slave nexus), to react to economic downturns, such as those caused by natural disasters, trouble in production, and so on (Crouch 2013, pp. 63–4). On the other hand, if we compare Sylvia's situation with the one of her colleague (who owns a field and a few cattle), we can notice that both are completely free in the first sense indicated by Marx, but the colleague is less free in the second sense – because she owns some private assets – and this renders her less commodified than Sylvia. The same happens with the worker who is a pure proletarian like Sylvia, but unlike her lives in a country with a sound welfare system, for even though this person is experiencing Marx's second freedom, state provisions do partially compensate for the lack of private assets by assuring him of some market-independent well-being. Thus, he is also less commodified than Sylvia.

The interesting question to ask, reading Marx, is: how did it occur that after pre-capitalist social asymmetries – stemming from aristocratic heritages, religious privileges and so on – had been levelled out, new social asymmetries emerged from the market logic, such that new relations of domination took the place of old ones? Marx's response is through 'merciless vandalism' (Marx 2013 [1867], p. 534). As soon as workers obtained an unencumbered title over their work performance, they prepared to become individual property owners. Had the social evolution that emerged from the dissolution of feudalism been limited to this first step, a society of small and divided property owners would have emerged. Nonetheless, Marx holds that this form of production is unmaintainable in the medium run. A myriad of small property owners prevents any form of cooperation or division of labour, and function as a barrier against the 'free development of the social productive powers' (Marx 2013 [1867], p. 533). Therefore, at a certain point the creative and productive forces within society start to swell, and the walls of the social system prove to be too oppressive. These new forces need a new division of natural goods, one in which individual labourers begin to work beyond their individual property (see Marx and Engels 1988 [1844], pp. 208–22).

The attainment by workers of the second freedom occurs through a form of 'accumulation', that is to say, the concentration of large masses of capital in the hands of a restricted social class. The latter, Marx (2013 [1867], p. 501) says, 'plays in Political Economy about the same part as original sin in theology'. The legend goes that a long time ago there were two different groups of people, those talented, diligent and hard-working, and those lazy and spendthrift. The former accumulated considerable amounts of money at the expense of the latter. These diverging attitudes, prolonged for years, created the two social classes that, once well defined, allowed capitalism to flourish: the owners of capital and the free workers. Marx provides a detailed historical analysis with the purpose of unmasking the myth of political economy. He wanted to demonstrate that it was state-backed violence, rather than laziness and productivity, which was the key element in explaining the existence of labour as a commodity:

> Hence, the historical movement which changes the producers into wage-workers, appears, on the one hand, as their emancipation from serfdom and from the fetters of the guilds, and this side alone exists for our bourgeois historians. But, on the other hand, these new freedmen became sellers of themselves only after they had been robbed of all their own means of production, and of all the guarantees of existence afforded by the old feudal arrangements. And the history of this, their expropriation, is written in the annals of mankind in letters of blood and fire. (Marx 2013 [1867], p. 503)

One of the points mostly emphasised by Marx is that these 'letters of blood and fire' were written through laws promulgated by the state. The laws were the main instruments employed to separate the workers from their means of production. The enclosures of the common land that occurred in England is the classic example. From the thirteenth century on, the feudal land law guaranteed that only lords, recognised as such by the king, could claim a property right over their estates. The remainder of the land was held in common (Wily 2012). The existence of common land prevented both the workers from achieving Marx's second freedom and a large amount of natural resources from becoming productive capital. Starting from 1730, the English Parliament began to pass laws that dispossessed commoners of the land. The process was subsequently sped up by the adoption of the General Enclosure Acts of 1836, 1840 and 1845 (M. Turner 1990). A good schematisation of the so-called 'enclosure movement' that lies at the basis of Marx's analysis of capitalism has been given by William Lazonick (1974). While the feudal social system was at its peak in England, between the twelfth and thirteenth centuries, there was an open-field system, in which almost every peasant cultivated a piece of land, thus being guaranteed subsistence, while another part of common fields was controlled by feudal lords who relied on serf labour. Already from this historical moment and increasingly from the fifteenth century, when slavery was abolished, smallholders exchanged pieces of common land among them and started consolidating their property rights. A second step towards the privatisation of the means of production took place when landlords autonomously turned arable land into pastures and negotiated enclosure agreements. The third step consisted in the British Parliament adopting, as noted above, national legislation to further speed up and enforce the acquisition by landlords of enclosed land (Lazonick 1974, p. 14).

In Marx's view, the state actively supports the dispossession of property from small owners because it envisions in this social process the only feasible way to obtain economic development (Roberts 2017, pp. 2–3). Accordingly, the capital that can be used to buy the labour commodity is not simply held by its owner; rather, it becomes a productive economic entity through the extraction of surplus labour. What has been discussed over the years is whether Marx was right in considering primitive accumulation as a historical event, as the dividing line between capitalism and pre-capitalist societies. Rosa Luxemburg (2003 [1913]), for example, has contested that capitalism continuously needs to invade non-capitalist societies, both as an outlet for its products and as basins from where to take wage labour and natural resources. While contemporary authors have emphasised that global capitalism determines the same forms of dispossession that Marx attributes to modern capitalism, for example in terms of land grabbing and privatisation of the commons, primitive accumulation should not be simply seen as the point of departure of capitalism, but rather as one of the features that define its functioning (Federici 2004; Harvey 2004; Nichols 2015). In Chapter 3, discussing the reasons why the responsibility for MDL should be global, I endorse this view, mainly relying on the recent work by Saskia Sassen (2014) on expulsions.

The problem with taking only this part of Marx's argument and renouncing his step 2 – namely his theory of exploitation – is that we take on the not-so-easy burden of proving that there continues to be something normatively wrong in capitalism even today. And we cannot rely on primitive accumulation alone for doing this, for three main reasons. First, the injustice suffered by the first proletarians may happen to be superseded today for all those people who get a reasonable wage-income (Waldron 1992). Second, even though we maintain that capitalism proceeds through dispossession (Harvey 2004), we have a normative argument that works well in some developing contexts and less well within developed societies. Third, not all capitalists accumulate their wealth through 'merciless vandalism'. Thus, my objective in the following chapters shall consist in justifying step 2.2, by elaborating an autonomy-based critique of the condition of labour commodification that can abstract from its contingencies – namely that applies to every proletarian, regardless of the specific facts that led her to become or to be born a proletarian. However, before pursuing this objective, I consider it important to briefly expound the other normative claim that it is possible to make, independently from the labour theory of value and from moral premises based on claims of distributive justice, step 2.3: labour commodification entails alienation – hence it is ethically wrong.

As many know, in the section on 'estranged labour' of the Economic and Philosophic Manuscripts of 1844, the young Marx envisages basically four forms of alienation of labour: the alienation of the worker from the product of labour, the alienation of the worker from the act of production, the alienation of man from his species being, and the alienation of man from man.[7] Within a capitalist society, Marx argues, the human being is estranged from the object of his work, which does not belong to him – thus, the more commitment and dedication the worker puts in to the realisation of the manufacturing process, the more he takes away from his person in terms of effort and life force. Moreover, the worker is compelled to invest his time and energy in an activity that 'neither depends on nor belongs to him' (Marx 1988 [1844], p. 75), and in doing this he does not unleash his creative and vital energies, nor does he act to fulfil his personal needs (as, for example, when you raise a cow to drink milk or you cook to eat a dish you crave), but instead he submits himself to labour tasks that are meaningless to him and are only instrumental to the fulfilment of his needs. Third, when the human being carries out transformative actions on the natural world, he objectifies his species life. Therefore, if you deprive the human being of the object of his labour, you are also tearing him away from his species life, and every free and spontaneous activity is turned into a means to satisfy biological needs – that is to say, a means to get a source of income necessary for his animal existence (Marx 1988 [1844], p. 77). Lastly, as a consequence of the previous three forms of alienation, the human being is also estranged from other human beings. The estranged worker ceases to look from a human perspective at the others with whom he enters into relation; rather, he wears the lens of the market nexus and considers others as mere workers or consumers (Marx 1988 [1844], p. 79).

From these arguments briefly outlined by Marx before the writing of *Capital*, it is possible to develop an ethical critique of capitalism, arguing that labour commodification is bad in itself, regardless of steps 2–4, because it determines a serious and unprecedented alteration of the human way of life, such that it suffices to raise a normative claim in itself. The first thing to point out in this

---

[7]   It is also worth looking at Marx's earlier reflections on money as 'alien mediator' and on the transformation of labour into 'labour to earn a living', as presented in his 'Excerpts from James Mill's Elements of Political Economy' (Marx 1975 [1844]).

regard is that, as I tried to suggest earlier, labour commodification and alienation are not directly proportional – previously I referred more generically to the pleasantness of the work activity, but the discourse can easily be extended to the more comprehensive concept of alienation. Accordingly, it is theoretically possible for someone to shift from a less to a more commodified condition while passing to a less alienating job. I made the case of Sylvia, who lost her job in the factory and started painting canvases. She experiences a higher level of commodification – for the reasons discussed in previous paragraphs – while performing a creative job in which she freely expresses her personality and enriches her artistic self. Obviously, this was just a theoretical case aimed at showing that labour commodification, on the one hand, and the harshness and alienation of the job, on the other, are conceptually different. But it would not be impossible to find other examples. Think of writers who are not best-selling authors and have no other way to scrape a living than to rush to publish the next novel. They are surely more commodified than a well-known notary, but in comparison with him they have the chance of performing a less alienating job, because in their works they can express their world view, leave room for imagination and say what they really want to say.

The second important thing is that claims 2.2 and 2.3 can be held together without incurring any contradiction. Besides, I am firmly convinced of the opportunity of pursuing the furrow of alienation traced by the young Marx to analyse what Jaeggi (2014, p. 15) has recently defined, in relation to Marx's view of alienation, as 'the problem of no longer having at one's command something that was once, and ought still to be, at our command (because it results from our own activity)'. That is why I would endorse the ethical challenge of regaining control over the estranged object, namely labour activities.[8] Nonetheless, in the rest of this book I shall set aside the theme of alienation and the ethical critique that comes with it, because I wish to develop a moral and political critique based on the phenomenon of labour commodification described by Marx as one of the fundamental preconditions of the capitalist mode of production.

---

[8]   For a historical reconstruction of the use that later authors made of the concept of alienation, also before the appearance of the *Economic and Philosophic Manuscripts of 1844* (which occurred only in 1932), see Honneth 2008; Musto 2010; Jaeggi 2014, pp. 3–50.

1.3 KARL POLANYI AND FICTITIOUS COMMODITIES

Labour commodification leads to domination and alienation, and Marx was one of the first thinkers to analyse these three phenomena together, in a comprehensive way. There is, however, a last question that we should ask to conclude this brief discussion on labour as a commodity. How far can the process of labour commodification be led? In other words, how close can a society get to the pole of complete commodification, the situation in which there is no longer any difference in the way we treat workers and non-human commodities? For even though the majority of people living in the countries that were the first to experience the Industrial Revolution are nowadays quite safe from falling back to the trials and tribulations of the nineteenth century economy, this question about the elasticity of the commodification process is still fundamental for understanding the situation of people living in developing countries, and the forms of exploitation to which they might be exposed.

An influential answer was offered by Karl Polanyi (2001 [1944]) in the mid-twentieth century. His great contribution to economic sociology is based on three notions that are deeply interlinked: fictitious commodities, embeddedness and the double movement. Furthermore, the debate on globalisation that emerged between the end of the last century and the first decades of the current one has renewed interest in his 'magnum opus', *The Great Transformation* (Stiglitz 2001; Fraser 2014, 2017). The centrepiece of Polanyi's argument is that the advent of the capitalist economy in the nineteenth century goes along with an attempt to disembed the economic system from social relations. This attempt is not the result of the autonomous forces that operate in the self-regulating market, as classic economists want us to believe, but rather it is the product of 'artificial stimulants' that are administered to the society in the form of legislation and administrative regulations (Polanyi 2001 [1944], p. 60). The process of disembeddedness is doomed to fail, or at least to remain incomplete, because even though it seeks to subject all the essential elements of production to the market mechanism, and it gets its strength in doing this, there exist three objects that cannot be transformed into real commodities: land, labour and money. The latter are the so-called 'fictitious commodities', and the fact that they can never be transformed into real commodities, without paying the price of annihilating whole societies, determines the double movement; that is, the struggle between self-regulating markets seeking to get completely disembedded from society, on the one hand, and human beings opposing the completion of this process for reasons linked to mere survival, on the other. This is in brief the description of the effects of the great transformation. But let's go more slowly, trying to analyse every step separately.

Economy has always existed. Every society needs to rely on an economy of some sort for survival. The same discourse holds true for the market that Polanyi (2001 [1944], p. 59) defines as 'a meeting place for the purpose of barter, or buying and selling'. But the point is that before the advent of the capitalist form of production, in the nineteenth century, the market's role 'was no more than incidental to economic life' (Polanyi 2001 [1944], p. 45). In order to better understand Polanyi's argument, it is useful to follow the distinction made by Charles E. Lindblom (2001) between the market and the market system. The former consists of the exchanges between commodities and/or services that can either be mediated through money (be it currency or financial products) or based on the bilateral transfer of commodities and/or services. The market pre-exists capitalism and goes even further, in the sense that also within socialist societies commodities and services are exchanged. On the other hand, a market system is a social system in which coordination is pre-eminently obtained through market interactions, rather than through other social factors or central planning. In this sense, a market system also presupposes the existence and the interconnection of a series of markets (Lindblom 2001, pp. 4–15). Accordingly, consider the case in which you offer me ten coins for cleaning your garden. This is a market. Yet, if you come to own your garden in virtue of your aristocratic status and I find myself excluded from controlling productive assets because of my lower social status, the market that occurs between me and you is not part of a market system, but perhaps it is an appendix of a feudal system. It might also happen that our respective social positions are the result of decisions taken by a central authority. Imagine that this authority decided that in spite of the different abilities that we can commercialise, we are both entitled to live in two identical houses with equal gardens, yet you value free time more than I do, and I value having some extra money to buy chocolate more than you do; hence, you decide to buy my gardening performance and I accept to sell it. Here our market is more likely to be part of a socialist system, rather than a market system. Lastly, imagine that as in the first hypothesis you own a garden because of your higher social position and I accept to clean it because of my lower position, but both our social positions are consequences of the different results that we have achieved in the single markets in which we have engaged and are still engaged – e.g. job markets, financial markets, commodity trading, and so on. In this case, our gardening market is part of a market system; that is to say, a social system in which our activities are shaped by the market mechanism, which we can simplify in the logic of supply and demand.

Obviously, not all market systems are equivalent. In different market systems there can be more or less unequal starting positions, more or less obstacles to the smooth functioning of the market logic – e.g. asymmetries of information, monopolies. However, the point that Polanyi seeks to emphasise is that in a market society everything is produced for sale, including labour, land and money, which become commodities. Their prices become commodity prices, respectively: wage, rent and interest. The market system seeks to bend to the market logic everything that previously belonged to the compact social sphere, or in other words it aims to ensure that no interference occurs with its self-regulation. 'Nothing must be allowed to inhibit the formation of markets, nor must incomes be permitted to be formed otherwise than through sales' (Polanyi 2001 [1944], p. 72). This is something new in the history of humanity, because before the consolidation of market society, the economy was 'embedded' in social relations. Politics, religion and social relations have always controlled the economy, determining the wealth of individuals and the way land, and natural resources in general, were to be managed and distributed (Block 2001, pp. xxiii–xxiv). The economy was subordinated to the rules of society, which were shaped at a superior level. Accordingly, once the economy begins to emerge from society, the latter, conceived so far as a solid sphere dominated by non-economic rules, splits into two separate spheres: the political sphere and the economic sphere.

Yet, the economic sphere that has just been released cannot survive detached from the political sphere – it needs to extend its dominion to the same social relations in which it was embedded before, and to the natural environment that surrounds them. If in pre-capitalist societies the economic system was embedded in social relations; in capitalist societies social relations are embedded in the economic system (Polanyi 2001 [1944], p. 60). The main consequence of this movement is the creation of a market for labour and for nature – that is to say, the commodification of labour and land. Polanyi engages in a detailed historical analysis of labour commodification. He writes that before the last decade of the eighteenth century the commercialisation of wage labour was so far from the political horizon that it had not even been discussed, either in France or in England. A real labour market emerged for the first time in England after the approval of the Reform Bill of 1832 and the Poor Law Amendment of 1834 that Polanyi (2001 [1944], p. 84) sees as the starting point of modern capitalism, in which labour is commodified, and the political attempts of de-commodification that characterised embryonic capitalism have been abandoned, and all remnants of paternalism have been swept away.

More precisely, from the Industrial Revolution until the 1830s, the commodification of labour was prevented in a first phase by the Act for the Relief of the Poor of 1601 (also known as the 'Elizabethan Poor Law'), successively amended by the Poor Relief Act of 1662 (also known as the Act of Settlement of 1662), and in a second phase by the Speenhamland Law of 1795. The Poor Law(s) reacted to the dissolution of the old medieval structures and the decline of monastery institutions, which previously took charge of the poor, by introducing a local administrative system whereby each parish had to protect those who were unable to work, the aged, the children and the 'impotent' poor, and to provide the means for work to the able-bodied who could not get into the productive process on their own, and it was funded through poor rates that were collected at the parish level (see also The Workhouse n.d.). According to Polanyi's historical reconstruction (2001 [1944], pp. 81–9), as soon as this system 'was loosened' in 1795, and hence a truly competitive labour market could have been established, the justices of Berkshire met in Speenhamland, at Pelican Inn, and decided to introduce subsidies in aid of wages, whose value was not fixed, but rather linked to the fluctuation of the price of bread. This practice of economic relief became law in most of England, and it was named the 'Speenhamland system', after the place in which it was adopted. In some way, the justices of Berkshire reacted both to the social distress caused by the loosening of Poor Law(s), as indicated by Polanyi, and to an increase in the price of bread caused by bad harvests, by setting up an economic threshold below which no labourer would have been let fall – and in this way they addressed those who were suffering from limited purchasing power even though they did not fall into the categories protected by the Poor Law(s).

From a historical point of view, the Speenhamland law was a backward-looking measure that attempted to resist the commodification of labour in a specific moment in which political power had wiped out the old paternalistic forms of social protection. Here we do not have time to delve into the specificities of this measure. But it may suffice to note that while Polanyi was critical of these magistrates' attempts to contain the advance of the market principle, because in his view it ended up driving down both wages and the productivity of labour, a recent study conducted by Fred Block and Margaret Somers (2003) has challenged the findings of the Royal Commission Report of 1834, the investigation that decreed the failure of subsidies in aid of wages and paved the way for the adoption of the New Poor Law a few months later, which somehow deceived Polanyi himself because of its ideological preset. In essence, the two scholars demonstrate that far from being a curse for the working class, the Speenhamland system functioned as a positive buffer against three negative trends: the growth of industrial production in the north of England with the relative decline in the south and in the east, fewer job opportunities in the farming sector, and the enclosures (Block and Somers 2003, pp. 300–308).

In any case, what is important for us to highlight here is that the abolishment of the Speenhamland system in 1834 represents the culmination of complicity between political power and the natural forces driving the disembedding process. As soon as aid-to-wage was put aside, the new economic sphere, driven by the market principle, and recently disembedded from the society sphere, came to dominate the last stronghold of society, labour. This point is particularly important because it allows Polanyi to demonstrate that the rise of market society[9] is based on a theoretical misconception of labour, land and money, for liberal capitalism seeks to disembed them from social relations and to subordinate them to the market principle – that is to say, to transform them into commodities. Nonetheless, differently from what happened with all the other elements of production, the commodification of labour, land and money cannot but be 'fictitious', because they are not created to become commodities. Polanyi defines a commodity as something that is created to be bought and sold on the market, and for him it is clear that 'the postulate that anything that is bought and sold must have been produced for sale is emphatically untrue in regard to [labour, land and money]' (Polanyi 2001 [1944], pp. 75–6), as labour is a human activity that cannot be detached from life itself, land is nature, and money is just 'a token of purchasing power'. I will leave aside money, because the reasons of its being a fictitious commodity are different from land and labour. Commodity money represents a threat to entrepreneurs and investors when prices fall because of the self-regulatory mechanism of the money market (Polanyi 2001 [1944], pp. 201–9). On the other hand, the commodification of land can be easily overlaid with the enclosures that occurred in England and that, as we have seen before, Marx links to the phenomenon of the primitive accumulation (Polanyi 2001 [1944], pp. 187–200). Thus, I shall focus, instead, on the commodification of labour.

If we look at labour from the Polanyian perspective of fictitious commodities, we can infer from it three different normative problems, which are all present, albeit with different levels of articulation, in Polanyi's work: one is moral and political and has to do with freedom, one is ethical and consists in a process of 'dehumanisation' (Özel 1997, p. 20), and one can be defined as functional and goes along with Polanyi's notion of the double movement. My particular interest is in the first problem, although I do not deny the relevance of the second one. With regard to the third, which I will outline in this chapter, I shall express reservations in Chapter 2 about its current relevance in a global context, and if my reservations are right, this should make the first problem even more serious.

The common premise of the three problems is that the attempt of the economic sphere to impose its regulating principle, the market principle, to land and labour is utopian, and at the same time it risks being highly destructive, because transforming human society into an appendage of the economic system means to make it vulnerable to the side effects of the adjustment between demand and supply. The price of this evolution is a dangerous social

---

9   For Polanyi (2001 [1944], p. 74) the two elements are indivisible: 'Such an institutional pattern could not have functioned unless society was somehow subordinated to its requirements. A market economy can exist only in a market society.'

dislocation (Polanyi 2001 [1944], pp. 171–86). As Gøsta Esping-Andersen (1990, p. 37) has rightly pointed out: 'Workers are not commodities like others because they must survive and reproduce themselves and the society they live in. It is possible to withhold washing-machines from the market until the price is agreeable; but labour is unable to withhold itself for long without recourse to alternative means of subsistence.'

The moral and political question that permeates Polanyi's works is whether the individual can be free within a society in which land, labour and money have been subjected to market rules. Polanyi's answer is negative (see also Buğra 2007, p. 185), and I think that the best explanation of this has been given by Esping-Andersen (1990, p. 37), when he defined the condition of the commodified worker as 'freedom behind prison walls'. This is an expression that not only synthesises well Polanyi's thought, but it also reflects the situation of the majority of human beings within a market society, because it combines two concepts that seem to be antithetical: freedom and prison.

The passing of the feudal system largely increases social mobility. When power and wealth were the prerogatives of a restricted class of people, in virtue of aristocratic origin, divine election and so forth, workers were relatively more protected from market fluctuations, but at the same time the social ladder was almost deadlocked. Thus, we may agree with Nancy Fraser (2014) when she emphasises that the transformation of labour into a commodity liberated oppressed social groups from subjection and allowed them to relate with others on a more equal basis, and the clear examples are women and slaves. At the same time, by submitting the organisation of society to the sole rule of the market principle, the newly disembedded economic sphere removed the formal ceiling that kept the lower classes from ascending to the higher steps of the social ladder, and in this sense, labour commodification and the conquests of the market principle in the field of society represent a source of freedom. Yet, the criticism that Marx first, and Polanyi and Esping-Andersen later, level against this freedom is that it is experienced in prison. If, on the one hand, the worker becomes the full owner of herself and of her labour, on the other hand her survival is no longer guaranteed a priori, but it becomes completely dependent on wage-income. Accordingly, the labour market functions as a prison from which the worker cannot escape unless at the price of her survival. Obviously, this prison can be a golden cage for some people, even for the majority of them, in comparison with previous social forms of organisation, but it remains a prison.

The ethical problem with labour commodification consists, instead, for Polanyi in what Hüseyin Özel (1997, p. 20) has defined as a process of 'dehumanization'. The separation of the human being from labour and from land is something that contradicts the very concept of humanness and it entails the dissolution of the 'totality' of life into specific components – religious, political, economic – and their subjugation to two simple economic motives: the 'fear of hunger' and the 'hope of gain' (Özel 1997, pp. 20–21). Moreover, it is important to stress that, in Polanyi's view, the appearance of the 'fear of hunger' was the result of a conscious activity performed by the state in order to facilitate market forces in their disembedding process. Besides, he maintains that we can get a plastic example of this by looking at how industrialised countries were administering the colonies at the time. Since in those new territories the economy was still embedded in society, establishing a market for labour was impossible. Without the fear of hunger, Polanyi (2001 [1944], p. 172) suggests, labour could have never been transformed into a commodity. Therefore, for the purpose of paving the way to the market principle, the coloniser had to dismantle pre-existing social structures. The means of subsistence had to become scarce before labour could be extracted as a commodity from that population. As had already occurred in Europe during the eighteenth century, the primitive human being of the colony was turned into a 'willing worker' with the application of 'nature's penalty, hunger' (Polanyi 2001 [1944], p. 173). Özel (1997, p. 23) argues that the commodification of labour and land forces human beings to live a 'perverse' life, because 'they are deprived of the very qualities that make them human'.

Lastly, the functional problem that Polanyi associates with labour commodification is related to the resilience of market society, and it also helps us to provide a more thorough answer to our initial question at the start of this section, i.e. how far the process of labour commodification can be led. As Block (2001, p. xxiv) has underlined, one of the most common misconceptions about Polanyi is that he is read as saying that the process through which the economy seeks to separate itself from society and to dominate it from outside – the disembedding phenomenon – was accomplished. This is deeply untrue. The strength of Polanyi's discourse lies exactly in the impossibility of completely disembedding economy from society. Block explains this point by quoting the first page of *The Great Transformation*, where Polanyi (2001 [1944], p. 4) writes: 'Our thesis is that the idea of a self-adjusting market implied a stark utopia. Such an institution could not exist for any length of time without annihilating the human and natural substance of society; it would have physically destroyed man and transformed his surroundings into a wilderness.'

In other words, market capitalism put human life in the hands of a 'blind fate in spontaneous progress' (Polanyi 2001 [1944], p. 79). This transformation in the organisation of society – its becoming an 'accessory' of the economic system – would have 'annihilated' it but for the spontaneous emergence of a counter-movement that aimed at protecting it from self-destruction. Historically, the counter-movement emerged in England in the 1830s, after the abolition of the Speenhamland system, when every obstacle to the commodification of labour was removed and capitalism assumed its modern form.

At that moment, society instinctively resisted its own dislocation by calling for state intervention. Therefore, for Polanyi, nineteenth-century society is characterised by a double movement. On the one hand, the market principle, which guides the economic sphere in its disembedding process, seeks to extend its rule to every sector of society, transforming every factor of production into commodities, even those factors – labour, land and money – that for constitutive reasons can never be turned into real commodities, but which are forced to become 'fictitious' ones. On the other hand, society starts to press for factory laws, tariffs, social legislation and the management of the monetary system (Dale 2010, pp. 60–61), in other words, for the state to intervene with the aim of holding back the marketisation of fictitious commodities, in particular labour.

Fictitious commodification is necessary for the market to function properly, but, as explained by Esping-Andersen (1990, p. 36), with this movement the market system 'also sows the seeds of its own self-destruction', because 'if labour power is nothing more than a commodity, it will likely destruct'. Therefore, the counter-movement not only protects human lives, left at the mercy of the market's volatility, but also saves the market system from its own destructive excesses. Polanyi hints that a laissez-faire economy can survive over time only if the counter-movement guarantees its stability by calling for state regulation. The existence of the double movement is the reason why complete disembedding is impossible. Block (2001, p. xxv) uses the clever metaphor of the 'giant elastic band' to explain it. The counter-movement prevents the market movement from reaching its final objective, the complete commodification of society. The market movement pushes ahead the elastic band, but the counter-movement holds it back. The combination of the two opposing forces determines a limit in the disembedding process, the limit of society's complete commodification. From here comes the functional problem with labour commodification: a social process that has led to an ethical deterioration in the living conditions of human beings, and which prevents them from experiencing full freedom, would seem to be bound up with strong resilience, thanks to a sort of elastic equilibrium, which is determined by the double movement, keeping the market mechanism from crossing the critical threshold of complete commodification.

Moreover, the functional problem is exacerbated by the fact that, since the disembedding process is doomed to remain incomplete, the supporters of a free market can keep on explaining periodic crises and failures of the economic system as a consequence of political resistance against the full implementation of their economic recipes. The typical example, Block (2001, p. xxvii) says, is the imposition of market capitalism on the former Soviet Union after the fall of the Berlin wall. Although the so-called 'shock therapy' worsened the living conditions of Russians and increased the rate of extreme poverty, supporters of the 'Washington Consensus' blamed the incompleteness of the reforms as the main cause of their failure. The only way for society, in Polanyi's view, to expose the inappropriateness of neo-liberal policies is to cut the 'giant elastic band', renouncing the counter-movement. But this theoretical checkmate would cost social dislocation, a price that society is not willing to pay.

2. Market and domination

The originality of Polanyi's economic theory lies in his interpretation of the project of market liberalism as something that can never be fully accomplished, and this marks his difference with Marx, for Marx envisions within capitalism the seeds of its own destruction, given that the social struggle triggers a revolution that in the end is supposed to lead to the re-appropriation of the means of production by proletarians (Marx and Engels (1988 [1848]). In contrast, Polanyi ties the fortunes of capitalism to a dynamic stability secured by the double movement. This leads Block (2003, p. 281), for example, to the conclusion that Marx considers a pure market society, in which every element of production has been commodified, as a historical reality, with all the inconsistencies and conflicts materialising at the end of the same capitalism, while Polanyi considers pure market society as empirically unattainable. Nonetheless, I would tend to disagree with this reading of Polanyi, for even though the disembedding movement activates the counter-movement, the latter is not a direct function of the mode of production, but rather is a consequence of the historical and spatial contingencies in which capitalism develops. In other words, the double movement should not be read as a functional characteristic of capitalism, but as a political process that depends on factors that are exogenous to capitalism. Accordingly, nothing rules out, at least theoretically, that the disembedding movement described by Polanyi does not encounter a counter-movement that is capable of containing it.

I shall maintain, in fact, that Polanyi was much more optimistic about market liberalism than we should be today if we extend the scope of our analysis to the whole world. The first forms of land and labour commodification, which he studied and observed, concerned the pioneers of industrialisation, wealthy countries that benefited from disparities of power on the international market and in which the working classes had managed to obtain political leverage (Polanyi 2001 [1944], pp. 138–40). Under these circumstances, the double movement was really balanced. The antibodies that society activated against complete labour commodification were successful. Accordingly, I think that Polanyi had quite good reasons to argue that the Western history of the nineteenth century could be read through the lens of the market movement clashing against the social counter-movement. Nonetheless, today the situation is much more complex. In many developing countries the advance of the disembedded market sphere over society is not encountering the political barriers that

Polanyi described in his analysis. Moreover, in the second era of globalisation, three factors have altered the equilibrium of powers that the double movement guaranteed during the first phase of modernity. They have done so by structurally weakening the mechanisms of social protection.

Firstly, capital can move freely across the globe, while work remains local. This means that entrepreneurs can now invest in the cheapest possible labour regardless of the geographical boundaries that characterised the first industrialisation. Capital can be easily relocated where the economic conditions – in terms of a cheap labour force and low taxes – are available. Work is becoming more and more fragile, and what was an exception is now a rule (Baldwin 2016, pp. 79–108; see also Beck 1999). At the same time, the relation between growth of production and growth of job opportunities that was positive until the 1970s is now negative. Economic growth does not mean more job opportunities – quite the opposite. In France, for example, in the period from 1981 to 1991, gross national product (GNP) increased ten times, but the volume of work available in 1991 was 57 per cent of that of 1981 (Bauman 1999, p. 179; see also Graetz and Michaels 2017). As a result of the ICT revolution, at first, and then of the new developments in robotics and artificial intelligence, this trend is becoming even more entrenched. Just think of how internet banking, the apps for managing your sim card, or internet-based retailers like Amazon have increased the level of transactions while at the same time reducing the personnel that such a volume of operations would have once required. This has been possible through eliminating intermediate figures between the company and the customers (Frey and Osborne 2013; Ford 2015; Manyika et al. 2017). Despite the fact that global wealth has increased between the end of the last century and the beginning of the current century as never before in history, unemployment has been rising (Maxton 2015; Ford 2016). The main consequence of these two phenomena – the fragility and decreasing volume of job opportunities – is that work is now extremely redundant (Bauman 1999, p. 175; see also Bauman 2003). Nowadays, Marx's reserve army is a global army, but asymmetrically global. Owners of capital can move much more easily across countries in search of a labour force compared to workers in search of capital.

Secondly, national mechanisms of social protection are now unable to effectively counter the risks to which commodified individuals are structurally exposed, because these risks are now global.[1] Either intentionally or unintentionally, decisions taken by corporations, financial funds and rating agencies have pervasive effects on the lives of individuals living in the most disparate

---

[1]   With regard to this, Ulrich Beck (1999, p. 13) has pointed out – correctly, in my view – that we live in a 'post-national cosmopolitan world order', which in practical terms means living in 'an age of side-effects' (see also World Economic Forum 2019).

places of the world (Bohman 2004, p. 339; see also Bauman 2003). No country can decide to gravitate outside the global market (Milanovic 2019, pp. 1–11), but at the same time no single country is able to regulate the global market alone.[2] As noted by William R. Nester (2010, p. 3), the exchanges that are carried out every day on the global financial markets amount to the value of around 2 billion dollars; that, in turn, correspond to approximately one-seventh of the value of goods and services that were produced in the USA throughout 2009 – and we may also add that it amounts to roughly the GDP of Brazil in 2017 and almost twice the GDP of Mexico in the same year. Obviously, financial markets play an important role in fostering growth, if only for the fact that they mobilise savings. Yet, the magnitude of financial flows exposes single individuals, and also single countries, to risks that are unpredictable and unmanageable. The two forces stretching Block's elastic band are clearly unbalanced.

Thirdly, not only are single countries structurally weakened in their capacity to develop resilience strategies – because, as we have seen above, risks are global while the reach of political agency remains local – they also suffer new limitations in their internal economic leverage. Capital being global means that countries are now required to attract and withhold this supra-national economic entity. Investors generally seek cheap skilled labour and low taxes. Miriam Ronzoni (2009, pp. 249–51) rightly highlights that in a deeply globalised world, states face a dilemma. Either they make their tax system more regressive – thus renouncing their capacity for implementing effective welfare policies and increasing internal equality – or they resist global pressure at the cost of losing both foreign investments and local skilled workers (see also Cassee 2019; Risse and Meyer 2019). We may also add that a third solution consists in shifting the tax burden from capital to labour, which has far fewer chances of eluding the demands of contributing to national revenues. When this occurs, inequality between classes increases and labour becomes ever more fragile (Avi-Yonah 2000, 2019; Genshel 2002).

If my argument is correct, and therefore the commodification of labour tends to be a social process that, in certain socio-economic contexts such as those of some developing countries, goes beyond the limits drawn by Polanyi's double movement, then this would make the moral and political problem that Polanyi associates with wage work even more pressing, i.e. a systemic obstacle

---

[2]   This is what David Held (2010, pp. 4–5) referred to, more generally, as 'the paradox of our time', stressing the fact that the challenges that hinge on humanity in this century are clearly global in scope – just think, for example, of climate change, poverty, development and security – while the solutions that single actors can deploy are structurally limited; therefore, everything depends on the ability to obtain global cooperation (see also Hale et al. 2013; Pirni 2017).

to individual freedom. Accordingly, my aim in this chapter is to explain and to discuss the systemic character of capitalist domination. At the same time, I shall maintain that we should be careful in distinguishing this condition of systemic unfreedom from all the other moral problems that descend from it – e.g. exploitation. In order to do so, I will resort to the analytical formulation of the concept of freedom that has been proposed by contemporary neo-republican philosophers, namely freedom as non-domination. This is because I believe, as I will argue in a moment, that the concept of freedom as non-domination manages to grasp some forms of subjugation, both systemic and individual, which escape a strictly liberal conception of freedom as non-interference.

The notion of freedom as non-domination was recently reintroduced in the philosophical debate by Philip Pettit (1997) and Quentin Skinner (1997). They were both inspired by each other, even though Pettit focused on the analytical formulation of the argument while Skinner focused on its historical evolution. According to the Irish philosopher and the British historian, the dichotomy (made popular by Isaiah Berlin) between negative freedom – interpreted as absence of a more or less intentional interference, enacted through concrete coercion or its threat – and positive freedom – conceived as self-mastery – is incomplete (Pettit 1997, p. 30). There is an intermediate possibility, freedom as the absence of domination, or alien control. Sticking to this third formulation of freedom, an agent exercises dominating power over another 'to the extent that (1) [he has] the capacity to interfere (2) on an arbitrary basis (3) in certain choices that the other is in a position to make' (Pettit 1997, p. 52).

The liberal theory of freedom as non-interference and the republican theory[3] of freedom as non-domination differ on two basic points. According to republicans you can be dominated and not interfered with. In this case you are unfree in the republican view but free in the liberal one. But, republicans say, you can also be interfered with but not dominated. In this second case you are free for republicans but unfree for liberals. More generally, for liberals every form of interference limits freedom. So, even the state's laws limit some freedoms, but we are happy to let it happen because by curtailing the freedoms of some individuals the state guarantees more freedom overall, whereas for republicans there is no such trade-off in terms of freedom. Laws are not limiting freedom if they have been freely consented to by the members of the community (Pettit 1997, pp. 65–6). Some examples might help to make clearer the divergence between the two theories.

---

[3]   Skinner (2008, p. 84) writes that he would prefer to call it 'neo-Roman' theory but he accepts to stick to the word 'republican' in order to remain in line with other authors.

Assume that a slave is subject to a master who is willing to exercise his power, forcing the slave to do what he, the master, wishes. A liberal, committed to the negative theory of freedom, would say that this slave is not free because the master clearly interferes with him, limiting his options for action. A neo-republican would come to the same conclusion, but for a different reason. He would recognise that the master is interfering with the slave, but he would not envisage in this simple fact the cause of his unfreedom. He would rather consider the slave unfree because he is dominated by the master, meaning that the two stand in an asymmetrical relation of power.

Up to this point, the debate between negative theorists and neo-republicans may seem an analytical dispute for its own sake. But things get more complex and interesting if you now imagine that the master is no longer willing to exercise his power over the slave. He is still the master, but he is not interfering with the slave. According to the logic of non-interference, negative theorists have to say that the slave is free as long as the master does not decide to interfere again. On the other hand, for neo-republicans the slave is always unfree, even when he is not interfered with, because he is permanently dominated. To put the idea of domination without interference in more analytical terms, imagine this other case. Agent B has three options: x, y and z. Agent A desires that B choose option x and is ready to interfere to bring about this result. Nonetheless, B is independently willing to choose x, hence A is not even required to interfere in order to satisfy his desire. Is B free in his choice? According to negative theorists, B is free in relation to his choice, while for neo-republicans B is not free even if he is not interfered with, and he is so because he is subject to A's virtual control (Pettit 2008, pp. 111–14).

Some negative theorists have tried to attack the neo-republican formulation of liberty as non-domination; in particular, they have maintained that freedom as non-domination has nothing to add to freedom as non-interference. Matthew Kramer (2008) has argued that the situation of the slave subject to the benevolent master can be described as a case of unfreedom also in negative terms. For individual freedom is largely determined by what Kramer (2008, p. 44) defines as 'the range of the combinations-of-conjunctively-exercisable-liberties'. Even if the slave is not physically interfered with by his master, he is deprived of the capability of conjunctively exercising two liberties: acting as he wishes and not being obsequious towards his master in order to prevent him from retaliating – or simply interfering. Skinner (2008) has responded to this objection underlining that the case described by Kramer does not exhaust all the situations in which the two theories diverge. It might happen that the slave is not deprived of the conjunctive exercise of the two liberties described by Kramer because there is no probability that the master will actually interfere. In this scenario the negative theorist would have to say that the slave is free, while for the neo-republican he will still be unfree. What negative theorists overlook,

Skinner (2008, p. 99) says, is that slavery is an 'existential condition'. In his own words: 'it is the mere fact that their master or ruler has arbitrary powers to intervene that takes away their liberty, not any particular degree of probability that these powers will ever be exercised' (Skinner 2008, p. 97).

The second important divergence between negative theorists and neo-republicans concerns the case of interference without domination, or non-alien control materialising with interference. Imagine that you want to give up smoking and ask me to hide your cigarettes. In the moment in which you will feel the need to smoke you will be clearly interfered with by me. Have you lost your freedom to smoke? A neo-republican would say that although being interfered with, you are still free. The reason lies in what Pettit (2008, p. 108) defines as 'the positionality of alien control'. If A controls what B does, but B is in a position to control A, A's control over B diminishes or disappears, because 'controlled or countered control is no longer a form of control'. The broad political consequence of this analytical argument is that for neo-republicans a government's interference is not curtailing any freedom if this interference is non-arbitrary, meaning that it has been invigilated and checked through constitutional mechanisms (Pettit 2008, p. 118). So, if someone is put in prison because he has violated some laws, a liberal would say that the state is limiting his freedom but at the same time would justify it on the basis that his imprisonment guarantees a greater freedom overall. A neo-republican, on the contrary, would maintain that the state would not be limiting anyone's freedom if the law that has been infringed had been previously approved in a non-arbitrary way, meaning under sound constitutional guarantees.[4]

Ian Carter (2008) has defended the validity of the negative formulation of freedom by rejecting the idea that there can be interference without domination. He maintains that either we adopt a very narrow interpretation of common interest, specifically in terms of Pareto-superiority, or we accept that personal interest will inevitably come into conflict with common interest. If the latter is true, Carter (2008, pp. 64–6) says, there is no reason, when dealing with limitation of freedom, to give priority to the common interest over individual interest, unless we fall into the trap of moralising the notion of freedom. That is exactly what, according to Carter, has been done by Pettit. Pettit, in his turn, rejects the claim that the neo-republican theory of freedom is moralised, arguing that his notion of 'non-arbitrary' interference does not bring with itself an evaluative dimension. The non-arbitrariness simply refers to a procedural mechanism that is morally neutral. A procedure is non-arbitrary, in Pettit's view, if it

---

[4] On the question of whether from a neo-republican perspective the law itself represents a limitation of liberty, see Pettit 1997, pp. 65–6.

'track[s] the avowed or avowal-ready interests of the interferee' regardless of whether these interests are morally valid (Pettit 2008, p. 117; see also Arnold and Harris 2017).

There are several reasons, in my view, that render the account of freedom as non-domination preferable to the one of freedom as non-interference in order to adequately frame the situation of subjugation to which commodified workers are exposed. The first reason is general. I agree with neo-republicans when they maintain that there exist some cases of unfreedom that count as such only on the republican account, and I also agree with them when they hold that invigilated control does not curtail freedom – whether this second claim can be accommodated within the liberal theory as well is irrelevant to the alleged preferability of neo-republican theory, given that I endorse the first claim (Maynor 2003, pp. 43–8). The second and more specific reason is that the systemic unfreedom experienced by commodified workers resembles the existential condition that Skinner (2008) attributes to the slave of the benevolent master and is compatible with diachronic improvements in well-being (see Buckinx et al. 2015, p. 2). Accordingly, even though in the transition from a pre-capitalist condition (or from a condition of self-production) to a wage-work regime that is not accompanied with welfare provisions, the individual is made better off in terms of capabilities, this does not alter the fact that she is less free than before in the exercising of her basic capabilities; the latter are now dependent on the willingness of someone else to rent out her labour performance. It might be objected that in the previous condition the individual was more vulnerable to economic shocks because, for example, a bad harvest or environmental hazards could have prevented her from obtaining the necessary resources for her livelihood from the means of production she controlled – thus, she is overall more secure of her basic capabilities now than before. This is true, but as we shall see in a moment, what interests us for the assessment of freedom are social rather than natural obstacles. Meaning that I do not lose the freedom to play soccer because it is raining and the field is flooded, but I lose it instead if someone locks me in the house or steals the money I would need to pay my share for the rent of the field. Furthermore, I lose my freedom to play soccer even if someone simply has the power to lock me in my house or take my money away, regardless of whether or not he decides to practise this kind of interference. That does not take away the fact that my chance to play the game is at his mercy.

The third reason why the idea of domination is more appropriate than interference with respect to labour commodification is that it is better able to interpret those forms of domination, both interactional and systemic, that take place at a global level between state and non-state actors. Even though this is not the direct target of my normative critique of labour commodification, it is fundamental both for explaining why state institutions are limited in their possibilities to 'countermove' against the fictitious commodification of labour, as I hinted at just above, and to maintain that it is unreasonable to propose a statist understanding of the responsibility for implementing MDL. The clear example is countries, especially developing countries, that are forced to adapt to 'business friendly' conditions for attracting investment. Here investors do not interfere with states, and hence with citizens, but still they exercise domination, for the latter anticipate the wishes of the former – basically in terms of lower taxes and regulations – without the former having to actually use the threat of interference, meaning divestment or non-investment (see Laborde 2010, pp. 54–8; Laborde and Ronzoni 2016, p. 280).

Fourthly, the idea of domination is better suited than the one of interference to be declined at the structural level that interests us here with regard to labour commodification. This is so because for a system of practices and norms to interfere with someone, it would be necessary for the system to actually limit someone's choices, compared to a hypothetical but still possible alternative in which the system did not exist or was different in some fundamental characteristics. Thus, for example, an international system of trade rules is Pareto inefficient in terms of freedom from interference, and hence classifiable as coercive, if it is possible to think of a hypothetical and possible alternative system in which, all the other things being equal or no worse for anyone, at least one agent is more free from interference than she is in the existing system (Valentini 2011). Nonetheless, the systemic domination that is inherent in labour commodification, and that I label more generally capitalist domination, does not necessarily result in a realised systemic interference. Accordingly, the shift from system S1 to system S2 might be Pareto efficient with respect to constraints on individual achievements (i.e. people might have more capabilities in a capitalist than in a non-capitalist society), while in S2 some people are more vulnerable to losing their new capabilities, for social reasons, than they were in S1.

Lastly, freedom as non-domination allows us to reconcile the idea of unfreedom with the fact that capitalist structural domination does not lead to interpersonal interference between those who possess the means of production and those who do not. According to this position, which I named exploitation without interpersonal domination and that in my view represents the correct unfolding of the neo-republican theory, commodified workers are unfree for the mere reason of being commodified, while any form of abuse of power that takes place in the relationship between employers and employees, and which derives from mere asymmetries in the bargaining positions – without any violence or deception – is a form of exploitation that takes nothing away from and adds nothing to the structural condition of capitalist domination.

In the following pages, I will argue about the strictly systemic nature of capitalist domination. Accordingly, I shall briefly compare the neo-republican position on individual freedom in the market with the labour republican theory, and then introduce the account of exploitation without interpersonal domination. Then, I shall defend this account of structural domination from two powerful objections. The first concerns the very empirical fact that job contracts are usually incomplete; hence, an employer might be said to practise arbitrary interference over an employee when the former provides the latter with a job contract less enjoyable than he could have reasonably expected. The second objection pertains to the alleged arbitrariness of a property system that allows for some people to be left without the means of production, against which the double counter-argument might be raised that property laws are not arbitrary in the republican sense if properly invigilated and that the borders of the proletarian group are permeable – namely, a person born in the proletarian group might rise above his initial condition through individual effort.

What I want to stress from the beginning, however, is that my treatment of the concepts of domination and freedom in purely structural terms should not be read as absolution for the stronger party of a market transaction that profits from asymmetries of power to impose ignominious conditions on the weaker counterpart. The former remains certainly blameworthy for undertaking exploitative practices. Yet, the responsibility for the unfreedom of the victim of an exploitative contract does not fall directly on the stronger counterpart of the contract, but rather on all those people who share the political responsibility for keeping in place a system of social norms, mainly concerning the distribution of private property, that deprives the weaker party of any acceptable alternative but to hire out her labour performance.

2.1   LABOUR COMMODIFICATION AND ALIEN CONTROL

From this point on, I shall leave aside the broad dispute between the two conceptions of freedom and the issue as to whether freedom as non-interference suffices to sanction all those cases that constitute domination for neo-republicans. I shall focus instead on the economic implications of the neo-republican theory of freedom as non-domination, and more precisely on the question entertained by Pettit (2006) in more specific writings, as to whether the market might hinder neo-republican freedom. He distinguishes between outright and social freedom. Assume you want to go to watch a football match but a hurricane hits your city and you cannot leave your home, or, alternatively, the football match is in London and you happen to live in New Delhi. In this case, you are constrained in your freedom to attend the match by a natural obstacle. If, instead, you are unable to drive to the stadium because someone has stolen your car, you are a victim of social interference. A theory of freedom as non-domination should only be concerned with social obstacles. An unequal distribution of property will surely put restrictions on what people wish to do. But these restrictions, according to Pettit (2006, pp. 132–40), are non-dominating ones, just as natural interference is non-dominating. His argument is:

> I may regret the fact that under the existing property regime you have more oppor-tunities than me to enjoy our common status as free persons, but the fact of that regret does not mean that you stand over me in the position of a dominating power. I may be just as well protected against your arbitrarily interfering with me as you are protected against my interfering with you. (Pettit 2006, p. 140)

In Pettit's view, an unequal property system is not in itself a source of domi-nation. But he recognises that this system might have 'the contingent effect of allowing domination' (Pettit 2006, p. 139). In the latter case, a neo-republican should seek social adjustments. The same thing holds true for market partic-ipation: 'there is no particular threat to people's freedom as non-domination associated with participation in the market' (Pettit 2006, p. 142). This is so because, for Pettit, there is a substantial moral difference between offering a reward, as happens in market interactions, and issuing a threat.

Assume that you have three options: A, B and C. If I offer you a reward for choosing A, your set of options becomes A *plus*, B and C. If, on the contrary, I threaten to punish you if you opt for B, your set becomes A, B *minus* and C. Adding a plus to one of your options does not amount to any of the three forms of alien control – reduction of the ability to choose, removal or replacement of an option – while subtracting something from the outcome of an option clearly does. Therefore, in a market system, I might offer you something in exchange for something you own – be it a standard commodity or your labour power – without exercising alien control over you. For, by doing so, I would be adding a plus to your set of options. As long as you are free to refuse my reward, you can go back to the status quo (Pettit 2006, pp. 142–4).

In a following article Pettit (2007) goes deeper in his analysis of the relation between market and neo-republican freedom, taking into consideration those situations in which even the fact of being able to offer a reward might allow for domination. He makes the case of there being many more employees avail-able than employers willing to hire them. If the employers are in a position to decide who should be granted a decent living condition and who should not, the employees 'would be defenceless against [. . .] employers' petty abuse or their power to arbitrarily dismiss [them]' (Pettit 2007, p. 5). Therefore, he ends up arguing that for freedom as non-domination to be resilient we need to introduce an unconditional basic income (Pettit 2007, p. 5).[5]

---

[5]   Conversely, Richard Dagger (2006, pp. 166–7) maintains that a neo-republican civil economy would include, among other things, either the introduction of a condi-tional basic income or the allocation of a one-time capital grant.

Alex Gourevitch is unsatisfied with Pettit's conclusion. In a first article aimed at reconstructing a labour republican position,[6] Gourevitch (2013) argues that his colleague misses the real point of the dominating power exercised on commodified individuals because he keeps interpreting it in the light of the old interpersonal relation of master and slave. Moreover, Gourevitch argues, neo-republicans mention only one part of the Roman interpersonal domination. The Roman slave was surely subject to the arbitrary control of his specific master, and this is the first relation rightly highlighted by neo-republicans. But the slave also stood in another relation to 'many masters', that is to say Roman citizens, who actively sustained a legal order that kept the slave separated from other citizens, thus allowing for his interpersonal domination by a specific master. Therefore, in Gourevitch's view, while the Roman slave, at a first superficial glance, might seem simply dominated by his master, he is also subject to a broader domination by many masters. Obviously, these many masters are not intentionally working to ensure that that specific slave is dominated by that specific master. The element of intentionality, at this second level, comes in through another door. Roman citizens intentionally introduced and maintained the division of free men and slaves that led to myriad interpersonal relations of domination, where a specific master intentionally dominated a specific slave (Gourevitch 2013, p. 11).

Even in the Roman master–slave relation, Gourevitch argues, there is a structural form of domination that has been overlooked by those neo-republican thinkers who have recently rehabilitated the notion of freedom as non-domination. Structural domination is the same form of domination that subjugates the commodified worker. For Gourevitch, this modern structural domination arises when a group of individuals excludes another group from the possession of productive assets: 'those who do not own are economically dependent on employers for jobs, wages, and thus their livelihoods [. . .] Non-owners are thereby *forced* by the legally protected distribution of productive assets to sell their labor to some employer or another' (Gourevitch 2013, p. 12). The difference between Pettit and the labour republicans Gourevitch refers to is that the former would certainly agree that a poor person, forced to sell herself on the labour market, is being subjected to domination, but he would ascribe it to the interpersonal alien control the specific employer is able to exercise on her. Conversely, labour republicans would go deeper and say that the worker is unfree, in the first place, because of being subjected to

---

[6]   Gourevitch (2013, p. 594) refers to a group of editors and activists who had formed towards the end of the nineteenth century around the so-called Knights of Labor, one of the first major labour organisations active in the United States. Among the prominent figures in this group, Gourevitch mentions Terence Powderly, George McNeill, William H. Sylvis and Ira Steward.

structural domination, arguing that an 'unequal structure of control over productive assets' (Gourevitch 2013, p. 12) forced her to look for basic income
in an employer–employee relation and made her vulnerable to minimal shocks
– illness, loss of a family member, or a reduction in production needs, for
example. She has thus entered an interpersonal relation of domination due to
being born in a structural situation that allowed for this – she was born without
any other asset to use in the market, or for self-sufficiency, except for her
own labour power. Therefore, for labour republicans wage-slavery consists
in three moments: structural domination, the inequality of power that allows
the employer to set the contract terms he likes, and the employer's capacity to
arbitrarily interfere with the employees once she has entered the work relation
(Gourevitch 2015, pp. 105–15; see also Cicerchia 2019).

I hold a different position. I agree with Gourevitch that the extremely
commodified individual undergoing wage slavery is subject to structural
domination, due to unequal access to productive assets. But I do not agree that
a specific individual is also a victim of interpersonal domination by a specific
employer, who hires him. That is to say, I believe that structural domination
results only in exploitation, not interpersonal domination. I also hold that,
when Pettit provides arguments in favour of an unconditional basic income, he
is misusing his own definition of freedom as non-domination. Pettit is right,
in my view, in holding that adding a reward to someone's option does not
amount to an exercise of alien control over her. But, if the latter is true, Pettit
cannot successively maintain that in a situation in which employees are more
numerous than employers willing to hire them and 'times are hard', employers
are in a position to arbitrarily interfere with employees. Being able to offer an
important reward to someone might entail being able to exploit her, but you
can exploit someone without exercising alien control.

In order to illustrate the idea of exploitation without interpersonal domination, I will firstly clarify the definitions and then proceed with an example.
Interpersonal domination is the form of domination in which a first agent (or
group of agents) stands in a position to practise arbitrary interference over
a second agent (or group of agents). Structural domination, on the other hand,
occurs when an agent (or a group of agents) is subject to a system of institutions, rules or practices that can arbitrarily interfere with her, because, as we
shall see later on in this chapter, these institutions, rules or practices either fail
to track her acknowledged interests or prevent her from taking part in democratic mechanisms to reform them – hence, the individual responsibility for
domination and possibly arbitrary interference is only indirect and consists in
contributing to keeping in place this system. Capitalist structural domination,
for example, occurs when a system of social and legal rules protecting private
property, and which is a precondition for the existence of the capitalist system
itself, deprives one or more individuals of the possibility of achieving basic

well-being outside of a market relationship. Instead, the structural arbitrary interference of capitalism occurs when individuals who are excluded from the means of production fail to obtain adequate basic sustenance in market relations.

As for the interpersonal cases discussed by neo-republican philosophers, structural domination can occur without structural interference, and structural interference can occur without structural domination. Accordingly, capitalist structural domination can occur without capitalist structural interference, as long as the commodified individual succeeds in realising through market relations those basic capabilities that he would have been guaranteed in a hypothetical world in which he was free from capitalist domination, just as the slave of the benevolent master is dominated but not interfered with, as long as he can do those things that he would have done if he had been free. On the other hand, capitalist structural interference can occur without capitalist structural domination when the system of norms and practices protecting private property has been properly invigilated; hence, it is not arbitrary in the neo-republican sense.

Lastly, a first agent (or group of agents) exploits a second agent (or group of agents) when he takes advantage of her unfreedom, regardless of whether it is interpersonally or structurally determined, to impose relational conditions that we could rationally expect she would have refused had she not been dominated. Accordingly, a first agent practises capitalist exploitation over a second agent, when the latter is structurally dominated in the capitalist economy (because she has been excluded from the control of any productive asset except for her labour power); hence, she is forced to accept an unfair contract, or more generally unfair relational conditions, or rather is obliged to remain in an unfair job relation at any cost due to the lack of 'exit options'. By unfair contract, or unfair relational conditions, I refer to an agreement that the stronger party is able to impose on the weaker counterpart in virtue of an inequality of power that derives from the structural domination suffered by the commodified worker. In this sense, the structural claim is strictly connected to the interpersonal one, in the sense that the latter gathers its normative force from the former, but not the other way around. In other words, I maintain that capitalist interpersonal exploitation presupposes the existence of capitalist structural domination, but capitalist structural domination represents a normative problem per se, regardless – and not because – of the exploitative relations that may follow from it.

I am adopting here a quite restrictive and non-moralised definition of exploitation, which does not encompass all the cases in which an agent might obtain an unfair advantage over another agent, but rather only those ones in which an agent takes advantage of the unfreedom – interpersonal or structural – of another agent. So, for example, a situation in which X, who could be living off the income, accepts to work under ignominious conditions for Y, who is the editor of a well-known magazine, only because X ardently wants to be recognised by the general public as an intellectual, does not involve exploitation, as it would if X accepted Y's conditions because pushed by the lack of any reasonable alternative. Thus, here we assume that living without the possibility of making one's intellectual qualities known to the general public is a reasonable alternative to being harassed, while not having basic needs met might not be a reasonable one. In this sense, the definition of exploitation I am referring to in this chapter is directly and exclusively linked to the notion of unfreedom. Accordingly, a case in which Y takes advantage of X's physical disabilities to extort an unfair contract would count as exploitation in so far as – and only because – X could claim to be a victim of structural domination, meaning that she has been deprived of any reasonable alternative but to hire out her labour. Conversely, a situation in which X has a reasonable alternative to engaging in a market transaction would not count as exploitation, according to the restrictive account I am adopting here, even though X gets a lower reward than would have been obtained by any other agent with no disabilities.

On this point, I disagree not only with the labour-republican position, represented by Gourevitch, but also with Nicholas Vrousalis (2013), when he maintains that when agent A exploits agent B, the former is also dominating the latter. For me, the relation goes in the opposite direction: given that the capitalist coalition dominates B (together with the other members of B's coalition), then A is placed in a situation in which he can exploit B. To be more precise, Vrousalis (2013, p. 138) describes economic exploitation in these terms: '(4) A economically exploits B if and only if A and B are embedded in a systematic relationship in which (d) A instrumentalizes B's economic vulnerability (e) to appropriate (the fruits of) B's labor'. And I can agree with this assertion, or at least I would say that it is correct. But then Vrousalis (2013, p. 139) gives the following definition of domination: '(5) A dominates B if A and B are embedded in a systematic relationship in which (f) A takes advantage of his power over B, or the power of a coalition of agents A belongs to, in a way that is (g) disrespectful to B'. Moreover, he maintains that he wants to demonstrate that '(4) implies (5)', that is to say, that exploitation implies (interpersonal) domination (Vrousalis 2013, p. 140). This is the point where I cannot follow Vrousalis, for two reasons. The first one is that, in my view, the two definitions he gives, respectively, of exploitation and domination – (4) and (5) – are substantially equivalent and correspond to exploitation only; hence, it does not make sense to me that one implies the other. The second reason is that neither of the two definitions contain one of the essential elements of the concept of domination, namely the subtraction of one or more options that the dominated agent had at his disposal before starting to interact with the dominant agent.[7]

Consider this case. Robert is incredibly poor. He was born in a slum and has never owned any productive asset. All of a sudden, he loses his job, and his mother is sick and needs urgent care. He really has no other option but to accept an exploitative contract offered by David. The new employer is aware of Robert's dire situation and takes advantage of it to exercise full control over Robert. David overburdens Robert with work, gives him very few breaks, decides what he should do during free time and even harasses him. I would say that Robert is surely a victim of a form of structural domination that infringes on his freedom (as non-domination). I also think that David clearly exploits Robert because he is able to impose such horrible conditions in view of Robert's difficult economic condition. But I think that, if we take for granted the definition of arbitrary interference given by Pettit and Skinner, David's interaction with Robert at the workplace does not amount to interpersonal domination.

Before Robert meets David on the labour market, Robert has only one option, A – starving and leaving his mother without medicine. By offering Robert an exploitative contract, David does not perform any of the three actions in which, according to Pettit's formulation (2008, pp. 106–7), arbitrary interference can materialise: (1) reduce the actor's ability to choose, (2) remove or seemingly remove an option, or (3) replace or seemingly replace an option. I think that David only adds another option to Robert, B – working for him in exploitative conditions. And he is able to make Robert opt for B by offering just a very modest reward for it. But David never subtracts anything from the only option, A, that Robert had before meeting him. Moreover, at any moment in their work relation, Robert is free to restore the status quo, eliminating B and remaining with A only. In short, I do not think that when David harasses Robert at the workplace, he is infringing on Robert's freedom. But David is surely responsible for sustaining an unequal distribution of assets, the main consequence of which is that, when Robert enters the labour market, his set of options is so incredibly limited that he can be easily exploited. So, in

---

[7] See also Vrousalis's more recent formulation of structural domination as a 'triadic relation' involving dominated agents, dominating agents and regulators. He makes this example: 'Structural domination – Regulator pushes women, and only women, into pits. Regulator pushes Woman into a pit. This enables Man to demand an extortionate price from Woman in return for extracting her from the pit', and he maintains that in this case 'Regulator confers structure to the domination relation' (Vrousalis 2020, p. 4). I would respond to this claim by saying that there is no relation of domination between the woman in the pit and the man who could rescue her. The regulator dominates the woman, and this allows the man *only* to exploit her.

my view, David is responsible for contributing to limiting Robert's freedom only in a structural way.

In a short essay on workers 'forced' to take hazardous jobs, G.A. Cohen (1988, p. 242) made an important point that is relevant for our discussion, although it seems like something we should take for granted. He held that when you are forced to do something, you are free to do that thing. We should distinguish, he says, between 'being free to do something' and 'doing something freely' (Cohen 1988, p. 243). If you force me to do something this means that I am free to that thing, but surely I will not do it freely. Now, assume that someone wants me out of a room, and consider two different strategies this person can adopt to reach his goal. He can drag me out by force. Or, alternatively, he can get me to leave by making a threat. For example, he might point a gun and tell me that if I do not leave immediately he will shoot me in the leg. The difference between the two scenarios is that in the first case I cannot choose to remain in the room, because I am not given the chance to do anything; I am just passively brought out. While in the second case, I am free to decide whether to remain where I am or to leave the room. The point, clearly, is that despite being free to remain, I could not do it freely because it would cost me to be shot in the leg. So, Cohen (1988, p. 245) concludes, 'whenever a person is forced to do something there is something else which he is free to do instead'. The problem is whether the alternative can be freely opted for.

These general observations can be easily transposed, as Cohen does, to a more specific debate on job contracts. Rightist thinkers would hold that, in my example, Robert is free to sell his labour power and by accepting David's offer he is merely exercising his market freedom. In contrast, Marxists would argue that Robert is forced to sell his labour power because of his dire condition. I agree with Cohen when he says that both 'bourgeois thinkers' and Marxists are right. The former would stress correctly that, differently from my case in which I am dragged out of the room by another person, Robert does have some alternatives. He might let his mother do without medicine and go begging, or, alternatively, might also slowly die. The problem with the employee accepting a hazardous job is not that he does not have other choices, but that he does not have any 'other choice worth considering' (Cohen 1988, p. 246). Therefore, the leftist claim that Robert is forced to sell his labour to David at shocking conditions should be read in the sense that there surely were other things Robert might have done but none of them were worth considering as acceptable. Cohen puts it in analytical terms:

> He who is forced to do A is free to do A, and is free to do some B different from A, but, and this is why he counts as forced to do A, is free to do no C which is an acceptable alternative to A. (Cohen 1988, p. 247)

An agent is forced to do A when he has as the only other available option B, that is not acceptable. So, an agent is forced to do A when he lacks any C – an acceptable alternative to A. When the agent is deprived of C, he suffers arbitrary interference, and the second agent, who practises arbitrary interference over the first agent, can be said to dominate him and violate his freedom. What we should not take for granted is that the person who benefits from the fact that the first agent has been left without C, is the same one who has deprived him of C. In the room case the two persons are the same. Before I meet the person with the gun I have option C – remain in the room and preserve my bodily integrity. When this person warns me, saying 'leave, or I will shoot you in the leg', he practises arbitrary interference on me by replacing C with either A (leaving the room) or B (remaining in the room and being shot). Conversely, in Robert's case, before meeting David, he is already lacking any C – having a source of income that allows him to survive and to buy medicine for his mother. David offers him B (a bad contract) and Robert is forced to accept it because of the lack of C. But who has deprived Robert of C; that is to say, who put him in a condition of domination? Surely, not David, or any particular person.

Labour republicans were right in holding that a person born in the proletarian group is victim of a form of domination, in the sense that she lacks any acceptable alternative to selling her labour in the market, and hence the exercise of her basic capabilities is contingent on the willingness of others to grant her access to the means of production. Furthermore, I would also stress that this domination may either result in arbitrary interference, as for Robert, when the individual falls short of achieving good living conditions within the market, or not result in arbitrary interference, when the commodified worker encounters a benevolent employer. Yet, both the facts that the commodified individual lacks a reasonable alternative to entering the market (domination) and that he may potentially end up in a condition of deprivation or mistreatment if he does not get a good contract (potential interference) are systemic contingencies. In the case of Robert, for example, it is a condition he inherits from birth. For all his life, in every interpersonal interaction Robert will have with employers, he will suffer the consequences of being a commodified worker (at least as long as he does not manage to leave the proletarian group), but the latter is not due to the arbitrary interference of any specific person or employer. Accordingly, it would be unreasonable to hold that someone can deprive Robert of something he has never had, C – a reasonable alternative to entering the labour market.

In the same way, I think that Robert Taylor (2017, pp. 50–54) is absolutely right when he holds that 'the absence of meaningful exit options for workers' constitutes a curtailment of freedom that should concern republicans. Nonetheless, Taylor (2017, p. 49) maintains that 'market power gives leeway for exploitation, discrimination, and domination', thus implying that the problem with workers lacking credible alternatives to engaging a market relation lies – also – in the fact that they are exposed to interpersonal domination by the firm; thus, he clearly says that under conditions of perfect competition 'no firm will be in a position to dominate workers, given the possibility of costless exit' (Taylor 2017, p. 52). On the contrary, I believe that the lack of costless exits accounts for domination in itself, because it is an arbitrary deprivation of options. Furthermore, I hold that structural domination never reverberates into interpersonal domination of the firm–employee kind, even when the employee lacks a reasonable alternative to the market relation; hence, everything that occurs at the point of production is simply a matter of exploitation.

Therefore, while Taylor (2017, pp. 54–62) concludes that a perfectly competitive market combined with free exit constitutes a sound anti-power to capitalist domination, as long as they prevent employers from arbitrarily interfering with employees, in my view free exit alone is the anti-power to capitalist domination, because it restores the lost option to not enter the market at any cost. Conversely, a competitive market can surely prevent exploitation, in the sense of allowing employees to resist disadvantageous job offers, which they would accept if there were no worthy and viable alternatives, but cannot do anything with regard to market domination; that remains a structural issue related to the distribution of the means of production.

In sum, my point so far in this chapter is that the whole issue of workers' unfreedom should be addressed structurally, and in the following pages I shall defend this argument from several objections that I imagine might be raised. Yet, before I do this, I think it is important to clarify the further implications that the account of exploitation without interpersonal domination might have beyond market interactions. In particular, am I arguing that no agent Y is ever dominating agent X as long as X is free to interrupt her relation with Y, independently of how costly this exit can be? Imagine, for example, a couple relationship in which partner Y mistreats partner X and consider two possible scenarios. In the first one, Y subjugates X through violence, hence X is not free to abandon the relation without losing something in comparison to her situation before starting the relationship, namely, bodily integrity. In this case Y is surely practising arbitrary interference over X and interpersonal domination is occurring – consider also that Y might practise arbitrary interference over X through deception or manipulation, rather than physical violence. In the second scenario, Y mistreats X as well, but X is free to say goodbye to Y without suffering any form of retaliation. Yet, Y knows that he can continue mistreating X for she will never leave, given that X does not know where to go and lacks any means to start a new life on her own. Here, assuming that X was in the same economic situation before meeting Y and that Y did not take any asset from X, we should conclude that Y is not practising any arbitrary interference over X and that the mistreatment of X does not account to domination. X is surely unfree and imprisoned in the relationship with Y, but differently from the previous example involving interpersonal domination by Y; here, what keeps X stuck in her relationship with Y is not any action performed or performable by Y, but rather the lack of any reasonable alternative to remaining with Y, which is, as I argued before, a structural rather than an interpersonal problem.

This change of perspective on the roots of X's unfreedom does not involve a modification, let alone a lightening, of the moral judgement we should have about the seriousness of her condition of subjugation. The only thing that changes is the moral judgement about the causal contribution of other agents to X's subjugation, which is no longer directly ascribable only to Y but is rather dispersed through the chain of individual contributions to the social structure that determines X's unfreedom. At the same time, saying that Y does not dominate X does not imply that Y bears no moral blame. On the contrary, Y exploits X's structural unfreedom to impose on her conditions that would never have been accepted had X been structurally free. In both scenarios Y is blameworthy for the bad things he does to X, but only in the first scenario is Y interpersonally responsible for the unfreedom that keeps X stuck in a relation based on mistreatment.

The same discourse holds true in the case that Y manages to keep X stuck in a relationship that is unfavourable just because of conservative family laws. Here the core of X's unfreedom should be identified in the laws, institutions and norms within which their relation is framed. These laws, norms and institutions deprived any X of the possibility of relating to any Y on the basis of equal rights and obligations. Whatever form of mistreatment a specific Y imposes on a specific X amounts to exploitation – deplorable exploitation, obviously, that does not alter the negative moral judgement we should have about Y. Yet, Y is not directly responsible for X's unfreedom, because when they meet, X is already unfree by virtue of the social structures within which their encounter takes place. Accordingly, the restoration of X's freedom would not consist in Y ceasing to mistreat X up to the limit permitted by conservative family laws, which would only amount to an act of benevolence by Y, while X would remain dominated in the republican sense, given that nothing would prevent another agent from practising on X all the exploitative actions allowed by the law. To the contrary, X's freedom could only be recovered – or obtained – through the reform of the conservative family laws that leave her at the mercy of the bad or good will of every Y.

In sum, whether X is structurally dominated because of property or family laws – or both – Y shares the responsibility for the unfreedom of X with all those other people who actively participate in keeping an unjust social structure in place. In this sense, the responsibility for change is twofold. On the one hand, Y is responsible for ceasing to exploit X, and this responsibility is interpersonal, meaning that any positive change would only concern X. On the other hand, all those other people who participate in the social structure to which both Y and X belong share the political responsibility to reform the norms and institutions that determine the unfreedom of X and of all the other persons in the same situation of structural domination. Obviously, the political responsibility for change is not shared equally between all the participants in the social structure; rather, it is a function of the power that every single agent has to impact on the definition of its underlying norms and institutions (see Young 2011, pp. 95–122).

2.2 THE INCOMPLETENESS OF CONTRACT AND THE BENCHMARK PROBLEM

The first objection I would like to consider with regard to the account of exploitation without interpersonal domination is the one according to which the job contract does not cover every aspect of the work relation. The employer retains a large discretionary power over the creation of working conditions. So, at the moment in which the employer makes his job offer, the employee might have formed an expectation that may later turn out to be incorrect. Regardless of what was written in the contract, the employer might successively demand extra work, allow very few breaks, prohibit his employees from reading certain newspapers or attending some political meetings, and so on. So, the person who raises the objection might say, every time the employer arbitrarily subtracts something from the hypothetical work relation the employee had imagined at the moment he received the job offer, the employer performs arbitrary interference over the employee and dominates him.

There are two ways to respond to this objection. The first one consists of challenging the universal character of its premise. Every contract is surely incomplete, but this fact does not automatically entail that when the employee accepts the job offer he is unaware of the actual terms of the work relation. Think, for example, of a case in which the employer calls the employee to his office and says: 'Look, here is the contract, but be aware that there are some other things you should know before you sign. You will be requested to work *n* hours more than you are officially required to, if you are a member of political party P you will not be allowed to participate in its meetings, and here is the list of the newspapers you are not allowed to read during lunch breaks' (and so on, until nothing of the prospective work relation is left unsaid). Alternatively, the prospective employee may happen to be fully informed of all the aspects of the work relation after having talked with current employees, or because everyone in town knows how that employer treats his employees. When the employee gets exactly the work relation he was expecting – in the light of the data he collected both formally and informally – he is just made an offer.

The second strategy consists of analysing the cases in which the premise of the objection holds true – the worker is unaware of the real terms of the work relation – and rejecting its conclusion – the employer dominates the employee. It may so happen that the employer does not clearly spell out the terms of the work relation, and more generally, even if he does, nothing prevents him from changing his mind in the future. My argument is that, even if the employer gives the employee a work relation that is less agreeable than what the employee had imagined, the employer is not exercising arbitrary interference. Consider the situation in which the employee signs a contract expecting not to be mistreated, but when work begins he turns out to be a victim of unpaid extra work. For the account of exploitation without interpersonal domination I am exploring here, it does not really make a difference whether the employee knew what he was signing on for or not. As long as the employer does not prevent him from taking a way out of their market relation, there is no interpersonal domination between the two. For even though there is no worthy exit option for the employee, this is a structural problem that cannot be directly ascribed to the employer.

In order to clarify this point, let us go back to the case of Robert (the employee) and David (the employer). We can assume that when Robert accepts David's job offer he expects to get B. But after Robert starts working for David, he realises that the new employer requires him to do extra work and wants to interfere in his private life. So, while Robert opted for B, when presented with a choice between A and B, he ends up with D, which is inferior to B. Does this amount to arbitrary interference? It does not, because no matter how inferior D is, compared to B, David never deprives Robert of A – the only option Robert had before they began interacting.

Robert is free to leave his new job at any moment. If David progressively worsens the terms of the work relation with Robert, shifting from D to E, then from E to F, and, finally, from F to G, but Robert does not quit his job, it would mean he still considers G better than A. David is able to make Robert accept progressively worse work conditions because the only other available option, A, is incredibly modest, but David is not directly responsible for A's meagreness, as he would have been, for example, had he earlier reduced Robert to starvation by killing his cattle or doing something similar. This does not mean the employer is cleared of all faults. He is responsible for sustaining an economic order that allows for such structural domination. He does not deprive the employee of any option at any specific moment, but he intentionally defends the unequal distribution of assets that leaves the employee commodified and exploitable. As Gourevitch rightly underlines:

> to be clear, owners do not need to intend the exact, empirical distribution of control over productive assets [. . .] They need only intend that property rights be respected even if the overall distribution of control over productive assets means that some will be forced to sell their labours to others. (Gourevitch 2013, p. 12)

I have been holding that the entire explanation of domination of employees (and the infringement on their freedom) should be unfolded in structural terms. In my view, we cannot maintain that capitalist structural domination does also lead to interpersonal domination between the employer and the employee unless we introduce a principle which, though desirable in itself, I find troubling to demonstrate: that the employer, for the sole reason of having capital available, has the duty to offer to the employee an option, 'ideal-C', whose terms are clearly stated. If David had the duty of providing Robert with an option that is at least equal to 'ideal-C', then we can interpret the replacement of 'ideal-C' with any inferior option – D, E, F and G – as a form of arbitrary interference that gives rise to interpersonal domination.

In his first book on freedom as non-domination, Pettit (1997) deals with the issue of the 'benchmark'. He holds – and I agree – that a person can interfere in the choice of another person not only by removing or replacing an option she happened to have in her set earlier, but also 'to the extent of worsening what by the received benchmark are the expected payoffs for the options [she] face[s]' (Pettit 1997, p. 54). He gives the example of a pharmacist, who agrees to sell an urgently needed medicine to a customer only at an exceptionally high price. I think that Pettit is right in describing this case as one of arbitrary interference, because the pharmacist does deprive the customer of something – the legitimate expectation that a person, who has a licence to run a pharmacy, will pursue her profession in line with national public standards.

But, now, assume that the pharmacist and his customer – who in this case is not an official customer but just Susan – happen to meet in a desert, where both are holidaying. The situation is the same. Susan urgently needs the medicine, and the pharmacist, who always carries with him a case full of medicines when he travels, is willing to sell it only at an exploitative price. Is the pharmacist practising arbitrary interference over Susan? That amounts to asking if there is any reasonable benchmark price that the pharmacist should respect. While I find it easy to say that when the pharmacist is in his pharmacy, he has to meet the standards set by the national health plan, I have some problems when the pharmacist is simply John, a tourist who is crossing the desert. This high price, surely exploitative and morally wrong, arises from the logic of supply and demand. When John acts as a pharmacist, he clearly has to respect some norms that take precedence over the market mechanism. But if we want to keep the notion of interference completely unmoralised, what is the alternative benchmark that John, as a private citizen, should respect when performing a market interaction in place of the one that emerges out of the market mechanism? I cannot find any.[8]

The entire discourse concerning the legitimate expectations of the parties of a market transaction revolves around the existence of regulations that go beyond the mere logic of profit. Consider, for example, a case in which a natural disaster determines an excess of demand for a medicine. It might be asked whether the pharmacist, in the exercising of his profession, would be curtailing the legitimate expectations of the customer in the case that he decides to increase the price of the scarce good. I think he would be doing so, because he would fail to treat the victims of the natural disaster (at least) as well as other citizens treated by other pharmacists under standard conditions. Thus, this second pharmacist would be on a par with the pharmacist of Pettit's example, the one charging the single customer a higher price only because she is in dire need of the good the pharmacist controls. Accordingly, the legitimate expectations of the customer here stem from the fact that the seller is acting within norms that have been set at a national level to constrain the job activities of those agents involved in welfare provisions, whereas no arbitrary interference would occur between a person who is willing to pay any price for the last stamp of his collection and another person who possesses the sought-after stamp and is willing to sell it only at 100 times its market value.

Similarly, the introduction of 'ideal-C' in the discourse on job contracts would require two moves that have little to do with the theory of freedom as non-domination, and which we cannot consider to be self-justifying. The first, and less troubling one, consists in demonstrating that, when the employer decides to hire someone, he has to place his offer above an acceptability threshold that is independent of the logic of supply and demand. But this alone, though difficult, would not be enough, because we would also need to demonstrate that, for the simple reason of capital being available to him, the employer has the duty of making a job offer, that is to say, providing a prospective employee with an additional option. Step 1 makes the undertaking of step 2 unavoidable. Let us assume that every person who has capital when making a job offer has to meet the 'ideal-C' standard. We have seen that David offers Robert option B, which is inferior to 'ideal-C'. But B is, surely, better than nothing. So, if we hold that, when David offers option B to Robert, he indulges

---

[8]   In this regard, I disagree with Richard Dagger (2006, pp. 158–9) when he discusses the situation of 'a person in urgent need of a good that can only be obtained from someone who has an effective monopoly on that good' and holds that the weaker party is 'trapped' in a 'state of dependency' on 'the good will of the stronger party' that accounts for unfreedom. More precisely, I agree that the weaker party is unfree, but I believe that it is due to systemic reasons, not to interpersonal domination by the stronger party.

in arbitrary interference as long as B is inferior to 'ideal-C', we should say the same about the other capitalist, who decides to spend all his money on crazy parties without building up any business. In fact, the interference by this party capitalist in regard to Robert is more severe than the one performed by David, because a bad contract is surely better than no contract at all, amounting to leaving Robert with option A only.

Therefore, if we really insist that a benchmark for a contract exists, we should also accept the troubling conclusion that those who happen to have capital available infringe on the freedom of unknown people if they do not use their money to offer an unlimited number of job contracts. But this would entail a sort of capital-slavery. Whoever has capital is not free to use it as she wishes; rather, she has to reinvest everything in the economy, at least as long as there is even one proletarian who has not been provided with 'ideal-C'. Such a conclusion is unacceptable, but, if we reject it, we have to give up the idea of an ideal benchmark for job offers that employers have to respect regardless of the logic of supply and demand, and, if we have no benchmark, we cannot hold that structural domination results in interpersonal domination.

2.3   THE ARBITRARINESS OF CAPITALIST STRUCTURAL DOMINATION

A similar point was made, from a Marxist perspective, by John E. Roemer, when he argued that:

> Marxists have often emphasized the coercion of the worker by the capitalist at the point of production, as it occurs at the locus of expropriation of surplus value. According to the property relations definition, the key locus of coercion is not at the point of production, but in the maintenance of property relations. The struggle at the point of production is, I think, of second order in importance; it is the struggle over the terms of a contract. (Roemer 1982, p. 311)

The difference between the Marxist interpretation of structural domination proposed by Roemer and the republican account of freedom in the market I am sketching here resides in the reasons as to why such an unequal distribution of property titles, leaving some people without a costless exit from market relations, is coercive. For Marx (2013 [1867], pp. 120–214, 501–42) the problem about some people becoming capitalists and others proletarians revolved around the fact that the first wage-workers were violently deprived of the means of production – the primitive accumulation – and then capitalists profited from this illegitimate expropriation to extract surplus value from newly created proletarians. Roemer (1982, pp. 310–13) rightly contends, in my view, that proletarians are exploited not because of employers extracting surplus value from their labour, but rather in virtue of the unequal access to the means of production. The latter renders employees exploited also when there is no attrition in the job relation – meaning that the terms of the contract have been clearly agreed and/or no extraction of surplus value takes place.

Nonetheless, as Roemer (2017, pp. 272–3) recognises, primitive accumulation is not enough for arguing ad infinitum that property relations are exploitative. After all, many people today enjoy the fruits of capital that they have honestly accumulated, and, in addition, the presence of a market for labour does not entail per se the extraction of surplus value (Roemer 2017, pp. 268–9). Therefore, Roemer's conclusion (1982, p. 312) is that property relations can be considered as exploitative by taking as a non-exploitative benchmark a fair allocation of resources, as, for example, the one described by John Rawls in his theory of justice. Indeed, also in more recent writings Roemer (2017, p. 309) has argued that 'socialism's ethical goal' should not consist in overcoming the market mechanism but in the achievement of distributive justice. In contrast, from the republican perspective I am embracing in this chapter, the problem with a property system that allows for the exclusion of a consistent group of people from the control of the means of production rests in mere domination, that is to say, not in comparison with a positive account of socio-economic justice as the one that Roemer ends up embracing, but rather in terms of a negative duty of justice to not pose avoidable constraints on the individual autonomy of others.

Yet, it might be objected that an unequal property system that allows for the exclusion of a consistent group of people from the control of the means of production is not arbitrary – at least in the neo-republican sense – as long as it is invigilated through democratic practices, to which every member of society is given access. In this sense, while Roman slaves were surely under a form of structural domination – because slaves were not given a voice in the law-making process that rendered them slaves – wage-slavery alone[9] cannot be considered as a case of structural domination in a democratic society. If this were true, we would have capitalist structural interference without capitalist structural domination.

At this point, it is inevitable to recall the distinction highlighted by Frank Lovett (2010, pp. 85–123; 2012, pp. 137–41) between the procedural and the substantive interpretations of arbitrariness. On the first account, an interference can be considered arbitrary as long as it is not constrained by rules and procedures that are both effective and known by all the agents concerned. On

---

[9]   Here I am postulating that capitalist structural domination does not result in interpersonal domination. Thus, differently from labour republicans, I cannot rely on the arbitrariness of the interference performed by the employer in regard to the employee; rather, I need to demonstrate that we can make sense of the arbitrariness of wage-slavery entirely at the systemic level.

the second account, an interference counts as arbitrary when it both falls short of the procedural proviso and does not track the avowed interests of all the agents involved in the interference. Lovett (2012, pp. 147–50) backs up the procedural account, while Pettit (1997, p. 55) has always leant towards more substantive qualifications of arbitrariness. In *Republicanism*, he wrote that 'an act of interference will be non-arbitrary to the extent that it is forced to track the interests and ideas of the person suffering the interference' (Pettit 1997, p. 55), while in the more recent *On People's Terms* he shifted towards a position that Samuel Arnold and John R. Harris (2017, p. 57) defined as 'control substantivism', according to which a government cannot be said to dominate citizens as long as its decisions can pass the 'tough-luck test', that is to say, as long as 'you and your fellows have good grounds to think that any unwelcome results of public decision-making are just tough luck' (Pettit 2012, p. 177).

Now, in which sense can we hold that the fact that some people are left without productive assets within a given property system amounts to a form of domination even when this property system is the outcome of a democratic legislation that is effectively invigilated by all citizens – including proletarians? Surely not in the procedural sense championed by Lovett, because from this perspective the existence of transparent property rules is enough to defuse arbitrariness.[10] From the purely substantial account proposed by the early Pettit,[11] on the other hand, it is possible to maintain that all those people who provide their political support to a property system that causes a group of citizens to be left with no valid alternative other than to seek their survival in a market relation, are failing to heed a basic interest of this disadvantaged group: the interest not to be forced, for lack of alternatives, to end up in an exploitative employer–employee relation.[12]

Yet, the solution is less clear from the perspective of control substantivism. After all, someone might contend, nothing prevents proletarians from seeking support in favour of a political reform that deletes private property and forcibly redistributes the means of production.[13] Therefore, if things remain unaltered it is because the majority has legitimately expressed its will in this sense, and proletarians should only consider their condition as a case of tough luck – in

---

[10] For a convincing analysis of the limits of a merely procedural interpretation of arbitrariness, see Arnold and Harris (2017, pp. 59–63).

[11] Arnold and Harris (2017, p. 57) define it as 'interest substantivism'.

[12] On the relation between responsibility and structural injustice, see also Chapter 4 and the 'social connection model of responsibility' proposed by Iris Marion Young. In her words, 'individuals bear responsibility for structural injustice because they contribute by their actions to the processes that produce unjust outcomes' (Young 2011, p. 105).

[13] In some cases it would be a constitutional reform.

the same way as a criminal might resent ending up in prison but he cannot maintain to have been arbitrarily interfered with by criminal law. This being the case, the idea of capitalist structural domination could find its justification only in interest substantivism, not in control substantivism.

I shall leave aside the general issue about what constitutes the more appropriate account of republican arbitrariness. Rather, I would make two comments regarding the possibility of defending the arbitrariness of an unequal property system also on 'control' grounds. The first one is very concise and concerns the peculiarity of capitalist structural domination. Consistent asymmetries in political power arise between those individuals who control productive assets and those who do not. Proletarians live in a structural situation of subjugation that limits many of the capabilities needed to effectively participate in the democratic process. In particular, they have fewer resources to invest in education and fewer opportunities to draw the attention of policy makers to their interests. Instead, those with higher political power are the same people who control the largest percentage of productive assets and they have a strong interest in preserving the status quo. From this, it does not directly follow that proletarians encounter the same insurmountable obstacles in invigilating property laws that the slaves faced in invigilating slavery laws. Yet, it should at least entail that radical inequality in access to the means of production would not entirely pass Pettit's tough-luck test, because it is not 'under an efficacious form of control that you share equally with others in imposing' (Pettit 2012, p. 178).

The second comment pertains to the relation between structural obstacles to freedom and the individual capacity to surmount them. Robert, for example, was born with option A only – starving. David exploits him by offering him B – an unfair job contract. Robert has suffered arbitrary interference at birth because he was denied C – an acceptable alternative to selling his labour power. But was Robert, though starting his life with a clear disadvantage, structurally unable to make up for this disadvantage and get an option C through individual effort? After all, literature, movies, music and chronicles are full of stories of people who start their lives in dire conditions but manage to accumulate some wealth through their work and industriousness, and raise themselves from proletarian conditions. If this is true, one might say the structural domination of proletarians might be mitigated through individual skills. This means, in a capitalist society, the boundaries of the class, subjected to structural domination, are not closed. Individuals are free to escape from it. Hence, the idea of capitalist structural domination would be watered down.

Also, in this case there are two possible ways to respond to such a strong objection. The first one consists of resorting to the distinction between individual freedom and collective freedom made by Cohen in another excellent essay on the conditions of proletarians. As per this first strategy, we accept the premise of the objection but reject the conclusion. The second way consists, instead, in rejecting both the premise and the conclusion in cases of extreme commodification of labour.

Cohen (1988, p. 266) made two arguments:

1. There are more exits from the British proletariat than there are workers trying to leave it. Therefore, British workers are individually free to leave the proletariat.
2. There are very few exits from the British proletariat and there are very many workers in it. Therefore, British workers are collectively unfree to leave the proletariat.

An individual worker can rise above the proletarian class and enter the 'petty bourgeoisie' as Cohen calls it. She is not individually imprisoned. She might patent a new app, sell it for millions of dollars to some big company and leave the labour market forever. Or, more likely, she might save part of her wage, invest it in a small enterprise, and slowly accumulate enough capital to get moderately de-commodified. The problem, Cohen argues, is that there are more workers stuck in the proletariat group than available exit points. The freedom to leave the proletariat, experienced by an individual worker, is conditional. She is free 'only on condition that the others do not exercise their similarly conditional freedom' (Cohen 1988, p. 263). To make the case clearer, Cohen proposes the room analogy. Ten people are blocked in a room. There are two doors and two keys. Once someone picks up one key and opens the corresponding door, photoelectric devices set by the gaoler will make it unusable again. In Cohen's example, only one person opens the door; all the others are disinclined to leave the room. This might happen for several reasons: they are too lazy, the room is not so uncomfortable, they think if they try to pick the last key the others will try to block them, and so on (Cohen 1988, pp. 261–3). Every one of the nine people who remain in the room is individually free to escape, but the freedom is contingent on other people not exercising that freedom. Despite being individually free, they are collectively unfree. Cohen gives this definition of collective unfreedom:

> A group suffers collective unfreedom with respect to a type of action *A* if and only if performance of *A* by all members of the group is impossible. (Cohen 1988, p. 268)

All proletarians enjoy individual freedom to escape their condition as long as they do not exercise it at the same time. Or, to put it more precisely, as long as the number of proletarians attempting to leave the group is less than the available exits. When the opposite occurs, collective unfreedom generates individual unfreedom (Cohen 1988, p. 270). Therefore, we can accept the premise of the objection – commodified workers are individually free to cease selling their labour power – without accepting the conclusion that commodified workers are not structurally dominated. In short, even if we pick a single worker and argue that she is individually free, although conditionally, to take a route out of the proletarian group, the capitalist arrangement does not allow us to empty this group completely.

When Cohen wrote his essay at the end of the 1980s, he was clearly analysing the conditions of British workers. His aim was to reach the conclusion that proletarians were unfree. But in order to do so, he had to concede right-wing arguments that the single proletarian was individually free. His argumentative strategy is incredibly useful, because it permits us to neutralise the right-wing objection to proletarian unfreedom in the context in which it is more powerful, in developed countries. Nonetheless, I think that if, today, we broadened the scope of our analysis to the global proletariat, we would not have to recognise the universal truth of the objection's premise – that a single proletarian is individually free.

At the end of his essay, Cohen (1988, p. 284) acknowledges that 'it could be that there is more crowding at the exits in other capitalist societies, and therefore less truth in the premise of argument 7 [our argument 1] when it is asserted of those societies'. This is certainly true, but the biggest problem with proletarians in the most destitute areas of the world is not a crowding at the doors towards the middle class, but rather the fact that they are so extremely commodified that they never manage to reach the door.

Just think, for example, of the notion of 'disposable people', recently introduced in academic debate by Kevin Bales (2012), referring to those people who are so poor and so short of any decent job opportunity, or any reasonable alternative to selling their labour, that they have to use their lives as debt collateral or voluntarily enter into a semi-legal relation of slavery for survival. It would be really hard to argue that these 'disposable' people are individually free to escape from proletarian conditions. I simply cannot see how the Brazilian farmer, displaced by deforestation and voluntarily accepting a slave contract, or a Thai girl sold to a brothel by her family for mere survival, described by Bales, might move to an upper class. They are selling their labour performance solely in exchange for being kept alive in unseemly conditions. They cannot save money from their wages. No matter how ambitious or industrious they might be, they will never be able to build any capital while in their work situation. Someone may try to object that they can simply look for a better job that allows them to make some savings. The first problem with this argument is that when you work for daily survival you do not enjoy any amount of freedom to explore the market, look for opportunities, apply, and wait for responses. The second problem is that if you are born in a state of extreme commodification, you are denied the opportunity of enriching your human capital. The job opportunities of a person who has spent her life in contract slavery or debt bondage are incredibly limited.

Surely, even for a 'disposable' person, it is theoretically possible to enter an upper social group if some events, independent of market dynamics, were to occur. If the Brazilian worker, stuck in contract slavery, happens to meet a wealthier person, marry her, and inherit her wealth, he can find a route out of proletarian conditions. The same would hold true if he happens to have some innate talent that is independent of schooling. But these are very rare cases. We can lightly hold that the persons experiencing extreme commodification of labour power are individually unfree to escape from the proletarian fold – their chances of doing so being so low that they would be considered insignificant.

In sum, I have sought to maintain that if we move from the definition of freedom as non-domination, we can neither hold that the problem with individual unfreedom in a market economy consists in the fact that under peculiar circumstances those who control capital can be said to dominate wage-workers, as neo-republicans have argued, nor that structural domination, of the kind described by labour republicans, leads to interpersonal domination at the point of production. Conversely, I have maintained that if we are committed to republican theoretical premises about liberty, we shall conclude that within a market economy the individual loses his freedom for systemic reasons, due to an unequal and unfavourable distribution of the means of production, while the imposition of obnoxious conditions on the weakest counterpart of a market transaction is a matter of exploitation, which is a consequence rather than a replication of domination.

This should not be read as an attempt to mitigate, let alone justify, the moral condition of the exploitative agent, who remains blameworthy for the abuses he practises over the exploited agent, in the same way as a Roman citizen was blameworthy for the abuses he inflicted on his slave, regardless of the fact that these horrible acts were the result of norms that rendered them possible. In this sense, by distinguishing between domination and exploitation, we can maintain that an exploitative action remains equally grave, whether it is a result of structural or interpersonal domination. The judgement as to how a person becomes exploitable does not necessarily alter the judgement about the seriousness of the exploitation she suffers and the moral responsibility of the exploitative agent. Moreover, by putting structural domination before exploitation, we have the advantage of extending the moral responsibility for the exploitation of the weaker party in a transaction far beyond those involved in that same transaction, thus raising a general obligation to intervene to change the rules within which exploitative transactions take place.

3. A minimum de-commodification of labour and global justice

I have argued that the privatisation of productive assets and their unequal distribution represent a problem of justice from the republican perspective on domination. Those people who are structurally deprived of a valid alternative to seeking survival in a labour contract are dominated in the neo-republican meaning of the term. This is not necessarily true in a diachronic sense – that is to say, taking a pre-capitalist moment in history as our baseline – but as I shall argue in more detail later on, the domination suffered by proletarians should be properly interpreted subjunctively, in relation to a hypothetical alternative that is achievable within capitalism, in which freedom from domination is preserved.

In order to render this discourse less abstract, it is sufficient to look at some data. In 2016, there were about 16 million people in forced labour in the global private economy. More than half of them were in debt bondage, meaning that they had been coerced into working to repay a debt in most cases due to an economic shock (ILO 2017a, pp. 10–11). In 2017, there were 1.4 billion people in 'vulnerable employment', that is to say in a condition in which they lack both social security and any form of bargaining power with their employers (ILO 2017b, p. 7). In 2019, around 470 million people in the world were either denied the opportunity to work *tout court* or were prevented from working the desired number of hours – on the basis of their personal life-plans. Moreover, many of the people in the world who have jobs, and they amount to about 3.3 billion, fall short of 'decent working conditions' (ILO 2020, p. 12). Another interesting perspective from which we can examine the phenomenon of labour commodification is through the data concerning the rising number of rural migrants in the world and of people living in urban slums. Market and trade liberalisation have mostly meant the privatisation of rural land, hence millions of workers who were previously relying on rural assets – either private or public – have been deprived of land and forced to look for a job contract in the industrial sector, thus populating the suburbs of big cities and megalopolises (Davis 2006, pp. 1–19). To this, we should add the impact that climate change, extensive farming and extensive agriculture are having upon the yield of rural land (Lister 2014; Thompson 2019). Lastly, we should also bring into the picture the fact that these people usually live in developing countries where they lack the social provisions that might help in absorbing the economic downturns they have to undergo.

Consequently, if it is true that a consistent number of people in the world enter the labour market in a condition of domination, the reasons for which are not only systemic but also global (as we shall see in a while), it is not enough, from the point of view of justice, to criticise the unequal allocation of global wealth only from a distributive perspective. We should rather consider that the majority of people who take part in social cooperation do not do so out of free choice. This fact entails two consequences. First, structural domination matters per se, because it infringes on individual freedom, and this accounts for the systemic claim that I briefly discussed in Chapter 2. Second, structural domination poses a further problem of justice when it paves the way for serious cases of exploitation and unjust enrichment, and this leads us logically to a second, relational claim. My aim in this chapter, and partially also in the next, is to discuss how to counter capitalist structural domination and to clarify who has the duty to contribute to this objective and to what extent.

In Chapter 2, I gave a definition of capitalist structural domination and of capitalist interpersonal exploitation. I shall now give a definition of a third concept, unjust enrichment, before proceeding further. Unjust enrichment refers, in my view, to the extra profits that those people who monopolise productive assets, and those other people who entertain market relations with them – e.g. as consumers, self-employed – are able to yield in the global market, in comparison with a hypothetical situation in which their salaried counterparts have been given a valuable alternative to seeking survival in a market relation (Calder 2010). Accordingly, unjust enrichment is not simply a prerogative of entrepreneurs, but also of all those people who benefit from interacting with someone who has obtained unjust profits. Consider, for example, a multinational company that exploits workers in country X and then gets partially taxed (hopefully) and offers well-paid executive jobs in country Y. People from country Y would have their welfare provisions and job opportunities financed – only in part, obviously – through extra profits that could not have been raised had everyone in country X been free from capitalist domination. The same holds true for the shareholders and for the people who unwittingly entrust their savings to banks which transfer the money to investment funds that buy the stocks of companies such as the one we are considering here. Similarly, a consumer is realising an unjust enrichment as long as he buys a product at a price that is kept low by paying a minimum percentage of the final value to the worker who made it, and the latter accepts the unfair pay because he experiences a structural condition of domination.

Moreover, also those who simply hire out their human capital can benefit from capitalist structural domination in the same way as entrepreneurs, investors and consumers. Consider this case. The pay that an architect gets for a given project should be read within a fixed budget that an investor has set for realising it. Assume that the investor has 100 coins available for building a palace. The architect asks for 20 coins to work on the project; this is her standard fee. If the investor is able to limit all other expenses – materials, workers, machinery, etc. – to 80 coins, the project is feasible. Now the question is this: is the investor able to limit all other expenses to 80 coins because the bricklayers, or the workers that realised the building materials, are experiencing a condition of extreme commodification? If the answer is yes, then we should conclude that the architect is able to charge 20 coins for her labour performance because other workers were violated in their freedom from domination – were victims of capitalist structural domination. Had all other workers employed in the project been free, two things might have happened. The architect could have remained unmovable in her fee, thus renouncing the project. Or she could have lowered her fee, to 15 coins for example, so as to make it compatible with the investor's budget. In both cases, she would have lost something, or, to put it differently, if some workers involved in the project are extremely commodified the architect gains something, unjustly.

Ultimately, unjust enrichment presupposes both structural domination and interpersonal exploitation, but it is not said that he who obtains an unjust enrichment is he who directly exploits the dominated worker – e.g. the consumer, the investor, the architect. Accordingly, the obligational claim of my argument unfolds on two different levels – structural and interactional[1] – with the interactional level unfolding on two sub-levels: exploitation and unjust enrichment. This means, first of all, that doing well on the interactional level does not suffice to dispel the structural obligation. For instance, it may happen that I do not exploit anyone nor do I obtain unjust enrichment, in the senses delineated above, yet I do nothing to change the unequal distribution of the means of production that allows for capitalist domination – and hence I allow other individuals to exploit and obtain unjust enrichment. Conversely, doing well at the structural level does not give me an unconditional green light at the interactional level. More specifically, a reformist slaveholder fighting for the abolition of slavery is still guilty of the use he makes of his slaves, just as a reformist capitalist actively engaged in the political battle for a fairer distribution of the means of production is not morally justified in saving on production costs through the containment of labour costs made possible by the

---

[1]   I have used so far the term 'interpersonal' for discussing the relations between employees and employers. I shall now use the term 'interactional' to account for the fact that exploitation and unjust enrichment can also be the result – as they often are – of the actions of companies, investment funds, consumer groups, and so on.

inequality of property that he wants to change.[2] Moreover, as previously noted, a person may be getting unjust enrichment without exploiting anyone, or vice versa – even though the latter is a rarer case, but it can occur in the uncommon situation where the exploiter registers losses instead of profits.

In Chapter 4, I will deal more directly with the question of how the causal responsibility for capitalist structural domination in itself, and the responsibility for the unfair individual benefits that structural capitalist domination allows, translate into practical obligations to redress. In this chapter, instead, I will introduce the notion of a minimum de-commodification of labour power as the correct 'anti-power' to capitalist structural domination. I will explain through which measures it can be achieved. I will argue in favour of a cosmopolitan interpretation of MDL and I shall clarify how MDL is grafted onto the broader political ideal of countering the more general concept of domination. I will then analyse the implications of MDL from a gender perspective. Lastly, I illustrate why MDL as a cosmopolitan principle of justice is different, and in my view preferable for normative reasons, to sufficientarianism, the capability approach and Pogge's GRD.

3.1   A MINIMUM DE-COMMODIFICATION OF LABOUR

In his seminal book on welfare capitalism, Gøsta Esping-Andersen (1990, p. 37) defined de-commodification as 'the degree to which individuals, or families, can uphold a socially acceptable standard of living independently of market participation' and he added that 'de-commodification should not be confused with the complete eradication of labour as a commodity'. The 'degree' and the notion of social acceptability are probably two of the most controversial issues in contemporary politics. A complete de-commodification of labour power would reduce, almost completely, the likelihood of someone being exploited on the labour market and would fully neutralise the structural domination stemming from unequal distribution of assets. But obviously this would prove to be unsustainable in economic terms. If we recur to a thought experiment and imagine what would happen if suddenly every member of a given society were completely de-commodified, we would probably be

---

[2]   At least unless the capitalist can demonstrate that he ended up in what elsewhere I have called an 'atypical dirty hands dilemma'. More explicitly, on the one hand he would like to convince all other competitors to give up exploitation, but if the others are not willing to cooperate he is obliged to keep on exploiting because the alternative would be worse both for him and for his employees, since he would go bankrupt (Corvino 2015). If this scenario occurs, then it is possible to reason about the fact that fulfilling systemic responsibility reduces relational obligations.

presented with a situation in which no one is prevented from enjoying the livelihood of the middle class of that specific society. The results would clearly differ in absolute terms according to which society we put through our thought experiment. The list of capabilities of the fully de-commodified individual would be much bigger if we imagined this process to take place in Norway rather than in Ecuador. But what would be true, regardless of the specific contingencies in which the thought experiment takes place, is that every person would be free to quit the labour market without falling below a substantially high welfare threshold.

Our hypothetical society D – a completely de-commodified one – would surely be more equal than society C (society D before full de-commodification) because those who were kept below the threshold by market contingencies would be brought near the centre of the social spectrum; hence, the gap between the top and the bottom would be reduced. But society D would not be fully equal because even if individuals were provided with the means for de-commodifying their labour performance, this does not necessarily entail that the market for labour would be abolished. Some people may choose to sell their de-commodified labour performance even if now they are provided with middle-level welfare anyway. I see three reasons why some people – probably the majority of people – may decide to remain in the labour market.

The first one is that someone may value the act of working for some purposes other than mere remuneration. For example, a person might be willing to keep on working, even if this does not substantially improve her livelihood, because she believes that her self-realisation depends on the satisfaction of seeing other people paying to buy her labour performance; or because a good job might grant her social respect, and social respect is the source of her self-esteem. Assume, for example, that in society D complete de-commodification is guaranteed through a substantially high universal basic income. In this scenario, Olivia, who has invested all her life in enriching her culture and might now opt for not commercialising her intellectual skills and enjoying the amenities of life, decides to work for a popular magazine at a very low wage – the magazine cannot offer more – because she really values being publicly recognised as an intellectual. Or, alternatively, assume that in society D the process of full de-commodification has been achieved through a mix of unemployment benefits and free public services. The unemployment benefit Olivia would receive for staying home is higher than the wage the magazine can offer her. Given these circumstances, we can imagine that Olivia's desire of being read and known is so important that she might actually renounce the unemployment benefit just to work, thus paying an economic price for entering the labour market.

Secondly, a person might deem the middle-level livelihood as unsatisfactory in absolute terms. Imagine that Leopold, an above-average skilled individual, craves for some luxury goods (e.g. an expensive car) that are unachievable at the welfare level that has been made independent from market participation. Leopold might decide to enter the labour market because he deems being able to buy expensive goods more valuable than being free to enjoy a middle income all day. Thirdly, a person might be dissatisfied with the middle-level livelihood in relative terms. Imagine, for example, Martin, a highly skilled person, who finds having the same welfare as less skilled persons unsatisfactory. Distancing other people on the wealth scale might be a sufficient reason for Martin to put his labour performance on the market.

In this hypothetical scenario, in which the achievement of a middle-level livelihood has been decoupled from market participation, market exploitation cannot occur, at least according to the non-moralised account that I am defending, provided that there are no market distortions. This is so because every individual would be free from capitalist structural domination; hence, no one would be in the position to profit from the structural unfreedom of someone else. Obviously, it is important to underline that I am only referring to market exploitation, while other forms of exploitation would still be possible. As an example, consider the case in which you come into possession of photos that may embarrass me with my loved ones and force me to do things that I would never have done if you had not had my photos. Labour de-commodification, no matter how extensive, cannot do anything against this kind of exploitation, because the leverage you use on me, my potential embarrassment, does not pertain to the market sphere. In cases like the latter, exploitation should be addressed through non-market measures, such as legislation prohibiting the use of personal material for the purpose of blackmailing. In some other cases, on the other hand, exploitation remains a private affair that pertains to individual ethics. Imagine, for example, that I fall in love with you and you know that you can never return my love but still you take advantage of the situation to burden me, knowing that I would do anything for you. Here everything hinges upon our private relation and your willingness to be fair with me, given the existing unbalance of 'contracting' power among us.

However, the point I would like to emphasise here is that even in a fully de-commodified society, people will nurture what we may call extra desires, that is to say the desire for something – be it some specific goods or the gratification of one's self-esteem – that cannot be obtained through the middle-level livelihood guaranteed by complete labour de-commodification. Another consequence of this, in addition to the inequality induced by the willingness of some to continue commercialising their labour performance, is that it may happen that someone feels that the realisation of a given extra desire is so indispensable for his well-being that, in order to achieve it, he is willing to trade off a considerable part of the protection guaranteed by labour de-commodification. Assume, for example, that Olivia is not sufficiently talented to collaborate with a magazine that is important enough to render her a publicly recognised intellectual, and the only way for Olivia to realise her dream is to work for a magazine whose editor would harass her continuously.[3] The editor has clearly set unfair, hateful and disgusting conditions for the job relation.[4] In general, we may say that the lower the level of Olivia's de-commodification, the higher the editor's chances of buying her labour performance at those conditions – meaning that were Olivia driven to seek that job contract to secure a minimum livelihood, it would have been much easier for the employer to exploit her. But what happens if these job conditions are offered in society D, where full de-commodification has been achieved? According to the non-moralised account of market exploitation, and given the circumstances of society D, the editor is not practising market exploitation over Olivia – even though he is morally guilty of reprehensible and punishable actions from the point of view of professional deontology, with possible and just criminal consequences. In broader terms, we may say that once a medium welfare has been unconditionally guaranteed, bargaining over extra desires cannot give rise to market exploitation, because this sort of bargaining remains morally neutral from the market perspective – and we should look for arguments of moral reproach in other moral realms.

Ultimately, capitalist structural domination has been neutralised in society D. People are still divided among those who own and those who do not own productive assets. But the de-commodification of society has mitigated, almost eliminated, the dominating effect of the division of private property. Exploitation is limited to non-market relations. Yet, an interesting question to ask regarding what I named extra desires is whether someone might claim to be dominated insofar as she is prevented from realising her extra desire in a way that is not related to the market. For example, Olivia could put forward the argument that she is victim of a derivation of capitalist structural domination because in a market society she is prevented from achieving self-esteem as an intellectual without being published in a magazine that is commercialised. Consequently, if the argument were successful, the editor could be said to practise market exploitation over her also from the non-moralised account of exploitation I am proposing. However, the problem with this kind of discourse is that it would shift the focus of capitalist domination from an objective evaluation, based on the access to a middle level of welfare that is proportionate to single societies, towards a more subjective evaluation that is sensitive to extra

---

[3]   This is the elaboration of an example that was sketched in Chapter 2, where I assumed the applicant publicist was wealthy enough to live without having to work.

[4]   Alternatively, we might say that the employer has set an unfairly low price for the labour performance offered by the employee.

desires. Accordingly, someone could claim to be structurally dominated as far as the establishment of the market principle as the main mechanism for regulating social relations prevent him from obtaining the right social prestige and respect he would deserve in virtue of his outstanding warrior skills. Therefore, for the sake of simplicity, I would tend to interpret both capitalist structural domination and capitalist exploitation in relation to a level of income that is valid for everyone, and that I identify in a medium level of welfare, which is what everyone would be guaranteed unconditionally in society D.

However, this is true at the theoretical level, but unfortunately the thought experiment that we have followed so far cannot avoid contemplating the very practical issue of how to finance full de-commodification of labour power in society D. More precisely, we should be careful in distinguishing between full de-commodification and a universal basic income. The former corresponds to a situation in which every individual can decide to leave the labour market while continuing to enjoy the medium level of welfare of her respective society. In this sense, the unit of measure of de-commodification is not diachronic, that is to say it does not correspond to the medium level of welfare calculated on that same society in a previous condition of labour commodification. Rather, the medium level should always be calculated with respect to the overall economic conditions of the society at the time the measurement is made. Therefore, if in the shift from society C to society D people become poorer because, for example, the full de-commodification of labour slows down growth and puts an unsustainable strain on public finance, the level of welfare that indicates the full de-commodification of any individual would progressively decline, possibly until the condition of full de-commodification amounts to poverty, because these are the redistributive possibilities of this society at this precise moment.

Inversely, the universal basic income corresponds to the payment of an unconditional sum of money to every member of the society, either through periodic instalments or a lump sum payment.[5] Even though Philippe Van Parijs (1992, p. 465) has famously argued that 'the introduction of such an unconditional income is to be viewed not as the dismantling but as the culmination of the welfare state, prepared by welfare state achievements in the same way as the abolition of slavery or the introduction of universal suffrage had been prepared, and made possible, by earlier partial conquests', there is little doubt that the whole discourse about the financial sustainability of the

---

[5]   Here I do not have space to linger on the different philosophical reasons that the proponents of a universal basic income propose in favour of this measure; hence, I simply discuss the policy tool. However, for an overview of the philosophy of basic income, see Cunliffe and Erreygers 2004; Raventós 2007; Widerquist 2013.

basic income hinges upon how many welfare provisions can be progressively replaced by it. In fact, many proponents of the basic income defend it on the grounds that it could be paid for through the money that is saved both on the performance of other welfare provisions and on the related administrative costs (see Arcarons et al. 2014; Standing 2017). Conversely, de-commodification of labour, be it more or less extensive, does not necessarily depend on the allocation of cash payments but, as explained in Chapter 1, it can also be obtained through welfare provisions. Accordingly, a person who receives a given basic income can be as de-commodified as another person who does not receive any market-independent income but who in return has access to a wider set of welfare provisions. Put more simply, whether an individual enjoys a given capability independently of her permanence in the market, as for example, going to an ophthalmologist for treatment, because she has been given an unconditional income that she can use to pay for the provision or rather because she can access the provision for free, does not make any substantial difference in the assessment of her level of de-commodification. This means that basic income is only one of the policies through which people can become de-commodified. Moreover, the condition of full de-commodification is different from the welfare regime centred on the basic income because the former guarantees protection from market vulnerability to a much wider set of capabilities than the latter, which could be correctly interpreted as 'a modest regular payment to each individual to help them feel more secure and able to purchase necessities for living' (Standing 2019, p. 5).

Hence, the general arguments that are typically used in favour of the universal basic income do not apply to a full de-commodification of labour power, which perhaps could only be achievable in a society that possesses abundant reserves of natural resources and redistributes the proceeds fairly among its members. But even in cases like this, the sustainability of the full de-commodification of labour would depend on the availability of natural resources, which, as we know, are not infinite in the case of non-renewables. A distinct argument is that in the future human beings could delegate the greatest percentage of the existing work to robots, thus progressively reducing human involvement in labouring activities while preserving economic growth. This is a fascinating vision that, as the Italian sociologist Domenico De Masi (2017) explains, could allow us to reproduce the ancient division between slaves and free human beings, with the former carrying out the bulk of productive work and the latter indulging in free activities that are instrumental to their human flourishing, but without incurring the ghastly injustice of human slavery (a possible futuristic scenario that deserves and would require another book).

Accordingly, I would here assume that a full de-commodification of labour power is desirable on normative grounds but infeasible in economic terms, so it is a hypothesis that should be dropped in practice. But what would happen, instead, if the full de-commodification of labour power were obtained through a generous unconditional unemployment benefit, namely a benefit that people receive when they leave – voluntarily or involuntarily – the labour market with no need to demonstrate that they are actively seeking to get back in it?[6] In this case, the sustainability of the system would depend on which percentage of people would prefer to opt out of the labour market. Obviously, the higher the benefit, the more people would prefer it to working. Personally, I think that in contemporary society the percentage of people who would accept enjoying life outside the labour market would not be excessively high. I also believe that Bertrand Russell (2004 [1935]) grasped a defining point of modern society when he argued that people would be unable to enjoy free time, even if it were technically possible to reduce the working time without a trade-off on economic growth, and to devote much of their time to either intellectual or physical activities that do not have an immediate impact on the productive sphere, because the imperative of rationality and efficiency has crushed every ability to enjoy the economically non-productive opportunities for human enrichment – and this marks the difference between the modern era and previous ones. A similar point was also made by John Maynard Keynes (2008 [1930], p. 23) when, committed to explaining why technological changes may in the long run allow human beings to solve what he called 'the economic problem', that is to say disentangling the satisfaction of subsistence needs from strain, he nonetheless warned that 'there is no country and no people, I think, who can look forward to the age of leisure and of abundance without a dread. For we have been trained too long to strive and not to enjoy.' Moreover, there is no doubt that social esteem and respect are things that contemporary people associate mostly with job positions. For all these reasons, I do not think that a large percentage of people would be able to feel satisfied and self-realised outside the labour market (see also McAfee and Brynjolfsson 2016, pp. 145–9). But these are complex hypotheses that can only play a marginal role in any theory of justice. For our purpose here, we can hold that an unemployment benefit that is both substantially high and unconditional would be impossible to sustain because the economic incentive to leave the job market for those whose income-wage was lower – or not much bigger – than the subsidy, is too large.

The fact that a full de-commodification of labour power is unsustainable in economic terms, or at least suspected to be so, makes it also undesirable

---

[6]   It is important to keep in mind that for an unemployment benefit to bring about a full de-commodification of labour power it should be unconditional. This is because the kind of subsidy that people lose after refusing a given number of job offers would only prevent them from falling below a decency threshold in the case in which labour demand outweighs labour offer. But it would not render anyone free to leave the labour market.

on normative grounds. The normative aim consists in countering extreme exploitation and domination within the structure of global capitalism, for, as we have argued before, the capitalist form of production has proved to be able to generate, absolutely, an unparalleled level of wealth. As stressed by Gourevitch (2013, p. 604), 'independence cannot mean radical economic autarky, a romantic, agrarian republic view out of step with the modern economy'. In our search for freedom we should stop at that point at which a marginal increase in non-domination would lead us outside modern capitalism. The reason is that we would pay for that marginal increase in freedom with the loss of a substantial set of capabilities that make our lives incomparably more enjoyable than in the pre-capitalist era. A full de-commodification of labour power is the most desirable social arrangement as far as exploitation and domination are concerned, but we should not embrace it normatively because its implementation would jeopardise the capitalist form of production.

I hold that we should rather opt for a minimum de-commodification of labour power (MDL), through which a basic set of capabilities is shielded from market contingencies and is guaranteed unconditionally to every human being. In the following section I shall explain why I interpret MDL as a cosmopolitan proviso, while now I shall stress that a basic set of capabilities includes access to food (in sufficient quantities to remain in good health and free from hunger), to housing, to health security, to education and the capability to relate to others without feeling shame (which is exercised in access to clothing, personal hygiene products and the like). Moreover, MDL can be obtained through any of the following provisions or a mix of them: universal basic income, social assistance, public services, community benefits, and unconditional unemployment benefits. Nonetheless, I would tend to set a universal basic income (UBI) apart for two reasons – one normative and the other empirical. First, given that the aim of MDL is to protect commodified individuals from structural domination, those who already happen to be more than minimally de-commodified (because they possess private or social alternatives to wage-income) do not have any claim to MDL, at least for the moment. Second, even though it might be argued that in general it is cheaper to make the basic income universal rather than shoulder the costs of targeting those mostly in need (Raventós 2007, pp. 124–8; De Wispelaere and Stirton 2011), MDL is such a low-level provision that it might make sense, even from the point of view of mere efficiency, to spend time and money in identifying those who are entitled to it.

Therefore, the proper way to implement MDL is to subordinate the provision to an extreme level of labour commodification – that is to say, to a condition in which the bond between the participation of an individual in the labour market and her welfare is strong enough for us to reasonably expect that, were this person to voluntarily or involuntarily leave the labour market, her well-being would fall below the threshold of decency. Moreover, the provision should be unconditional. The unemployment aid that you lose after declining a given number of job offers – a conditional unemployment benefit (CUB) – does not fully counter the negative consequences of what we have identified as the most undesirable effect of structural domination: the subjection of survival to market participation. With a CUB in place, you might still be forced to accept an unpleasant job offer for the simple fact that structural domination made you extremely commodified. If under the threat of losing your minimum income, you accept a lousy job offer that you would not have accepted had your minimum livelihood been unconditionally guaranteed, CUB has not met the requirement set by MDL.

The idea of MDL much resembles that of the basic needs approach. Although both approaches share many practical aspects, there are substantial differences with respect to the philosophical justification, the moral objective and the scope of the correlative duty to provide the means for fulfilling basic needs. The basic needs approach contends that there exists a set of basic rights, mainly pertaining to basic nutrition, shelter and basic health care, that it is a priority to guarantee to every human being. Honestly, very few people, and even less political and moral philosophers, deny the moral urgency of basic needs, at least in practice. Yet, what characterises the basic needs approach is the recognition of the non-instrumental importance of the latter. Thus, for example, a utilitarian may agree that when some people are in dire need, it is morally compelling to distribute resources to them, but she would say so in view of the broader moral objective to maximise aggregate utility. In the same way, a contractualist may say that, given certain moral premises, it is in the interest of a rational agent to accept a principle of distributive justice that indirectly favours the worst off, either in terms of democratic equality (Rawls 1999a, pp. 47–72) or of a basic floor, below which no one should be allowed to fall (Brock 2009, pp. 45–83). Conversely, a basic-needs theorist would maintain that basic needs are compelling per se. Some, like David Copp (1992), hold that the enjoyment of basic needs is intrinsically valuable for the individual insofar as it is an unavoidable condition to exercise 'rational autonomy', that is to say to set oneself life goals that are the result of a free choice. Others, Henry Shue (1996) for example, maintain that basic needs exercise an autonomous claim to prioritarian fulfilment because they are the practical precondition to the enjoyment of any other social or political right.[7]

---

[7]   In my view, Shue (1996) can be considered a proponent of the intrinsic value of basic needs only insofar as we recognise that there exists a right to have rights, or in other words that justice matters per se, regardless of the moral and political theory in which it unfolds – be it utilitarianism, contractualism, libertarianism, and so on.

However, what all basic-needs theorists have in common is that they move from the hypothesis of the clean slate. They simply acknowledge that some people – actually many people – fall short of exercising their basic rights. They maintain that this contingency is morally inacceptable, because of some of the reasons that we have seen above. Accordingly, they defend the cogency of basic rights and propose political models for allocating the corresponding duties – either to single individuals, to states or to the global community – with more or less refined schemes of subsidiarity. Conversely, MDL rejects the hypothesis of the clean slate and contends that the fact that some people do not meet their basic needs is the side-effect of the capitalist mode of production, and more specifically of the system of private property that subtends it, which in turn is not a morally neutral baseline but rather the result of a social transformation that is subject to both moral and political analysis. Accordingly, while basic-needs theorists end up arguing that it is morally deplorable not to transfer some wealth to those who cannot meet their basic needs, when this is economically feasible without someone else falling into severe poverty, MDL holds that it is morally wrong to support a system of private property that causes some people to be insecure in the fulfilment of their basic needs. This is the same difference that exists between arguing that it is morally wrong not to help the victims of a flood, thus considering the flood as a morally neutral fact, and saying that it is morally wrong not to help the victims of a flood for those who destroyed the forest vegetation thus causing the flood. The latter moral duty is much more stringent than the former, because it incorporates a negative claim of justice.

Another important issue is my reason for holding that countering capitalism's structural domination requires disembedding only a basic set of capabilities from the market. Keeping aside the problem of economic realism, someone might object, on purely normative grounds, that freedom from capitalist structural domination requires more. I think that here we have no other option but to be counterfactual. I have maintained that extremely commodified individuals are structurally dominated insofar as they are excluded from the ownership of any other productive asset except for their labour power. Countering this structural domination means leading these individuals to a condition they would have experienced had they not been deprived of access to productive assets. The crucial point here is this: what is the welfare level that defines this condition we should restore?

My response is a set of basic capabilities, relating to food, shelter, wealth, education and basic relational opportunities. Protecting freedom from capitalist structural domination does not allow for more. It is surely true that had a specific person not been relegated to the proletarian group, she might have obtained a higher livelihood through her talent and effort, but the contrary might also be possible. It is obviously impossible to analyse the potentiality of every single living individual and tailor a personalised de-commodification. But even if it were possible, which point of her life would we take as a reference for measuring her productive potential? MDL solves all these problems by allowing us to restore an initial neutral situation.

It is important to note that MDL is not a compensation stemming from a diachronic conception of harm.[8] In other words, I am not holding that proletarians should be compensated for something that they had before capitalism, but rather for something they could have within capitalism. Karl Polanyi adopts a diachronic conception of harm related to labour commodification when he says that before the market principle got hold of the disembedded economic sphere, individual survival was not at risk because it was guaranteed by social norms, regardless of how unfair and undesirable these norms were. Within such a view, it would be possible to be much more trenchant than I am and hold that the advent of capitalism has produced an unparalleled absolute level of wealth at the cost of the most vulnerable individuals systemically losing something: namely the capability to survive without offering their labour in the market (Polanyi 2001 [1944], pp. 171–3). Therefore, those who benefit from the existence of capitalism have to compensate extremely commodified individuals by restoring the safety net they had before capitalism.

I accept Polanyi's thesis that proletarians are harmed in a capitalist society, but I remain neutral with regard to the diachronic nature of such harm, both because I think it unnecessary to insist on this second point and because I want to avoid the historical objection that there is much less misery today than in the past (see Risse 2005). The proper way to interpret the harm stemming from labour commodification is through what Pogge (2008, p. 25) defines as a 'moralized subjunctive baseline' – not in relation to what the extremely commodified individual might have had as her worst-off outcome, had capitalism never appeared, but rather in relation to the worst-off outcome she might have, were capitalist profits so redistributed as to neutralise the effects of capitalist structural domination. In sum, MDL should be interpreted as a capability standard below which it would be unjust for any individual to be allowed to fall. The standard indicates the point at which the commodified worker could be considered as compensated for the domination she suffered in being excluded from the control of the means of production. The MDL standard is similar in its logic to the threshold(s) advocated in the capability approach and by sufficientarian thinkers. Yet, as we shall see later on, what really marks the

---

[8]   For the difference between negative duties invoking a diachronic conception of harm and negative duties invoking a subjunctive conception of harm, see Pogge 2008, pp. 19–26. On the more general issue of diachronic, subjunctive, and combined conceptions of harm, see Meyer 2003.

peculiarity of the policy claim I am proposing here is the fact that it should be read in the light of the structural claim. In this regard, MDL does not emerge from a positive account of justice, but rather from the need to compensate the victims of domination. Moreover, and apart from the justification, MDL differs from the classic formulation of the capability/sufficiency threshold in that it is not simply supposed to give us a static point of reference with regard to freedoms and (or) well-being; rather it also takes into account whether freedoms and (or) well-being are sufficiently independent from market participation. In Section 3.5, I shall also discuss whether this feature of the MDL standard could be reconciled within a set of multiple capability thresholds.

3.2   WHY LABOUR COMMODIFICATION SHOULD BE A GLOBAL CONCERN OF JUSTICE

MDL should be conceived as a cosmopolitan principle of justice; it should be moulded so as to respect the three general tenets of cosmopolitanism: individualism, universality and generality (see Pogge 2008, p. 157; Heilinger 2020, pp. 23–7). First, the addressees of MDL are individuals, not social organisations such as states. Second, every living human being should have the right to MDL, regardless of gender, ethnicity or nationality. Third, the duty to contribute to MDL falls upon every member of the group that has not been excluded from the control of productive assets; the degrees of their contribution would vary depending on how much they benefit from the existing capitalist order. Why so? Could we not simply think of MDL as a principle of justice that holds at the state level? No, because the source of capitalist structural domination is global. States are no longer able to control it, and even if they were able to implement MDL nationally, thus successfully countering structural domination, to limit to fellow nationals the duty of contributing to MDL would be unfair, for the owners of capital who contribute to and benefit from the existence of extremely commodified individuals in a given country might be resident in another country.

I shall start from this last point. As I mentioned earlier, capital is now global while labour is still local. Or, at least, labour is much more local than capital. Owners of capital can explore the world labour market and search for the best place to temporarily invest – the place where the ratio between productivity and cheap labour is optimal, or just the place where labour is cheaper. Meanwhile, proletarians are mostly dependent for their survival on someone who invests capital to hire their labour performance. But the point is that in the global economy, owners of capital are able to move their productive assets out of the reach of proletarians, thus exacerbating the consequences of the fact that proletarians are not autonomous in producing for basic sustenance. Just consider closely the case of delocalisation. Industries can yield huge profits because they are able to keep costs constantly low by chasing the lowest available labour on a global scale. However, commodified workers cannot follow the capital as easily. When the industry delocalises, they usually have no alternative but to remain where they are, look for something else, or wait for another job offer, possibly coming from another foreign investor. Their state can even try to attract capital by offering a better environment for business through lowering taxes – in other words, cutting down on social expenditures and welfare.

In the case of delocalisation, the owner of capital exploits extremely com-modified individuals to get high profits as long as he benefits from their condi-tion and from the asymmetry in the freedom of movement of capital vis-à-vis labour to impose on them an unfair contract in terms of remuneration and job conditions. Nonetheless, when the foreign investor arrives with his money, he does not deprive local workers of any available option they had before. He simply makes an offer – a clearly unfair one – that they are perfectly free to decline. Moreover, we can also expect that he contributes to local social expenditures by paying taxes on his profits. So, an objector might argue, the investor already pays his part in guaranteeing basic services to the workers he interacts with. Why should he also be required to contribute to MDL for individuals living in countries with which he has never had business, or for the workers living in a country from which he has just delocalised?

He has to do it because a consistent part of the profits he is able to raise is due to the possibility of lowering costs in the global labour market, which is a consequence of the existence of a world class of people living in a condition of extreme commodification. At the time of contracting, the investor manages to get his exploitative and non-arbitrary offer accepted because the counterpart has previously been made vulnerable by a form of structural domination and because the counterpart knows that were he to refuse the offer, there is an indefinite number of extremely commodified people in other countries that might accept those same contract conditions.[9] Both contingencies are the result of a capitalist global order that the investor clearly supports by implic-itly accepting the privatisation of global productive assets and their unequal distribution.

The second reason we cannot delegate the implementation of MDL to single states is that they are no longer as free as they used to be in the Westphalian epoch. As rightly explained by Cécile Laborde and Miriam Ronzoni (2016,

---

[9]   In other terms, following Miriam Ronzoni (2009, pp. 253–5) we might also say that, within a globalised economy, transnational competition among poor workers poses a problem of 'background injustice' as long as labour transactions are no longer conductible 'according to the normative criteria that apply to the morality of those very transactions'. On delocalisation, see also Robertson et al. 2010; Capik and Dej 2019.

p. 279), in the current global order, states suffer domination by other state and non-state agents. States are forced to be a part of a global order governed by supra-national institutions that have been shaped by powerful states in their own interest and that now reflect the imbalance of power that lies at their origin. The power that the global system exercises over weaker states is thus dominating because it is unchecked (see also Laborde 2010). On the other hand, non-state actors are sometimes economically more powerful than the states they interact with. They can invest, delocalise, move capital in and out, buy public debt, and bet on states' default (see also Khanna 2016). Both kinds of power are dominating because they clearly limit states in their capacity to fully implement national decision-making. In the words of Laborde and Ronzoni (2016, p. 281), 'even ostensibly democratic and independent states are often unable adequately to shield their domestic decision-making processes from such forces'. Moreover, James Bohman has correctly stressed that economic globalisation has created 'deterritorialized and denationalized forms of authority' that operate in the financial market, mainly through financial institutions, which have completely inverted 'principal/agent relations' with states. These institutions are no longer accountable to states – quite the opposite. And the people they represent, on the contrary, usually have no influence on their functioning and encounter insurmountable difficulties in questioning the 'experts' that rule them (Bohman 2004, pp. 346–9). Rainer Forst (2001, pp. 165–7), in turn, has insisted on the fact that the current global context is marked by 'multiple domination', to emphasise that in many cases transnational domination is grafted onto forms of domestic domination. And he makes the case of individuals that are dominated by corrupt elites and governments and who live in developing countries which in turn are dominated by other states and non-state actors.

The structural domination of states by other states, by financial institutions and by non-state agents is a different matter from the structural domination stemming from the capitalist separation between owners and non-owners of capital. The two forms of domination should be dealt with separately and in different ways. The first form of domination can be eliminated by institutional adjustments at the inter-state level. Laborde and Ronzoni (2016) have argued for republican internationalism. They hold that states are called to counter basic domination wherever it occurs, guaranteeing to all people the capacity of setting up and maintaining a republic. Basic non-domination, the object of international republican justice, is the prerequisite to optimal non-domination, something that the individual can only achieve within her republic. Basic domination can be countered, Laborde and Ronzoni maintain, through five strategies: power countering (the building of coalitions of the weak or the neutralisation of powerful states); global redistribution of economic resources; democratisation of international organisations; global constitutionalisation of fundamental rights; and global regulation of taxes, labour and transnational companies (Laborde and Ronzoni 2016, pp. 288–93). In contrast, Bohman (2004, p. 351) insists on the fact that we can expunge international domination through establishing a 'transnational and democratic political community', provided that it is backed by coercive juridical institutions that are 'democratically accountable'. On the contrary, the second form of domination – capitalist structural domination – cannot be eliminated;[10] rather, we can seek to neutralise its negative effects through redistributive mechanisms. Nonetheless, the first form of domination is linked to the second, insofar as it serves as one of the justifications for making these redistributive mechanisms global. For the first form of domination limits the economic capacity of single states to correct the negative effects of the second form of domination.

Third, states and non-state agents are often responsible for the unequal distribution of assets in other states. When capital is free to flee across borders, it also contributes to making foreign people more commodified. The most typical case is land acquisition in developing countries by foreign public and private investors. In her excellent book on expulsions, Saskia Sassen (2014, p. 80) reminds us that between 2006 and 2011, more than 200 million hectares of land were acquired by foreign actors, both states and private funds. The most severely hit areas are Latin America, Africa, former Soviet countries and East Asia. The buyers are mainly rich Gulf states, China, Japan, India, South Korea, the United States, Europe, and private companies scattered all around the world, from China to Sweden (Sassen 2014, p. 108).

A relevant part of existing land has now been commodified and financialised. Millions of smallholders have been evicted from their natural environment, given modest compensation, and turned into rural migrants. On the one hand, the international commodification of land has also meant the commodification of human beings. Thus, a farmer expelled from his land and forced to move to a city slum becomes dangerously tied to wage-income. On the other hand, when land is only treated as a commodity that is used for raising huge profits, no care is provided for its inextricable natural component. Land commodification has so far gone hand in hand with a rise in the level of toxicity and pollution. As Sassen explains:

> One outcome has been hunger in areas where there used to be little if any hunger even if they were poor: soya has replaced black beans, which were a source of income and food for poor farmers. And many of them have had no option other than to migrate to the slums of large cities. The new hunger is further accentuated by the toxicity that large plantations bring to the surrounding area, making it difficult for

---

[10]   If not at the cost of threatening the capitalist form of production.

the households of plantation workers to use their small plots to grow food. (Sassen 2014, p. 82)

Sassen goes further. She attributes responsibility for the high level of land acquisition we are witnessing today to the restructuring and adjustment programmes designed for the Global South by the International Monetary Fund (IMF) and the World Bank during the 1980s. According to the Dutch-American sociologist, the main effect of such policies was the implementation of a sort of 'discipline' that kept states well anchored to free trade and privatisations, the same that is happening, 30 years later, in the Global North. The main aim of what she defines as 'regimes of discipline' is to restructure the role of the state so as to subordinate every internal decision – including those on health, education and poverty reduction – to the repayment of foreign debt. National states have been so weakened and debt-burdened that acquiring foreign land in developing countries has become very easy (Sassen 2014, pp. 83–9). The advantage of an approach based on capitalist structural domination is that we do not need to go so far to justify countering it. It suffices to note that foreign actors play a determinant role in commodifying people globally for the sake of profits. This simple fact makes those who benefit from 'expulsions' responsible for disentangling the survival of the 'expelled' from wage income. Moreover, it is important to stress that the economic advantages obtained by those states and those funds that buy up arable land abroad, thus turning foreigners into rural migrants, spill over to all the people who benefit from their countries or their funds having more resources than they would have, had the smallholders not been deprived of any means of production.

As we have seen in Chapter 1, there are good reasons to maintain that the process of the primitive accumulation is not simply a historically circumscribed phenomenon, but rather a recurring feature of the capitalist mode of production, which has been exacerbated in the neo-liberal form of capitalism. In other words, the tendency of the market principle is to continuously expand its dominion over the atolls of society that have remained immune from it. Thus, instead of primitive accumulation it would make sense to talk of what David Harvey (2004, p. 74) has defined as 'accumulation by dispossession'. Evidently, capitalist dispossession proceeds, in the majority of cases, through contracts and agreements that are perfectly legal.[11] On the other hand, some people even contend that phenomena such as land grabbing are positive insofar as they promote aggregate growth in developing contexts (World Bank 2011). But this sort of argument fails to figure out the self-reproduction cycle that

---

[11]   On the continuing nature of accumulation by dispossession, see also De Angelis 1999, pp. 16–25; Federici 2004.

is inherent in labour commodification. The fewer alternatives people have to engage in market relations, the more vulnerable they are to offers to make non-market assets marketable. And the more they renounce commons or sell the land that was previously controlled by small owners to large farms that use it for extensive cultivation, the more they become dependent on wage-income.

The fourth reason for justifying a global implementation of MDL is that, if not implemented, individuals living in developed countries would run the serious risk of benefiting from the exploitation of poor workers, made possible by capitalist structural domination. Think of a person in Amsterdam who goes to buy a cheap t-shirt produced in a Pakistani sweatshop. The consumer is paying a very low price because the owner of the company producing t-shirts was able to get his exploitative job offer accepted. This fact alone does not account for alien control. But if the worker who has produced the t-shirt was working for survival – that is, he was not minimally de-commodified – he was suffering the consequences of capitalist structural domination. This means that there is a direct link between the low price paid by the consumer in Amsterdam and the unfreedom of the Pakistani worker. If, on the other hand, the Pakistani worker were minimally de-commodified, the consumer would have only benefited from his exploitation, but not from his unfreedom.

Obviously, someone might say, another way to avoid benefiting from workers' structural domination consists in selective consumption. Would it not be easier to avoid the kind of t-shirt described above instead of minimally de-commodifying every person in the world? No, I do not think so, for the cost of tracking the origin of a cheap item to capitalist structural domination is incredibly high. If we were simply to assess whether the item is exploitation-free, our task would be relatively easier. We might simply distinguish between items that are produced in sweatshops and those that are not. But assessing whether an item is domination (structural)-free would require us to distinguish, among the items that are produced in sweatshops, between those that are realised by extremely commodified individuals and those that are not. This is clearly impossible. It might happen that the same company is selling some exploitation-free t-shirts and some domination-free t-shirts in the same collection. Then, basing selective consumption on the company alone – as usually happens with sweatshops – or even on a single collection would not be enough, for in the same sweatshop there might happen to work some persons who require MDL and others who do not.

Against the four arguments in favour of a global interpretation of the duty to contribute to MDL, it might be objected that not every member of the global group who controls productive assets is an entrepreneur, lives in a state that benefits from international domination, is responsible for the commodification and the financialisation of land, and buys clothes that have been manufactured abroad by very poor workers. In response to this objection, I shall firstly underline that those cases illustrated here are only some of the most representative among the argumentations that can be used to demonstrate the causal global connection between the economic benefits of some people and the structural domination of others, but they do not suffice to exhaust the whole discourse. Then, it is equally important to stress, as I did at the beginning of this chapter, that the principle of unjust enrichment extends the chain of responsibility for benefiting from capitalist structural domination way beyond those agents who directly carry out the market transactions that give rise to unjust extra profits – i.e. marginal profits that could not have been raised had the counterpart not been structurally dominated. Accordingly, we can identify four different categories of people who achieve unjust enrichment without engaging in direct exploitation: workers in multinational companies, people receiving social services paid partly through taxation on unjust enrichment, consumers looking for cheap products, and self-employed workers.

Lastly, we should never lose sight of the fact that the obligational claim I am making is twofold: structural and relational. Therefore, even if a person were able to demonstrate not being involved in any unjust enrichment at the expense of commodified people – who are in turn victims of structural domination – there could remain her political responsibility for contributing to keeping in place a global system of economic rules that brings about structural domination. Accordingly, the obligational claim is structural in proportion to the cultural, political, social and economic power that every single person has to neutralise the negative consequences of capitalist domination – that is to say to bring about MDL (Young 2011, pp. 142–51). Furthermore, the relational in proportion to the unjust enrichment every single person obtains, in more direct or indirect ways, from economic transactions in which the victims of capitalist domination are involved.

3.3   LABOUR DE-COMMODIFICATION FROM A GENDER PERSPECTIVE

Over the last century, the feminist cause has focused on the need to ensure that women have as fair access to employment as their male counterparts, that they are free from violence and abuse in the workplace and that they are acknowledged, either in monetary terms or in terms of paid absence from work, for the care work that they usually do at home. The political effort has been therefore addressed in two directions. Some have insisted on the need to reform working structures so as to ensure that a certain number of jobs are reserved for women, that the possibility of career advancement is safeguarded for those who are already working, or that women and men are paid in the same way for the performance of the same functions. In addition, much emphasis has been placed, thankfully, on overcoming rigid and conservative social structures that prevented female employees from pursuing their life goals on an equal basis with men. In more practical terms, the politics of empowering women within the workplace has declined in different ways, but the most significative policies are those that enable women to share fairly with men the care work that has traditionally fallen on the former, while also ensuring that employers do not discriminate against women because of non-working needs, such as having to devote time to their children, during pregnancy or immediately afterwards (van der Gaag 2014).

Others have emphasised, instead, the need to pay a universal basic income (UBI) to everyone, including women, so as to guarantee the right to say 'no' to unacceptable job offers, to resist, at least partially, exploitation and harassment in the workplace, and to give remuneration to those who are obliged to leave the labour market to carry out care work (Alstott 2001; Flanigan 2018). Moreover, UBI is also praised for enhancing the living conditions of women in developing contexts. Being a measure that directly targets the individual, UBI is expected to correct for male bias within families, to provide young women with a basic set of resources to invest in their education or in entrepreneurial activities, and to counterbalance the so-called 'bad habits' that many people believe male recipients of unconditional cash money cultivate (Jhabvala 2019). We might determine this strategy as empowering women before they enter the market, so as to secure more and better market entrances for them once they decide to hire out their labour performance or to invest.

The approach of labour de-commodification to the gender issue differs from both these two classic political accounts, although sharing some important points with the second one. The underlying assumption of those who want to empower women within the workplace is that the easiest way to guarantee independence to women, thus breaking down the narrow bounds of patriarchy, is to allow them to compete fairly with men in achieving wage-income. Yet, the limit of this political strategy is to overestimate the emancipatory character of the market and to underplay the compulsion of seeking sustenance in a market relation when lacking any other productive asset except for your own labour performance. Accordingly, while the politics of empowering women within the workplace ends up replacing one form of domination with another, or more correctly fails to defuse capitalist structural domination, MDL aims to guarantee the real unconditional enjoyment of a basic set of capabilities, free from family ties, from market bonds and from any sort of domination that can arise from living within a market society in a position of structural weakness due to the unequal distribution of private property.

On the other hand, MDL and UBI share two fundamental characteristics that are relevant in the gender discourse, namely individualism and unconditionality. The fact that MDL directly targets individuals, instead of being filtered through intermediate social structures, guarantees that the disentanglement of a basic set of capabilities from the market is effective and equal for everyone, regardless of their geographical location, the cultural orientation of the families they belong to and the type of sentimental relationships in which they are involved. More simply, as we shall see in more detail in Chapter 4, the mechanism of MDL does not allow welfare provisions to be accumulated for the exclusive benefit of only a few members of the household, and this represents an enormous advantage for women, and more generally for those who are subject to asymmetries of power within families, especially in developing contexts. Obviously, this discourse holds true in theory, for in practice MDL cannot do anything, in a patriarchal system for example, to prevent dominating subjects from appropriating the resources allocated to the dominated counterparts. Nonetheless, clearly establishing the principle that every individual is entitled to MDL and allocating it directly to everyone is the best that can be done, at least from the perspective of MDL, to guarantee its effective enjoyment. Then, the preservation of individual property titles, with respect to the unconditional provision of MDL, is a matter of local management of interpersonal relations.

On the other hand, the unconditionality of MDL means, as for UBI, that the recipients do not need to demonstrate a willingness to enter or re-enter the labour market; hence, both measures yield an individual sphere of independence from market society. Yet, many proponents of UBI insist on the instrumentality of market-free income, arguing that it is an effective macro-economic strategy to sustain economic growth in the face of rising unemployment – not least, technological unemployment – (Jackson 1999; Pulkka 2017; Clifford 2018), to replace heavy and paternalistic forms of welfare state (Zwolinski 2019), or to remunerate those who carry out work that is not directly productive but nonetheless instrumental to capitalist production (Baker 2008). These points are particularly important for our discussion, given that in the majority of cases it is women who face more difficulties in maintaining stable and acceptable working relations and who are asked, or have been asked in the past, to take care of the house and of the children so as to allow men to hire out their labour performance or to invest their capital (Benería 2007). Thus, although both UBI and MDL may converge in terms of their practical effect on women, they differ substantially in their philosophical justification. This is because UBI aims to shore up market society so as to ensure its smooth functioning despite downturns and structural unemployment, and it is no coincidence that the discourse on UBI has regained momentum in the era of automation, that is to say, when full employment seems to have become an old form of utopia belonging to the past.

Conversely, from the perspective of capitalist structural domination, every human being, whether male or female, is entitled to a market-free existence, even when everyone could live within the market, that is to say even when full employment is achievable. Proponents of UBI generally maintain that it would be magnificent if everyone could live a decent life relying on wage-income, yet this is a difficult objective, and given that it would be unreasonable to inhibit through regulations a mode of production that keeps on creating economic growth, thanks also to technological advances that in many cases replace human labour, the easiest way to guarantee well-being for everyone is to redistribute wealth from those who remain active in a prosperous labour market towards those who are excluded from it, and the same discourse holds, more specifically, for women. Since someone has to take care of offspring, women are often discriminated against in the workplace for this, and since nowadays it is not possible to employ everyone, it would be worthwhile providing UBI for all the members of society. Inversely, capitalist structural domination moves from the assumption that wage-income is compulsory for the individual who lives in an extreme condition of labour commodification; hence, the domination that under these conditions is inherent in the work relation should be neutralised through MDL. More specifically, women should not be guaranteed market-free provision to remunerate submerged work within families or to empower them vis-à-vis oppressive employers, but rather to free them from the dominating effect that the exclusion from the control of productive assets has on them.

Obviously, if women were minimally de-commodified, they would not be simply shielded from capitalist structural domination, but they would also be empowered both in their private lives and in their 'freely chosen' work relations.[12] As members of the family, they would be free from the ties that bind them to other people through fear of losing the means to lead a minimal and decent existence. As workers, they would gain greater bargaining power and they would be minimally shielded against gender-based discrimination. As human beings, they would conquer a small sphere of freedom in which they could cultivate their real life interests, regardless of any form of work compulsion, whether remunerated or related to care. Accordingly, MDL represents a truly intersectional measure for promoting women's freedom, because it addresses both the gender issue and market domination. More precisely, MDL allows us to take into due consideration what Leslie McCall (2005) has defined as the 'intracategorical complexity' of 'lived experience'. Within a market society, those women whose labour performance has been commodified belong to two basic social categories that reflect entrenched inequalities of power, one of which is pre-capitalist and one is the product of the market society. First, women are women, and this entailed, and in many contexts

---

[12] By 'freely chosen' work relation I refer to one the renunciation of which does not entail the loss of the basic capabilities guaranteed by MDL.

still entails, a long march of emancipation from traditional and conservative social structures that took them away from the emerged part of productive life. Second, they are proletarians, and as such they are denied any acceptable alternative to either commercialising their labour performance or subjecting themselves to a condition of dependence on another person (or more persons) who receives wage-income or has capital to invest.

The intra-categorial complexity of commodified women can be exacerbated when gender and class intersect with other categories incorporating unequal relationships of power or forms of discrimination, as in, for example, race, religious affiliation, disability and so forth (Henry 2018; Loretoni 2018). MDL cannot do much in relation to these categories of disadvantage. In other words, while MDL can empower those subjects who are victims of asymmetries of power within family relations, by providing them with a feasible economic way out of these relations and hence containing within certain limits the asymmetry of power, MDL cannot rebalance the social disadvantage of those who, for example, are victims of religious discrimination. Yet, under the latter circumstances, MDL can provide a sort of economic safety net for those who suffer the combined effect of intra-categorial discrimination, namely, to a young woman who cannot get a job because the employer fears that she may get pregnant, or because she is Muslim, or because she comes from southern Italy and seeks work as a teacher in a northern region but the director of the school denies it because the parents of the children do not want them to be educated by a woman from the south.

3.4 A MINIMUM DE-COMMODIFICATION OF LABOUR VS. SUFFICIENTARIANISM, THE CAPABILITY APPROACH AND CAPABILITARIAN SUFFICIENCY

In the last two sections of this chapter, I wish to deal with the issue of what the minimum de-commodification of labour power (MDL) has to add to the global justice debate. Isn't MDL an abstruse way of putting forward something that has already been proposed in other theories of justice? I will begin with the first doubt that I had when I started thinking about the subject of this work. Isn't sufficientarianism enough? After all, sufficientarianism is the theory according to which justice only requires everyone to have 'enough' (Frankfurt 1987; Huseby 2010; Shields 2016), and MDL means, quite similarly, preventing every human being from falling below a modest well-being threshold. Moreover, the same doubt can be extended to the capability approach. Isn't MDL just a wordy discourse around the fact that, as Martha Nussbaum (2000, 2006, 2011) has brilliantly argued, we have cogent reasons for protecting basic capabilities regardless of national affiliations?

Sufficientarianism and the capability approach have some things in common, but they also differ in other fundamental theoretical aspects, both related to the philosophical justifications of the two theories of justice and to their structures. What both accounts share somehow is the idea of the threshold. In Nussbaum's work, the threshold relates to the situation in which an individual enjoys the set of the ten combined capabilities that she deems as basic, as the precondition for a human life to flourish. For Nussbaum, there are ten different thresholds related to each of the basic combined capabilities, and each threshold must be respected for an individual to live with dignity, because she does not allow for any trade-off between these central capabilities (Nussbaum 2000, pp. 78–81), whereas in sufficientarianism, the idea of the threshold has been used in many different ways. There are, on the one hand, subjective thresholds that are supposed to indicate when a person can be said to have enough according to a subjective evaluation. This subjective evaluation can be personal, as for Harry Frankfurt (1987, pp. 39–43) and for Robert Huseby's maximal sufficiency threshold (Huseby 2010, pp. 181–2), or based on the evaluation of an impartial spectator, as postulated by Roger Crisp (2003, pp. 755–63). The difference between these subjective sufficientarian thresholds and the conception of the threshold employed by both the capability approach and MDL is clear, for the former indicates a maximal level of welfare above which duties of justices expire,[13] while the latter is supposed to indicate a bare social minimum – the minimum, according to Nussbaum (2000, p. 5), for living life with dignity, the minimum, according to MDL, for being free from capitalist structural domination – that does not exhaust the discourse on socio-economic justice. Above all, subjective thresholds are based on a personal evaluation of contentedness and satisfaction, while basic capabilities can be easily measured in an impartial way.

On the other hand, in sufficientarian theories, we also have objective thresholds that refer to that social minimum demanded by Nussbaum and by MDL, and that can be measured in terms of capabilities. I am referring, for example, to Huseby's minimal threshold (Huseby 2010, p. 180)[14] or to the theory of capabilitarian sufficiency proposed by David Axelsen and Lasse Nielsen (2015, pp. 407–13) and based on the concept of 'freedom from duress' in central areas of human life – that is to say, in a basic set of capabilities.[15]

---

[13]   This is the reason why, for example, Paula Casal (2007, p. 311) criticises sufficientarianism for being unable to prefer progressive to regressive taxes in all those cases in which both can guarantee sufficiency.

[14]   Huseby differentiates vertically between a minimal and a maximal sufficiency threshold.

[15]   See also Nielsen and Axelsen 2017. Note, however, that the thresholds employed by Axelsen and Nielsen are not minimal like Husbey's first minimal threshold, for

With regard to sufficientarian objective thresholds, including capabilitarian sufficiency, and to Nussbaum's theory, I owe a somehow deeper explanation about the aspects in which they differ from the MDL threshold. In providing this explanation, we can narrow down my initial doubt about the originality of MDL theory in the following question: what is the difference between decoupling the enjoyment of a capability from market participation and simply guaranteeing the enjoyment of that same capability? That is equivalent to asking what the difference is, for an individual, between meeting an MDL threshold and meeting a capability threshold.

Assume that we choose a given set of capabilities – having a decent house, being able to complete high school education, being granted basic health care – to identify a basic threshold. Then imagine that we use the same set of capabilities to identify a de-commodification standard, meaning that the standard is met when the achievement of those capabilities is made independent from labour market participation. It might happen that a person who meets the sufficiency threshold falls short of the de-commodification standard. For the de-commodification standard is not simply met when a person enjoys some given capabilities at a given moment, but when that person is sure of being able to continue enjoying those capabilities even if she opts out of, or is excluded from, the labour market.

This problem is usually overlooked within the capability approach, particularly when it is used as a method for evaluating well-being. Amartya Sen (1999, pp. 26–31), for example, is perfectly right in holding that market freedom is valuable in itself, and that if it were possible to yield the same amount of wealth from either a centralised system of production or free market, we might have good reasons for preferring the latter to the former because in it we would enjoy additional capabilities related to free choice. Yet, the problem is that the mechanism does also work the other way around. As long as the individual remains in the market, human capabilities are surely enhanced, but once participation in business transactions is no longer possible, there is a risk of losing them. Accordingly, in evaluating individual freedoms to achieve things that we may value being or doing, we should also take into consideration how precarious these freedoms are.

Enjoying some capabilities is not enough to achieve human security. The latter presupposes that the enjoyment of those capabilities is reasonably guaranteed over time (see UNDP 1994, p. 23). In the same way, at time t a person is

---

Axelsen and Nielsen distinguish horizontally between basic thresholds related to basic capabilities, and their sum meets all the demands of socio-economic justice, in the sense that when a person reaches all the central thresholds indicated by Axelsen and Nielsen, she exhausts all her claims of positive justice.

above a capability threshold if she is enjoying those capabilities in that specific moment, but she is meeting the corresponding de-commodification threshold if at that specific moment the enjoyment of that specific set of capabilities is independent from labour market participation. That is to say, for a person to be de-commodified with respect to a given set of capabilities at time t, she needs to be sure that she will continue to enjoy that set of capabilities at time $t + n$ regardless of whether she will opt in or out of the labour market. In contrast, the assessment of whether a person is meeting a capability threshold at time t is completely independent of whether she will still be able to meet it at time $t + 1$ or $t + 2$.

It might be argued that both capabilitarian sufficiency and the capability approach as proposed by Nussbaum might accommodate my demands for resilience through incorporating them within a scheme that is based on multidimensional thresholds. Accordingly, justice may require everyone to be above a series of horizontal thresholds, one of which might be being sufficiently de-commodified. If we introduce the further clause that there should be no trade-off between the horizontal thresholds, we might maintain that person A, who has a level W of welfare, is below sufficiency, whereas person B, who has a level W1 < W of welfare, is above sufficiency, provided that both A and B meet all the other thresholds, but B is sufficiently free to leave the labour market without suffering a substantial loss in welfare, while A is not. The only problem with this form of amended capabilitarian sufficiency consists in explaining why the de-commodification threshold matters both for descriptive and for normative purposes. If person A is able to get a better living than B from work, should it matter in terms of assessment of well-being that A's well-being is less secure than B's? Probably yes, if we consider the discourse I was alluding to before considering human security. Yet, from the social justice perspective, the very existence of the sufficientarian de-commodification threshold might be contested. After all, it might be argued, why should it matter for positive distributive justice whether A and B get their welfare from a job contract or rather from self-production?

The most rational way to defend the normative relevance of a de-commodification standard is by relying on a negative duty of justice. Yet, both sufficientarianism and the capability approach are based on a positive thesis. The freedom from duress advocated by Axelsen and Nielsen (2015, p. 407), for example, is based on the assumption that 'bringing people above some threshold is especially important'. In this view, justice requires enabling people to succeed in central aspects of human life – such as health, schooling, or having shelter. The correlative duty is of a positive kind. Those who are supposed to pay for realising freedom from duress are provided no other reason for doing it than embracing a peculiar definition of justice; a just social order is one in which no one is left below a given threshold of well-being.

The capability approach is also based on a positive thesis but, differently from sufficientarianism, it springs from the Aristotelian tenets that the human being is 'both capable and limited' and that practical reason is an 'essential necessary condition of humanness', on the one hand, and from Marx's description of humans as beings in need of different opportunities for activities, instead of mere commodities, on the other (Nussbaum 1995, pp. 118–20; see also Nussbaum 2006, pp. 74–5). Accordingly, in Nussbaum's view, we do not have to redistribute to those in dire conditions simply because justice presupposes everyone having enough of something, but rather because human life can only flourish when the individual develops a minimum set of combined capabilities. The latter are structurally unachievable by the single individual unless social external conditions compensate for his limitedness.[16] Hence, all members of society bear the duty to provide every individual with the right conditions for living with dignity. The capability approach relies on a more refined philosophical argument than sufficientarianism because it refers to a specific conception of humanness, but it remains centred on a positive interpretation of socio-economic justice. In contrast, MDL finds its justification in the violation of individual freedom – interpreted as non-domination. Here, the reasons for paying for redistribution are much stronger. We have a group of people that have been excluded from the ownership of productive assets and who are thus enslaved to wage by systemic reasons. We have a second group of people that benefits disproportionately from the artificial vulnerability of the first group and actively contributes to sustaining the system that makes the first group vulnerable.

In the end, de-commodification represents a way in which capabilities are held. It indicates that capabilities are secure over time because their enjoyment does not depend on the holder taking part – or continuing to take part – in a market transaction, be it a job contract, a sale, and so on. Potentially, any sort of economic capability could be put in de-commodification terms. Yet, MDL only recommends disentangling a very limited bunch of capabilities from market participation, for reasons that, as we have seen, stem from the structural claim I am defending in this book; hence, nothing prevents both the capability approach and sufficientarianism (even more so, capabilitarian sufficientarianism) from recognising the existence of negative duties of justice and incorporating the concerns for freedom from market domination that are raised by MDL, in addition to their positive claims of social justice. On the other hand, MDL is, like the capability approach, only a non-exhaustive minimum account of justice; hence, it is perfectly reconcilable with broader

---

[16] For the distinction between 'basic', 'internal' and 'combined' capabilities, see Nussbaum 2000, pp. 84–5.

theories of socio-economic justice. Moreover, MDL has the advantage over the sufficiency principle of not remaining indifferent to the causes and the responsibilities that lie behind insufficiency. Furthermore, it also overcomes the most significant limit of Nussbaum's account of justice: the link between her fascinating description of combined capabilities and the indiscriminate assignment of duties to sustain the development of these capabilities to humanity as a whole.

3.5   A MINIMUM DE-COMMODIFICATION OF LABOUR VS. POGGE'S THEORY OF GLOBAL JUSTICE

Lastly, as I began the book, there is nothing particularly new in talking about negative duties of global justice. Indeed, Thomas Pogge was the first philosopher to use the idea of negative duties for developing an articulated account of global justice. In order to understand Pogge and the reason why he feels the need to elaborate his own theory of global justice, we have to start from an important premise. He is not morally distant from thinkers like Peter Singer, Nussbaum, or their prioritarian and sufficientarian colleagues. In fact, he writes that 'my moral sympathies are with those who are appalled by how the vast majority of affluent people ignore the massive underfulfilment of human rights in the present world' (Pogge 2007, p. 19). Besides this, in more recent writings he has stressed that he is still committed to the global egalitarianism that marks his long dispute with Rawls on the scope of his principles of justice (Pogge 2010, pp. 194–5). Nonetheless, he recognises that severe poverty is not a human rights violation in itself, in fact adding: 'yet, my intellectual sympathies lie with those who hold that an agent's failure at a low cost to protect and to rescue others from extreme deprivation, however morally appalling, is not a human rights violation' (Pogge 2007, p. 19). He is even clearer on this point when he stands back from the extreme conclusions reached by act-utilitarians:

> An affluent person who, in order to save $80, fails to respond to an invitation to sponsor a child in Mali with the predictable result that this child dies – such a person is not morally on a par with an affluent person who kills a child for a $80 benefit. (Pogge 2007, p. 22)

This kind of assertion may sound like an absolution for the wealthy people of industrialised countries in the face of extreme poverty coming directly from one of the most renowned theorists of global justice. Yet, this interpretation would be misleading. What Pogge seeks to do with all his work on negative duties of global justice is to demonstrate that also his libertarian colleagues, who deny the existence of positive obligations of global justice, have cogent reasons to be concerned about world poverty in virtue of the widely accepted principle that it is wrong to cause avoidable harm to others. To put it in other terms, far from denying his well-known global interpretation of Rawlsian justice (Pogge 1989, pp. 240–80), he maintains that even though libertarians might have arguments to resist the conclusions reached by global egalitarians, utilitarians, sufficientarians and so on, the same premises of their libertarian philosophy should lead them to accept a theory of global justice that is entirely built on negative duties of justice (Pogge 2010, pp. 195–6).

Pogge's basic idea is that the current global order is harming the poor, not necessarily from a diachronic perspective, nor because the poor are treated in a sub-optimal way, but rather in the very restricted sense of causing human rights deficits that could be avoided without incurring unsustainable costs. An alternative, and more just, global order can be easily achievable at a very low cost for the richest, but affluent countries have as yet failed to make this desirable change. Therefore, people from the countries that might play a pivotal role in pursuing global reforms are indirectly violating their negative duty not to harm the poor, for the simple reason of supporting their governments and not penalising them for their indifference towards the victims of global injustice. This is the reason why the world's rich owe compensation to the world's poor (Pogge 2008, pp. 23–32).

The compensation envisaged by Pogge is the Global Resources Dividend (GRD), a global redistributive scheme that consists in those states owning natural resources – especially those owning a relatively huge amount of them – contributing to building up a fund to eradicate extreme poverty by paying a dividend on the value of any given resource every time they decide to use it for economic purposes. For example, every time an oil-rich state sells a barrel of oil, a small percentage of the money earned through this economic transaction should be put into the GRD fund. The owner of a given natural resource retains full control over the decision about what to do with it. Accordingly, if a state decides to use oil barrels for artistic purposes, erecting them as street sculptures, or, more realistically, decides not to extract oil in the first place, it is completely free to do so and is not responsible for paying anything. The dividend has to be paid every time the natural resource brings some profit (Pogge 2008, pp. 202–21).

MDL and the GRD are similar in their logic. The normative strength of both schemes derives from negative duties of global justice – although the GRD refers to the negative duty to not cause avoidable harm to others, while MDL appeals to the neo-republican ideal of preserving freedom from domination. Moreover, both MDL and the GRD resort to a compensatory method that calls for the participation of all those people who are blameworthy for indirectly contributing to sustaining a form of systemic injustice that is global in scope. Yet, the GRD is much narrower in its scope as a redistributive tool because it is limited to natural resources. More precisely, in arguing in favour of the GRD, Pogge holds that the mere existence of radical inequality at the global level does not represent a violation of negative duties of justice. An 'impervious', 'pervasive' and 'avoidable' global inequality, such that for those at the bottom it is almost impossible to ameliorate their tragic conditions, and those at the top could change for the better the lives of those at the bottom without incurring substantial costs, requires something more for invoking the violation of a negative duty of justice.

We have three options, Pogge says, three different additional facts that we can add to the empirical evidence of radical inequality to denounce the violation of negative duties of justice. First, we can demonstrate that the current global order is among the causes of this pervasive global inequality, that people living in developed countries sustain their governments in shaping the global order in their interest, and that a shift to a better global order for those at the bottom can be achieved without those at the top incurring unbearable costs. Second, we can add to the facts about global inequality that some people benefit disproportionately from the use of natural resources without compensating those who are excluded. Third, we can appeal to historical wrongs that still burden developing countries – think, for example, of colonialism (Pogge 2008, pp. 203–10).

The GRD is 'a moderate proposal' because it rests on the second option: natural resources.[17] Yet, I believe that if global inequality is so 'impervious' – using Pogge's word – that it determines the extreme commodification of some individuals, this means that the unequal distribution of resources deprives some people of an acceptable alternative to whatever proposal they are made, including selling their labour performance on the market at exploitative conditions. In a few words, I see a direct connection between inequality and unfreedom, because I consider the option of deprivation suffered by extremely commodified individuals as a form of domination that accounts for the infringement of a negative duty of justice and that calls for an immediate corrective action. Obviously, in developing the MDL theory, I also rely on something similar to Pogge's first ground of injustice. I argue that some people are responsible for sustaining a global economic system that keeps some individuals in a state of extreme commodification and, hence, of structural domination. But the justification for a form of global redistribution resides in the simple fact that unequal access to the means of production – or more generally of sustenance – has pervasive consequences on the freedom of individuals.

---

[17] Pogge (2008, p. 210) tells us that he opts for the second alternative because the other two grounds of injustice would support any measure that ameliorates the conditions of the global poor.

In sum, what really renders MDL different from the 'moderate proposal' in which Pogge's approach finds its concretisation is that the former calls for a global redistribution of resources to preserve freedom from domination, while the latter does it to restore justice in acquisition. Since Pogge renounces the first and third grounds of injustice that, in his view, could be added to the fact of global inequality to invoke the violation of negative duties of justice, modelling his GRD only on the unjust appropriation of natural resources, he encounters the same limits of Georgist left-libertarianism. The only difference between the two approaches is that Pogge (2008, pp. 208–9) follows Robert Nozick in the restrictive interpretation of the Lockean proviso, according to which natural resources are initially unowned and can be unilaterally seized on the condition that the appropriator leaves the non-appropriators in a situation that is no worse than before the appropriation took place (then diverges from Nozick in holding that current inequality represents a violation of this proviso), while left-libertarians maintain that natural resources are initially equally owned (Vallentyne 2000, pp. 5–10; see also Steiner 2009).

It is for these reasons that, like left-libertarians, Pogge lacks arguments for giving his GRD to those who are not victims of under-appropriation, or to those who have already been compensated for it. Let us consider, for example, the first case. Imagine a person who is not penalised by the current allocation of global resources in comparison with a hypothetical situation in which the Lockean proviso, in its restrictive interpretation, was respected. It is not so difficult to find such a person because I think you would only have to consider a person that is not struggling for survival. Now, assume that this person, despite having started his life with an acceptable amount of resources, ends up in dire poverty, and hence is forced to look for his means of survival in a market relation. He is dominated and exploited in a terrible manner. This could have happened for any reason – because he has mismanaged his few resources, because he has taken risky gambles, because of an unpredictable economic shock, because of a natural disaster, because of an economic down-turn, and so on. I guess that Pogge would be sympathetic with this person. But what arguments would Pogge have at his disposal to maintain that this person is entitled to GRD? I think none, because this person is not entitled to compensation deriving from a violation of the Lockean proviso.

It might be rebutted that my remarks are somehow specious, because it is obviously impossible to go through the personal history of every poor individual in order to assess whether he originally was an under-appropriator. We can just choose a threshold of well-being and hold that all those below it are entitled to a redistribution. The objection might continue that this is what Pogge had in mind when he held that states should pay a dividend on natural resources in order to eradicate extreme poverty. This is probably true, but if it is true, it means that there is an irreconcilable contradiction between the functioning of the GRD and the normative argument that supports it, for the GRD would be invoked in the name of an entitlement that cannot be evaluated. Every extremely poor person would be allocated the compensation, regardless of whether he was penalised in the restrictive Lockean sense, from the distribution of natural resources.

In conclusion, the advantage of focusing on domination rather than individual entitlements to resources consists in having a very elastic philosophical justification of redistribution. It does not really matter, from the perspective of MDL, why a person is now in a state of extreme commodification, whether she has fallen into the proletarian group or rather has always been a proletarian, and whether she has already received a sort of de-commodification. Whoever happens to experience a state of extreme commodification is entitled to a minimum de-commodification, simply because this person has been deprived of any acceptable alternative for staying alive than entering into a market relation. This option-deprivation is a form of domination, and domination is a form of injustice per se.

Such an approach to justice allows us to target all persons that are in a condition of extreme poverty, without falling into theoretical contradictions. This is why I believe that, differently from the GRD, MDL can render people minimally resilient to the risks stemming from global capitalism. At the same time, it can render minimally sustainable a social arrangement in which individual destinies have been subjected to competition governed by the market principle. With MDL in place, there would be a little sphere of individual autonomy that is kept separated from market dynamics. Just as when you go climbing a very steep wall in a training centre, you know that you might fall at any moment, but you do not care, because there will always be a safety harness to keep you from falling to the ground; when you put the harness on during training, you experience the freedom of trying the most hazardous and dangerous moves, safe in the knowledge that the consequences will never be drastic. This is why I think that among the supporters of MDL there should also be the defenders of unfettered market capitalism, because MDL is the harness that can allow one to bring forward market experiments without incurring human dislocation, with all the social and political consequences that they would entail.

4. Statist objections to a cosmopolitan minimum de-commodification of labour

In Chapter 3, I presented an alternative theory of global justice based on the idea of a minimum de-commodification of labour power (MDL) as the remedy to the structural domination enshrined in global capitalism. I highlighted the source of capitalist domination, explained why it is systemic, sought to detail the idea of a minimum de-commodification of labour power, showed why it should be considered as a global principle of justice and lastly discussed what this approach to global justice has to add to – and in what it is different from – the classic theories of global justice briefly presented in the Introduction.

In this final chapter, I shall deal with four of the most pervasive objections usually levelled against any cosmopolitan account of justice. Two objections are theoretical: the compatriot priority principle and the coercion view: how do we reconcile global principles of justice with national allegiances? More specifically, how do we reconcile general and special responsibilities once we move out of ideal theory and are presented with concrete choices in a scenario of limited resources? Secondly, can a cosmopolitan theory of justice resist the attack of those thinkers who argue that principles of distributive justice only hold when in presence of the coercive apparatus of the state – and that social justice is actually required as a justification for the individual to accept the state's coercion? Two other objections are empirical: the allegations of uselessness and infeasibility. Even assuming that a given theory of global justice overcomes these conceptual obstacles, and that we manage to assert the existence of global principles of distributive justice, what is the point in spending time and energy in demonstrating the existence of political principles of justice that the majority of people will not be willing to follow? Lastly, if we put aside the political obstacles, isn't the concrete implementation of global justice – as the activation of global redistributive mechanisms – likely to encounter an array of insurmountable practical obstacles?

My aim here is to demonstrate that a theory of global justice based on MDL can stand up to both the theoretical and the empirical objections. With regard to the former, I shall maintain that MDL can accommodate the compatriot priority principle, and more specifically that it is compatible with the 'split-level ethical position' presented by liberal nationalist David Miller (2007, p. 44). At the same time, if we adopt a wider conception of coercion, we can find in global capitalism a justification for a theory of justice based on MDL. With regard to the empirical issues, I will argue, relying on Lea Ypi's notion of a global political avant-garde (Ypi 2012), that political and moral ideas can have a concrete effect on society, and also lead to substantial changes in the long run, when even a numerically restricted group of people champions them. Lastly, I will discuss the very practical issue of levying and spending taxes at the global level.

Before proceeding to the theoretical objections to cosmopolitan justice, I deem it important to briefly expose the general argument for moral universalism presented by Simon Caney (2005). Every account of cosmopolitan justice is based, more or less explicitly, on a linear argument of this kind, hence stating clearly its components will help us later to correctly individuate the parts of cosmopolitan morality that the conceptual objections seek to challenge. Caney (2005, pp. 35–6) rattles off the argument in these terms:

(P1) There are valid moral principles.

(P2) The moral principles that apply to some persons apply to all persons who share some common morally relevant properties.

(P3) Persons throughout the world share some morally relevant similarities.

The first assertion is rather uncontroversial. There might be people who argue against the existence of any moral principle but we can put this issue aside, because it has nothing to do with the conceptual objections usually levelled, from the liberal field, against cosmopolitanism. The same holds true for basal moral equality of human beings. Every liberal account of morality would reject as unreasonable moral differences based on ethnicity, gender, religion and suchlike. The third assertion, P3, is the most important and at the same time the most controversial one. If we take it as correct, thus holding in line P1, P2 and P3, we arrive at what Caney (2005, p. 107) calls 'the scope2 claim':

The scope2 claim: the standard justifications of principles of distributive justice entail that there are cosmopolitan principles of distributive justice.[1]

---

[1]   Caney gives it the number 2 because the scope1 claim is about civil and political liberties: '*the standard justifications of rights to civil and political liberties entail that there are human rights to these same civil and political liberties*'. He discusses this argument at length in another section of his book, but the issue goes beyond the argumentative scope of this text (see Caney 2005, pp. 63–101).

If we arrive at the scope2 claim without challenging any of the three passages that lie behind this conclusion, we are obliged to revise our whole account of morality, for the same ideas of national taxation and national distribution as interpreted and practised in every country would violate what we have identified as the correct principles of justice. We would end up maintaining that the same arguments that we have always employed to sustain and justify domestic principles of redistribution should lead us to embrace a cosmopolitan account of justice. At this point only a truly universal formulation of distributive justice, as a global difference principle à la Beitz (1999), or a global utilitarian redistribution à la Singer (1972, 2009), or a universal set of capabilities à la Nussbaum (2006), would pass the test of logical coherence.

Given the stringency of Caney's argument for universalism, which I consider correct in its formulation, the only way to resist its radical conclusion is to challenge P3. This can be done in two different ways. It can be said that human beings are not worth the same from a moral point of view, because ethnicity, or religious belief, or rather the colour of the skin do create a moral hierarchy among individuals. Or, alternatively, it can be argued that human beings are all worth the same from a moral perspective but there exist specific political circumstances that create special duties, and that the latter should in some cases take precedence over general duties towards humanity as a whole. The first solution is clearly unacceptable. It entails a misinterpretation of human nature, is based on a strong form of discrimination and racism, and goes against any credible account of moral and political philosophy. On the other hand, the second solution follows a powerful argumentative line, and it is the only point in which Caney's argument for moral universalism can be seriously challenged.

The two theoretical objections to cosmopolitanism that I will consider in this chapter do exactly this. They seek to demonstrate the existence of special duties among members of national political communities that prevent the implementation of global principles of distributive justice. The nationalist objection recognises the source of special responsibilities towards fellow nationals in the intrinsic value of nationality, while the coercion view hints at the fact that fellow nationals share subjection to the coercive power of the state, and it maintains that this coercion must find its justification in national principles of socio-economic justice. I shall start, in the following section, with the first conceptual objection.

4.1   THE COMPATRIOT PRIORITY PRINCIPLE

At this point in the book, an objector might pose the following question. In upholding the universality and generality of MDL am I not underestimating the ethical significance of national membership? That equates to putting the issue in these terms: assume that I am right in maintaining that the neo-republican idea of freedom as non-domination should be broadened to take into account economic systemic domination. And also assume that I am right in saying that justice requires us to neutralise this form of systemic domination and that the correct 'anti-power' is MDL. Why should I not first realise justice at the domestic level, thus giving priority to co-nationals in the process of labour de-commodification?

According to liberal nationalists, national membership is a relation of ethical significance, whose intrinsic value suffices to create special duties among members. David Miller (2007, pp. 23–50) explains it well when he makes the difference between relations that are instrumentally valuable and those that are intrinsically valuable.[2] Both kinds of relations can give rise to special duties among participants, but only intrinsically valuable relations can create what Miller (2007, p. 35) calls 'ground-level special duties', that is to say, duties that stem directly from the relation in itself and not from the cooperative practices it contains or from contracts and promises.

Imagine a group of people who decide to create an amateur biking team. When they go on the Sunday bike excursion, they surely have special duties towards each other that go beyond the general duties they owe to non-members. If, for example, a biker gets a flat tyre, her mates have a stronger moral obligation to help her than the other people who happen to be on the street. This kind of relation is instrumentally valuable. The special duties it creates among members are dependent on the collective practice entailed by the relation and are extinguished once the practice is over. If one of the team-mates experiences economic problems it would be unreasonable to hold that other mates have a special duty to help her, because in this kind of relation special duties depend on the practice of biking. Friendship, on the other hand, is an intrinsically valuable relation because people attach importance to the relation itself, independently of any practice involved. As Miller (2007, p. 35) rightly underlines, 'people's lives go better just by virtue of being involved in this kind of relationship'. If there is nothing troubling in the dissolution of the biking team – former members can easily decide to find new mates – 'when friendships dissolve for one reason or another, this is a loss'. When you end an instrumentally valuable relation you can replicate the lost practice elsewhere, while with friendship you lose something irreplaceable.

Only intrinsically valuable relations give rise to ground-level special duties. Nationhood, Miller says, is a relation of this kind. 'The way that most people think about their nationality reveals that its value for them is indeed intrinsic. They would, for instance, profoundly regret the loss of their distinct national

---

[2]   A relation can also be valuable in both senses.

identity, even if they were guaranteed the other goods that nationality makes possible, stable democracy, social justice, and so forth' (D. Miller 2007, p. 38). Obviously liberal nationalists are not claiming that nationhood is the only kind of relation that gives rise to 'ground-level special duties', to use Miller's expression. Also friendship, as we have seen, and the family would count as intrinsically valuable relations. The point that liberal nationalists raise against cosmopolitans is that we cannot dismiss national membership as ethically insignificant, in particular when we discuss distributive justice.

So, an objector might be tempted to say that MDL is irreconcilable with the liberal-nationalist position on distributive justice. The liberal nationalist might rebut that I am wrong in considering on a par all those human beings who happen to be below a minimum de-commodification threshold, since in so doing I would overlook the ethical significance of nationality. Yet, I shall argue that given the peculiar justification and the non-comparative nature of MDL, it can also be embraced by those who believe in the existence of special duties towards compatriots. When I propose MDL as a general duty towards all human beings, I am not denying the existence of a wider set of distributive principles, nor am I necessarily holding, as global egalitarians, that this wider set of distributive principles has to be global in scope. It is possible to argue that a general (global) duty to MDL should be combined with special (local) duties of justice. That is to say, someone might argue, for example, that every human being has the right to be minimally de-commodified – for the reasons discussed in previous chapters – but that fair equality of opportunity only holds among members of the national community – either for the cooperative reasons given by Rawls or for the nationalist ones given by Miller.

But what happens when national resources are limited and we are required to make a choice between the general duty to MDL and special duties of justice? Is there a hierarchy between general and special duties? This question is fundamental once we move out of the area of ideal theory and discuss the implications of principles of distributive justice in a real world of limited resources and limited choices. But it is impossible to give an answer without considering the nature of the general duty towards humanity – whether it is a positive or a negative one, or whether the negative duty is weaker or stronger than other existing negative duties. In order to do so, I consider it useful to start with the more analytical elaboration of the compatriot priority principle offered by Miller (2007, p. 46) through what he calls a 'split-level' view of agents' responsibility, or in his precise words a 'plausible split-level ethics'.

In order to respect the intrinsic value of the relationship of nationality in the face of inevitable trade-offs between the well-being of compatriots and that of foreigners, Miller (2007, p. 50) says it is necessary that the person in a position to make a choice takes into account both the urgency of the demand for justice made by the agents involved – regardless of nationality – and his causal connection with it. Accordingly, Miller maintains that the negative duty to refrain from directly causing avoidable harm to someone else does not allow for national prioritisation – meaning that it would be morally wrong to sacrifice the lives of five foreigners to save four compatriots. If we have to choose between meeting either the urgent needs of a group of compatriots or of a group of foreigners we are responsible for – e.g. because we are more or less directly responsible for their low living conditions – a looser equal treatment applies than with respect to negative duties. When the urgency of the positive demands of justice advanced by the two groups is equal, we have to favour compatriots. Yet, when the urgency of the demand advanced by the group of foreigners is more stringent, this can be used as an argument for outweighing the demand advanced by compatriots. Miller, for example, says that it would be morally fine to sacrifice our compatriots' need for basic education to save starving foreigners we are responsible for. Nonetheless, as soon as the element of responsibility ceases to exist, the split-level ethics diminishes progressively. Accordingly, there might still be margins for sacrificing compatriots' non-urgent needs to prevent some foreigners from inflicting harm on other foreigners (e.g. for financing a military intervention to prevent abuse of human rights abroad). But there seem to be almost no margins for trade-off when we have to balance the basic needs of compatriots, on the one hand, and the basic needs of foreigners who are directly responsible for their situation, on the other hand (D. Miller 2007, pp. 46–50).

Now, I would keep aside the validity of the complex balancing mechanism that the split-level ethics imposes between the different types of positive duties. And I shall emphasise, instead, that within this model, which can be taken as a sound and credible analytical scheme of the liberal-nationalist objection to 'strong' versions of cosmopolitanism (D. Miller 2007, p. 28), it is morally right to recognise strict equal treatment when dealing with negative duties of justice. Therefore, given that MDL is based on a negative duty of justice, it does not fall in direct contradiction with the compatriot priority principle, and since it goes straight back to the idea of freedom's inviolability, MDL is even more urgent than a redress due to simple harm or misappropriation of resources.

The unequal distribution of the world's resources systematically leaves a large group of people with no other acceptable alternative option but to take part in the labour market – usually under exploitative conditions. An extreme level of labour commodification represents a form of domination – though enacted at a systemic rather than interactional level – and in the split-level scheme illustrated by Miller any unjustified infringement of individual freedom would correspond to the violation of the duty to respect basic rights. As explained above, if we are able to keep the justification for a global redistribution at the top of the split-level pyramid, we remain in a field in which even liberal nationalists recognise strict equality of treatment between co-nationals and foreigners, and hence we can circumvent the nationalist objection while remaining neutral on the validity of the compatriot priority principle. Once the minimum de-commodification has been accepted as a general duty towards humanity, we can remain silent on issues as to whether or not Norway should invest less in national research in order to contribute to more equal opportunities for youngsters in Congo.

The only problem with the reconcilement between MDL and the split-level position is that the 'infring[ement][of] basic rights by our own actions' (D. Miller 2017, p. 47) appealed for by MDL is not so evident and direct as in the examples usually discussed by liberal nationalists. Miller (2007, pp. 48–9) clearly recognises that 'if we think about cases modelled on the trolley problem made famous by Judith Thomson, I do not think it would be justifiable to switch the trolley from a track on which it was hurtling towards a compatriot on to a track on which it would hurtle towards a foreigner'. Unfortunately, the situation with capitalist systemic domination is not so linear. As I emphasised in previous chapters, the arbitrary interference suffered by those who are excluded from the control of productive assets is not performed by a specific person. The extremely unequal distribution of property, a defining feature of capitalism, is systemically responsible for labour commodification of the most dangerous kind. In this case, the individual action that leads to the infringement of freedom consists in the active participation in a social system that can determine arbitrary interference over a large group of individuals.

In a situation in which agent A directly injures agent B we have no trouble in seeing a clear violation by agent A of the negative duty not to infringe the basic rights of agent B. Yet, when the violation of B's rights occurs systemically, we have to make a greater cognitive effort to see how agents A, C, D, E and so forth, are responsible for the existence of the system. But this asymmetry between interactional and systemic violations of basic rights should not divert our attention from the fact that both kinds of violation represent the infringement of a similar duty. Take, for example, the case of the Roman slaves proposed by Gourevitch (2013). Roman slaves were victims of a systemic domination stemming from the Roman legal arrangement that divided the population into freemen and slaves. 'Of course', Gourevitch (2013, p. 600) says, 'Roman citizens had no knowledge of and no direct hand in determining which specific slave would be subject to which specific master [. . .] but they *intentionally* created and maintained the institution of slavery.' In other words, in order to maintain that agent A is responsible for the systemic violation of B's basic rights it is not necessary to demonstrate that A intentionally dominates B, and not even that A is aware of who B is. It suffices to argue, as I did in Chapter 2, that A is responsible for – and also benefits from – the existence of a social system that determines the violation of someone else's basic rights.

The minimum de-commodification of labour power (MDL) as a principle of global justice appeals to the structural infringement of a negative duty not to harm others on which even liberal nationalists recognise equality of treatment among all humans. Therefore, embracing MDL normatively does not require a rejection of the liberal-nationalist assumption that national affiliations are intrinsically valuable relations and hence give rise to 'ground-level special duties' among compatriots. Differently from the theories that argue in favour of global positive duties of justice, MDL does not even enter in direct contradiction with the compatriot priority principle in those cases in which resources are limited, and hence we are required to make a choice between fulfilling special obligations towards compatriots and honouring general obligations towards humanity – this is an advantage that MDL shares with other theories of global justice based on negative duties. Lastly, it might be worth stressing that MDL can be included in the field of 'weak' or 'moderate' moral cosmopolitanism, because it does not bring in a comprehensively global conception of justice (see Scheffler 2001, pp. 114–15; D. Miller 2007, pp. 27–31). After the minimum de-commodification has been discharged, it is possible to remain neutral, from the perspective I have proposed so far, as regards whether a developed country is justified in retaining the huge majority of national economic resources for increasing even further the welfare of compatriots, or whether it should rather use it to provide better life opportunities for poor people living abroad. All the MDL requires is that the neutralisation of capitalist structural domination be given general – and global – precedence over less urgent issues of domestic socio-economic justice.

4.2   THE COERCION VIEW

The second objection usually levelled against cosmopolitan accounts of justice is based on the fact that state institutions exercise a form of coercion on individuals (subject to them), which stands in need of justification, otherwise it would be arbitrary coercion (Blake 2001; R. Miller 2005; Nagel 2005). For state coercion to be justified to all the individuals who are subject to it, we cannot ask everyone to express their individual acceptance of the social agreement, for several reasons. There might be some individuals who find themselves in specific contingencies in which it would be rational for them to renounce state coercion, as, for example, those who are going to commit or have already committed crimes. But it would be even more difficult to obtain the continued consensus of new members of a social group. Thus, the only possible solution we have to assess the justifiability of state coercion is to check whether the institutions exercising this coercion can pass a hypothetical acceptability test. One necessary, but not sufficient, component of the hypothetical social agreement that we may use to test the legitimacy of existing state coercion is that the distributive differences between the parties involved be contained within acceptable limits. Otherwise, if one were to consider the possibility that some subjects accumulate much more economic power than others to the point of being able to dominate them, it would be impossible to demonstrate, under all circumstances, the preferability of the hypothetical social agreement to a pre-social scenario of anarchy.

Accordingly, if the purpose of social justice is to make state coercion justified, then the absence of state-like coercion at the global level compels us to maintain that duties of relational justice – e.g. egalitarian justice – only hold between fellow nationals, while duties of absolute justice – e.g. those based on sufficiency – can also hold among foreigners, but the latter would arise out of humanitarian reasons rather than political ones (Blake 2001, pp. 293–4; R. Miller 2005, pp. 145–6; Nagel 2005, p. 130). As we can see, if we place the requirement of coercion alongside the classic Rawlsian requirement of cooperation for mutual benefit as *sine qua non* conditions of socio-economic justice, then it becomes very difficult to unhinge the statist conception of justice. It is no longer enough to appeal to the empirical evidence of transnational economic flows to show that the basic structure of society has gone beyond national borders, but it is instead necessary to play a complex theoretical game in terms of the coercivity of international institutions and norms, taking into account the obvious fact that at the international level no institution exercises a monopoly of force in support of these norms. To be more precise, although both Nagel and Blake develop their theories about the circumstances in which duties of justice arise as not necessarily Rawlsian, that is to say, not contingent upon the previous acceptance of Rawls's theory of justice, they both argue that the coercion view is also part of Rawls's theory of justice; hence, his cosmopolitan critics should do more than simply focus on the mutual advantage inherent in economic globalisation (Blake 2001, pp. 284–9; Nagel 2005, pp. 122–6). Here I will leave aside this Rawlsian interpretative question (see also Abizadeh 2007), and I will look at 'the coercion view' as a general objection to the cosmopolitan conception of justice.[3]

With the previous objection, the liberal-nationalist one, I remained neutral on the main argument – that national membership has an ethical significance that justifies special obligations – and I sought to demonstrate that a theory of global justice based on a minimum de-commodification of labour power (MDL) is compatible with the liberal-nationalist position. Here, on the contrary, I shall take a slightly different position. If, on the one hand, I shall tend to

---

[3]   The expression 'coercion view', which provides the title to this section, was proposed firstly by Laura Valentini (2011, p. 205). I use it interchangeably to refer to what Nagel (2005) defines as the 'political conception' of justice.

remain neutral regarding the premise of the 'coercion view', namely that coercion is a necessary component of the conditions of justice, on the other I also want to say that Laura Valentini (2011) has proposed convincing arguments, at least in my view, against the conclusion that the 'coercion view' draws with respect to global relations, that is to say, that something akin to state coercion cannot characterise the relations between individuals or institutions that are located in different countries, hence the scope of justice is doomed to remain statist – at least until we create cosmopolitan institutions with prerogatives compatible to national ones. More specifically, I believe Valentini (2011, pp. 214–16) made a serious point when she argued that the statist inference obtained by the anti-cosmopolitan proponents of the 'coercion view' only works insofar as they rely on what she defines as the 'narrow' and the 'interactional' conceptions of coercion, that is to say, a form of interpersonal coercion in which A (which can either be an institution or an individual) restricts the freedom of B through foreseeable but either intentional or non-intentional constraints, in comparison to before A and B began to interact (Valentini 2011, pp. 209–12). Conversely, if we employ a broader conception of coercion, which Valentini (2011, pp. 212–14) defines as 'systemic', we can maintain that not only institutions and individuals but also 'systems of rules' can limit the freedom of one or more individuals, in comparison to an alternative system of rules that would render at least some individual less unfree. By applying the account of systemic coercion to international norms (e.g. trade rules), we can stretch the scope of justice. In Valentini's words:

> What we have to look at is the WTO [World Trade Organization] as a system of rules supported by a plurality of states. The constraints it imposes on its members' (and third parties') conduct are certainly non-trivial, and no matter what our chosen baseline for comparison is – be it a WTO', WTO'', WTO''', or no global organization at all – we can plausibly (but not conclusively) assume that at least some agents' freedom would be greater in the alternative scenario than in the existing one. The WTO would then correctly qualify as systemically coercive and therefore as a subject of justice. (Valentini 2011, p. 218)

However, for the purpose of my argumentation, I shall address the 'coercion view' objection in a different way from Valentini. Rather than seek to demonstrate that the coerciveness of global social structures might indicate that there are normative reasons for upholding some global principles of positive justice, I will simply argue that the form of systemic coercion inherent in the distribution of private property in the capitalist system suffices to demonstrate, also from the perspective of the 'coercion view', that there exists a global duty of negative justice to realise MDL. Apparently, it might seem almost pointless to defend my argument in the face of the 'coercion view', because all its proponents clearly recognise the existence of a humanitarian duty regardless of any coercion. Nagel (2005, p. 131), for example, says: 'the minimal humanitarian morality governs our relation to all other persons [. . . , it] does not depend on the existence of any institutional connection between ourselves and other persons'. Blake (2001, p. 294) writes that 'while the existence of a coercive network of law is a precondition of a concern with relative deprivation, a concern with absolute deprivation seems not to have any such institutional precondition'. Richard Miller (2005, p. 145) holds that 'in addition to duties to help the foreign poor that depend on the nature of relationships and interactions with them, there is certainly a *prima facie* duty to help others just because they are suffering'.

Nonetheless, while all these authors relegate the redistribution of resources towards the extremely poor foreigner to a mere humanitarian duty, MDL appeals to an issue of justice. More specifically, the supporters of the 'coercion view' recognise that the respect for negative duties of justice should take priority over domestic issues of socio-economic justice. But then they fail to see that a violation of these negative duties is systemically occurring within the structure of global capitalism. Nagel (2005, p. 127), for example, writes that 'negative rights like bodily inviolability, freedom of expression, and freedom of religion [. . .] set universal and pre-political limits to the legitimate use of power, independent of special forms of association'. Notwithstanding this theoretical point, Nagel limits any eventual global redistribution to humanity alone because he overlooks, as do the other proponents of the 'political' conception of justice, important facts about the current economic structure.

There are two possible ways to make proper sense of capitalist coercion. The first one is systemic and calls into play all those who contribute to preserving a social system in which some individuals are excluded from the control of the means of production, and they do so by providing their implicit political consent. The second one focuses, instead, on those individuals, groups or institutions that either simply control large amounts of capital or also take a direct role in dispossessing other individuals of the means of production – in Chapter 3, I gave the example of land grabs, but we could easily extend it to the conquest of market segments by multinationals, to the privatisation of public goods and services, in general to all those actions and policies that force the individual to seek the means for the realisation of their needs within a market relationship.

Moreover, another important issue is that de-commodification is a dynamic concept, while poverty alleviation is a static one, hence minimally de-commodifying someone means more than simply giving her food because in that moment she is starving. And this is fundamental to understand why the normative argument in favour of MDL is immune to the coercive objection also in those cases in which the exclusion from the means of production does not result in unemployment. Consider, for example, the case of a peasant who is hired by the same people who bought the land he used to cultivate, and who as an employee has a higher income than he had as a self-producer. From the perspective of MDL this person is entitled to the decoupling of a basic set of capabilities from market participation, because of the normative urgency of restoring his autonomy that has been infringed by his exclusion from free use of land, regardless of whether he wants to profit from this decoupling or whether he chooses rather to continue entertaining a market relation with his new employer. What matters for negative justice to be respected is that the peasant is given an exit option from this market relation – and as I have argued in previous chapters, this is important both in absolute terms, for preserving autonomy, and in a relational perspective, insofar as an exit option guarantees a margin for saying 'no' to indecent working conditions. Conversely, welfare-sensitive concerns for the worst off, as those embodied in the humanitarian duties upheld by the proponents of the 'coercion view', fail to bring back into a normative dimension the conditions of salaried workers, such as the peasant in our example. Or, more precisely, they may sanction the moral behaviour of the employer as long as he exploits the peasant, but they do not have many arguments to extend the scope of responsibility for exploitation to the framework of power asymmetries in which exploitation is made possible.

4.3   IDEAL THEORY AND THE COSMOPOLITAN AVANT-GARDE

Having discussed two strong theoretical objections levelled against cosmopolitan justice, with specific regard to my idea of a minimum de-commodification of labour power (MDL), it is now time to deal with a common objection moved against any research in normative political theory, and in particular in international normative political theory, by those who lay claim to concreteness in social life. The whole argument could be summed up in the following simple question. What is the point of spending time, energy and money in researching something such as global redistributive justice that does not exist?

A typical reaction by both academics and non-academics in front of normative theories of global justice is something like 'Ok, that's interesting, but is it really useful to write about something that powerful countries do not have any interest in realising?' And I also believe that, although they never say it explicitly, many people wonder what the point is of paying salaries and scholarships to someone who spends time thinking about the right way to do something that we know will never be done. I think that all these questions cannot be simply put aside. They are very precise, and they deserve a serious answer. Among all the branches of political philosophy, international normative political theory is the most vulnerable to these observations. For let's also assume that what I have said so far is correct, and that starting from free-standing moral premises, we can demonstrate that a first group of people is causing harm to a second group of people. What is the point of having demonstrated this if the second group is the one that dictates the rules of the game and does not have an active interest in changing them? It is as if at the time of Ancient Rome someone invested time in demonstrating that slavery was an unjust violation of individual autonomy. Roman slave holders would have never accepted losing their privileges merely in virtue of a normative dissertation about what is just and what is not.

My first answer is that old-style slavery no longer exists – with a few old and minimal exceptions (Bales 2012). We could say the same with de-colonisation, gender equality, European integration, and so forth. And it would have been impossible to achieve these ambitious goals without prior social practices being subjected to normative criticism. My second answer is that insisting on the criticism of capitalist domination is at the same time difficult and necessary, under some aspects even more than with the other forms of injustice mentioned above, because usually the same victims of capitalist domination strive to reckon with the unfreedom that their condition of wage-labourers entails. And it certainly does not help, in this sense, that much of the criticism conducted against capitalism has been focused so far on the concept of poverty rather than on the concept of commodification.

Nonetheless, the problem remains that dominant countries have no short-term interest in shifting to global rules that subtract something from their economies to transfer that something to poorer counterparts. And I also think that those who believe that in the following decades the world will remain unjust, or that at least will not become completely just, have good reasons to be pessimistic. So, once we have set aside the issue of creating new institutions, the objection about pointlessness might be narrowed down in these terms: why shall we persist in judging and criticising a world order that perhaps will never meet the normative standards that we use in our analysis? There are two possible answers to this question. The first one consists in holding that even if a complete change will never occur it is still extremely important to keep in mind why justice does require us to reach a moral goal that we lack the motivation to reach, because that same justification can – and should – lead us towards intermediate, and more achievable, moral goals. The second argument is that the normative analysis and criticism of existing global practices can inspire a global avant-garde capable of triggering a transformation process that in the long run will bring humanity somewhere close to the normative ideal, as has happened with slavery, the death penalty, gender issues, and so on.

The first approach is the one embraced by a radical utilitarian thinker like Peter Singer. Since his first works he has been proposing a moral standard that nobody is able to fully respect, not even himself, because it requires the individual to redistribute all he owns until a marginal redistribution would make him worse off than the potential recipients, taking into account the fact that the majority of people are unwilling to redistribute – hence, there is no chance of splitting the burden of redistribution among non-poor people in proportion to their wealth (Singer 1972, p. 234). Singer's utilitarianism is a clear example of ideal theory that leads to extreme consequences. He starts from a free-standing moral premise – 'if it is in our power to prevent something bad from happening, without thereby sacrificing anything of comparable moral importance, we ought, morally, to do it' (Singer 1972, p. 231) – and argues that the real world, the one in which we live, is unjust, because its social practices and institutions are based, among other things, on a distinction between duty and charity that is untenable from a normative point of view.

Singer is not imagining that the world will ever get close to his moral standard (he is obviously aware of that), nor is he trying to devise a concrete policy.[4] He is simply saying that we are all living by moral and political principles that will not pass a normative test. The point of making this argument is to render society aware of the fact that it is going in the wrong moral direction and to indicate the correct path to follow. 'Over many years of talking and writing about this subject, I have found that for some people, striving for a high moral standard pushes them in the right direction, even if they – and here I include myself – do not go as far as the standard implies they should' (Singer 2009, p. 151). In this sense, the first aim of an ideal theory of justice is to help people to revise their thoughts about life affairs in the light of ideal principles that they are willing to accept when posed in abstract and impersonal terms, but that they systematically violate in everyday life. The second, on the other hand, is providing people with the indications for reconciling their life with their abstract ideas, knowing that the farther this reconcilement can go, the better for the theorist, and more generally for everyone.

MDL, in turn, represents a quite different compromise between ideal and non-ideal theory.[5] It starts from an ideal principle of individual freedom but then it accepts existing practice as unchangeable in the non-ideal world, and hence it proposes the introduction of a form of global redistribution within existing practices in order to reconcile them with the normative ideal. I tried to explain how we can preserve freedom within a system that systemically

---

[4]   Accordingly, Singer (2009, p. 151) has also recognised that 'asking people to give more than almost anyone else gives risks turning them off'.

[5]   For a definition of non-ideal theory, see Ypi (2012, p. 50): 'Contrary to ideal approaches, nonideal approaches are importantly constrained by practical agency in assessing the ability of theories to articulate social and political problems from a normative perspective [. . .] In the case of non-ideal approaches, it is the interpretation of specific social and political practices that provides the first step with reference to which the normative territory is explored and principles are further articulated.'

violates it. My conclusion has been that we can do it by rendering people more resilient to shocks. Does it mean that all people will become minimally de-commodified in the future? Probably not. But it means that we have sound normative reasons for working in that direction. We know that justice requires us to reach a demanding goal. We can move towards it step by step, regardless of whether we will ever take the last step. We could do it, for example, by rendering our trade and investment policies more just. In this regard, MDL offers us a convincing response to those such as Blake (2001, p. 292) who think that trade is 'a matter [. . .] of offers, not of threats'. Or we could give a higher share of our GNP to development projects in developing countries. Or we might push for existing international agencies to better target people in need. And so on.

In sum, MDL provides us with the normative arguments for challenging the dominant view about our relation with foreigners, according to which the only reason for being concerned with their welfare is a duty of humanity and not a duty of justice, and these arguments can be used in the political debate to justify a compromise between the two opposite approaches to foreign relations (i.e. statism and cosmopolitanism). But in so doing we also yield another important result; we foster the creation and the development of what Lea Ypi (2012, p. 154) has defined as 'a cosmopolitan avant-garde', whose aim is not simply to fight for intermediate changes but to promote a final and complete change of the status quo.

The real obstacle towards a complete implementation of a minimum de-commodification of labour power, or of other redistributive proposals, such as Pogge's GRD or Nussbaum's capability thresholds, is not mainly of an accounting nature. There would surely be organisational problems with the withdrawal and the redistribution of resources at the global level, in particular at the beginning, but we do not lack the technical knowledge to fix them. What we really lack, instead, is the political motivation to start these processes. The majority of people are currently endorsing the view that all that we owe to foreigners, we owe in virtue of humanity, hence it should be given to the needy through national or international agencies that intervene in cases of dire straits, such as famines, crises, floods and so on. Within this framework, a permanent scheme of redistribution to safeguard justice beyond borders would be unacceptable. And if a progressive politician, who has been persuaded by thousands of articles on global justice she has read, were to propose or to implement such a scheme, she would obviously pay a high price in electoral terms.

Before realising global justice, we need to persuade people that this kind of justice exists. This is the role that Ypi attributes to the cosmopolitan avant-garde. The term avant-garde has been originally used in art to indicate those movements that transformed existing practices following new projects. Ypi makes several examples: Russian avant-gardists of the beginning of the nineteenth century, such as Malevich, Lissitzky and Rodchenko, then Futurists and Dadaists, and also Picasso. We could obviously broaden this list *ad libitum*, but without opening here a digression into modern and contemporary art, what really matters to us at this point is that avant-gardists usually start from a study and an analysis of previous works, considered as 'classics', and then develop new expressive paradigms that break with the past and the tradition. Ypi gives the example of Picasso, who firstly studied and absorbed the modern classics that we can now find when visiting El Prado museum in Madrid – El Greco, Velasquez, Rubens, Titian and so on – and then proposed a new painting style that strongly influenced contemporary art (Ypi 2012, pp. 158–9).

I said that I will not digress into art, and so I shall not, but I think that it is important and useful to add an artistic example of the avant-garde, namely the French pre-impressionists of the second half of the nineteenth century, to the examples offered by Ypi. Up until the 1870s figurative art was still dominated by neoclassical canons. Artists were supposed to paint in their studios, representing with great accuracy mythological or historical scenes, putting drawing ahead of painting, and the custodian of these rules was the influential Académie des beaux-arts. After Eugéne Delacroix (1798–1863, the author of *Liberty Leading the People*) and Gustave Coubert (1819–1877, the author of *L'origine du monde*), the first artist to openly challenge neoclassical canons was Édouard Manet (1832–1883). With *The Absinthe Drinker* (1859), he consecrated on canvas a gloomy, drunk man, drawing him in the same position that was usually reserved for venerable people from the past, while in *The Luncheon on the Grass* (1853), he brought nudity out of myth and directly into contemporary life. In both cases he adopted a different technique from the one usually employed by his colleagues, because he gave priority to colours over portrayal.

The Académie refused to exhibit *The Luncheon on the Grass* at its most important show of the year, The Paris Salon of 1863, as it also did with the works by James McNeill Whistler, Camille Pissarro and Paul Cézanne. This decision created some tension between the Académie and the most innovative artists, so Napoleon III gave his consent to the creation of a second show, the Salon des Refusés, in order that the public could see both approaches to art and judge for itself. Unconsciously, Napoleon III revolutionised modern art and paved the way for contemporary styles. As stressed by Will Gompertz (2012, pp. 11–30), the BBC's current arts editor, the Salon des Refusés represented a fertile environment for artistic counter-culture to grow, and gave the pre-impressionist Manet the opportunity to inspire following impressionists. These latter began to work *en plein air*, reproducing scenes from everyday life with rapid and rough brush strokes that replaced neoclassical perfection.

This historical passage is fundamental for seeing how at a certain point a small group of artists decided to openly challenge the dominant view about art, strongly supported by the custodians of the tradition, and for understanding how we have gone from Raffaello to contemporary conceptual art à la Damien Hirst, where the artist's 'manual skill' is completely missing. Ypi sees the role of avant-garde political agents as similar to that of counter-cultural artists. In Ypi's work, this link between art innovation and political change is based both on a historical observation of past events and on a normative assessment about how cosmopolitan avant-gardists should act (Ypi 2012, p. 161). Avant-garde social movements challenge the status quo and strive for the concrete implementation of a different vision of the future, usually inspired by normative principles. This is the connection between the abstract analysis that we have in ideal theory and avant-garde agents. The latter translate normative principles into political practices that can be actuated in the real world. As usually happens both in art and in politics, avant-gardists are initially a very small minority that is systematically attacked and criticised by the supporters of those same practices they want to challenge. Their mission will be successful if the avant-gardists manage to trigger a transformation process that leads, in the long run, to the passing of old practices.

I think that Ypi's conception of the cosmopolitan avant-garde is interesting. She holds that a cosmopolitan avant-garde already exists. She counts among its members international networks and agencies campaigning on specific issues (migration, sweatshops, climate change, new slavery, trade rules, and so on), political parties (mainly from the socialist/social-democratic field), trade unions, non-governmental organisations (NGOs), and also such organisations as the World Social Forum, the annual meeting of no-global movement, and so on (Ypi 2012, pp. 166–72). The cosmopolitan avant-garde depicted by Ypi is quite variegated, but we should not make the mistake of interpreting it as a political front that opposes globalisation *tout court*. There surely are, among the members of the groups listed by Ypi, some people who hold more radical positions, but the majority of them stand in favour of better and fairer globalisation. Consider, for example, Pogge (2008, p. 18) when he says: 'I do not complain that the WTO regime opens markets too much, but that it has opened *our* markets *too little* and has thereby gained for us the benefits of free trade while withholding these benefits from the global poor.'

In addition to the cosmopolitan avant-garde, I would also emphasise the importance of those people who make up what I would define as cosmopolitan second and third lines, respectively. With the expression cosmopolitan second line, I refer to all those people who are seriously concerned with global justice, are familiar with the ongoing debate, and would be willing to support some initiatives that go in this direction, but nonetheless do not take part actively in the political actions of the cosmopolitan avant-garde. The members of the cosmopolitan third line are those people who are not very informed about the injustices denounced by the avant-garde and do not pay as much attention to international politics as they do to domestic affairs, but at the same time do abstractly embrace the cosmopolitan tenet of universality – all individuals are of equal moral worth.

This is to say that the borders of what Ypi calls cosmopolitan avant-garde are porous. We do not simply have cosmopolitan citizens on the one side and statist citizens on the other. In the middle there are several intermediate categories that might have a propensity for either of the two poles. The role of the cosmopolitan avant-garde also consists in working on the cosmopolitan second line to gain its active engagement and on the third line to increase its awareness about problems of global justice. Sometimes people simply need to be better informed to start getting indignant. In this sense, the second objective of a theory of global justice based on a minimum de-commodification of labour power is to offer new inspiration to the already active members of the cosmopolitan avant-garde and to shed some light on the market dynamics that bring about economic domination. Political scientists, economists and journalists do surely make a great contribution to the cosmopolitan cause when they describe new slavery, sweatshops, violence, harassment, and more generally the dynamics of extreme poverty. But all these, if not supported by a sound normative apparatus, can only trigger initiatives that are based on a duty of humanity or simply on compassion. The task of cosmopolitan theorists consists, in my view, in demonstrating that we have more stringent reasons of justice for being concerned with what happens to vulnerable foreigners.

4.4   LEVYING AND SPENDING COSMOPOLITAN TAXES

Here we come to the last of those that I deem the most powerful objections that might be levelled against cosmopolitan justice, and more specifically against a cosmopolitan MDL. Let's assume that what I have just argued above is correct, and that we can actually find a way to motivate a substantially large group of people to implement a global minimum de-commodification of labour without giving up classic conceptions of national socio-economic justice. How do we concretely convince states to cooperate in a global scheme of taxation for funding MDL and what is the specific kind of wealth that they should tax? Moreover, once a global fund has been created, how do we spend these taxes in a cosmopolitan way, that is to say, directly targeting individuals in need instead of states?[6]

The idea of a global tax is not new; it has been proposed in many different versions and for different reasons. But what the majority of these proposals

---

[6]   Here we are interested in cosmopolitan justice, not in inter-state justice.

have in common is the assumption that the funds for aid and development should be collected by introducing a new tax that should target a specific form of consumption or a specific kind of transaction. A first example is the Global Resources Dividend (GRD) proposed by Pogge (2008, pp. 202–3) and that I discussed in Chapter 3, but in addition to this, there are proposals for taxes on financial transactions (Tobin 1974; Wahl 2016), polluting emissions (Harvard Magazine 2014, pp. 53–4; Swiss Federal Office for the Environment 2017) and air travel (Douste-Blazy and Filipp 2017), whereas others have proposed contract-related mechanisms to protect developing countries selling natural resources from exploitation by multinational companies (West 2016), or they have advocated the creation of a global tax authority (Tanzi 2016).

Yet, the basic question here is the following: are global taxes like those on airlines or on carbon, more stringent rules on international economic operations, or new international authorities the correct means for raising the money needed to finance a minimum de-commodification of labour at the global level? Surely focusing on something specific to be taxed, such as flying or greenhouse emissions, is an easier way to funnel money into a global fund. Nonetheless, the objection that I levelled against Pogge when he centred the taxing part of his theory of justice on natural resources holds true here as well. It is an arbitrary restriction of compensatory responsibility that while helping the theory to be transformed into a concrete policy, risks being unfair. The same discourse holds true for strategies aimed at correcting the imbalance of power inherent in some precise practices such as extraction contracts, or recovering some money from tax evasion.

Extremely commodified individuals are victims of a form of systemic domination that infringes upon individual freedom. Why should we hold responsible for compensating for the negative effects of the unequal distribution of resources only those who happen to own a specific kind of resource (e.g. natural resources), those who consume more CO_2, or those who use an aeroplane instead of trains or cars? The responsibility for capitalist structural domination can be ascribed, as mentioned earlier, to three kinds of agents: those who grant implicit or explicit political support to an economic order that allows for some people to fall below a minimum threshold of de-commodification, those who actually control significant amounts of capital (thus excluding non-owners) and those who are directly responsible for dispossessing non-owners (in Chapter 3, I gave the examples of land grabs, privatisation of public goods and so forth). For the sake of simplicity, we might distinguish between supporters, owners and dispossessors.

The three groups do not necessarily overlap, but perhaps a good way to look at them is in terms of concentric groups, for a dispossessor is very likely to be both an owner and a supporter, whereas an owner is very likely to be a supporter, even only indirectly, but he may not necessarily be a dispossessor. And a supporter may be neither an owner nor a dispossessor, and the example might be a person who is just above the MDL threshold and still offers unconditional support to political parties and governments that strive to preserve the status quo. This can happen, for example, within the 'social connection model' proposed by Iris Marion Young, according to which the individual responsibility for structural injustice can be discharged (only) through collective actions, that is to say by 'joining with others' in those political activities that aim to reform unjust social practices (Young 2011, pp. 111–13). From this perspective on responsibility, it would be possible to maintain that someone (be he an owner or not) is not a supporter only insofar as he is engaged in political activities that aim to de-commodify people. I shall leave aside here the discussion as to whether it is right to interpret responsibility for systemic justice in entirely forward-looking terms (see also Sangiovanni 2018). What I want to say, instead, is that the systemic responsibility for capitalist domination is peculiar. On the one hand, it requires owners and dispossessors to engage in reformative collective actions. On the other hand, the aim of these collective actions is to create institutional mechanisms that can withdraw resources from them for MDL purposes. Accordingly, the structural problem is a function of the amount of resources that each of them controls, and this matters both in terms of individual responsibility and for calibrating the taxing part of MDL.

To make the discourse even more basic, the more resources you own, the 'more' you are preventing extremely commodified individuals from restoring their freedom. Therefore, the scheme that I imagine for financing MDL is a tax on wealth to be levied nationally. This form of taxation would fall short of targeting those who are supporters but not owners or dispossessors. Yet, this should not worry us, because it would not make sense to ask non-owners to contribute what they do not have, and, more importantly, also proletarian supporters would remain responsible for pushing those political reforms that can render owners and dispossessors economically accountable for capitalist domination. Accordingly, the first thing to do is fix an approximate target of the resources we need to achieve a minimum de-commodification of wealth for the first time, and it might be measured in dollars. Pogge (2008, p. 211), for example, tells us that the amount of money that prevents 2.5 billion people from escaping severe poverty is $300 billion annually, 0.67 per cent of the 2005 global product – 'a little over half the annual defence budget of just the US alone, about half the 2007 "peace dividend" of the high-income countries [...], and about one-seventh of the market value of the current annual oil production'.[7] An MDL threshold would be slightly higher than the severe poverty

---

[7]   But consider also that in 2007 we could have made up for the consumption short-fall of all human beings living below the World Bank's extreme poverty line ($1.25/

line to which Pogge refers, because it requires that those who are excluded, or who decide to opt out of the labour market, are guaranteed a minimum liveli-hood in terms of food, housing, health security, education and the capability to relate to others without feeling shame. Obviously, it is reasonable to assume that after the first investment, the amount of money required every year would get progressively smaller. A minimum de-commodification of labour power would restore individual autonomy over a basic set of capabilities, and this would surely help some people to escape the poverty trap. If you are no longer daily striving to keep your family alive, you can start making medium-run projects for your life, you can learn a trade, try to build up a small business, send your children to school without losing a fundamental source of income – child labour – and so on. In other words, after you bring all individuals above the MDL threshold, it is very likely that for the first time some of them would manage to remain above this threshold on their own for subsequent years.[8] Thus, I assume that the amount of resources required every year to finance the MDL would get progressively smaller.

Once we know the approximate cost of MDL per year[9] – I will say more about how we calculate it on the basis of individual needs later – we have to divide it fairly among the agents who are supposed to pay for it. Given that I presented MDL as a cosmopolitan principle of justice, it is supposed, at least *prima facie*, to respect the three tenets of cosmopolitanism: individualism, universality and generality (Pogge 2008, p. 175). Since now we are discussing how to raise money for MDL, and hence how to allocate the compensatory responsibility for capitalist structural domination, the principle that interests us here is the one of generality, according to which individuals should be equally considered as 'ultimate units of moral concerns' by everyone, not simply by those who belong to the same group, be it familial, local or national. Obviously, we cannot expect individuals to correct for capitalist structural domination on their own, bypassing existing institutions, or rather through world institutions that do not exist. Thus, it would be illogical and counterpro-ductive to split the cost of MDL directly among individuals. I rather think that the cost of MDL should be divided among states according to their economic capacity, which can be easily measured through GDP. Then every state would

---

day, a lower threshold than the severe poverty line employed by Pogge) with the rela-tively small investment of $38 billion annually (Pogge 2008, p. 306).

[8]   Even in a hypothetical scenario in which every human being meets the threshold, the principle of MDL would still be valid. The redistributive mechanism that under-lies it would just become 'dormant'. It would be reactivated in the case of even just one individual falling below the threshold. The MDL is a safety net that is supposed to prevent the market mechanism from reducing individuals to a state of domination.

[9]   But we might also think of it in terms of longer-term plans (e.g. five or ten years).

be free to collect the money required by the MDL scheme in the way it prefers. This strategy would partially violate the tenet of generality, since by allowing national governments to make decisions about MDL taxes we run the risk that some people might be treated unfairly in this respect. After all, not every state is a liberal democracy, and even among liberal democracies there are radically opposed views about taxation. Yet, this is another point at which MDL meets non-ideal theory. We live, for the moment and also for the future I think, in a world of states that retain full sovereignty over their tax systems. Companies and individual agents are free to move across these systems, but their organisation remains a national prerogative, and we should deal with it.

Accordingly, every country is assigned a sum to be paid for MDL. Governments can decide to introduce a new domestic tax, to increase existing ones, to sell public assets, or to increase public debt. Imposing on states the method of collection would be unrealistic since we lack an international authority that can do so. But the obvious question remains: why should countries agree to adhere to a scheme like this? After all, the majority of countries simply seek the realisation of their self-interests and do not really pay much attention to normative reasoning at the international level. This is not completely true as programmes of international cooperation have been activated almost everywhere. International programmes of direct intervention in crises, such as the UN's World Food Programme, are regularly financed by states that are not involved in those crises. During recent years there has been great emphasis on Millennium Development Goals, even though they have remained partially unfulfilled, and the same is occurring nowadays with the Sustainable Development Goals. On the other hand, it is also clear to everyone that ruling politicians are usually more focused on short-term than long-term strategies. Adhering to the MDL scheme would involve a government introducing an additional tax – either directly or indirectly – one of the most unpopular things a politician can do. So, if the MDL scheme were really introduced, it is reasonable to assume that only some countries would accept it with immediate effect, probably a minority. But every participation represents a step forward and can put pressure on other members of the global community to join in. This is the linchpin around which the cosmopolitan avant-garde can play a pivotal role.

Assume, for example, that European countries decide to redistribute into a global fund for MDL the amount that has been ascribed to them, while the United States does not. American citizens who share a concern for global justice can ask their government to justify its choice to remain outside the MDL. In the same way as happened during recent years with green parties and associations that have pressed their governments for action in response to climate change, the cosmopolitan avant-garde might bring the minimum de-commodification of labour into the political debate. It is important to note that once MDL is started, even just by a small number of countries, and the quotas are assigned, those governments that are unwilling to join it would no longer be simply blameworthy for the vague reason of not helping the world's poor; rather, they would be explicitly refusing to compensate the victims of capitalist structural domination. And they would have two ways of justifying it to a cosmopolitan avant-garde: either entering into the normative argument and challenging the whole MDL theory, or accepting it normatively – or simply not falsifying it – but maintaining that they want to grant extreme priority to their citizens regardless of what justice would require. In both cases the government, and the majority of citizens that support it, would have to take a clear position on the issue. This alone is a clear result, because it paves the way for the same political processes that led the concerns of minorities – gender equality, anti-racism, sustainable development – to be absorbed in the political programmes of the majority.[10]

Not every country in the world is a liberal democracy, it might be objected. Thus, this process that involves a free and vital cosmopolitan avant-garde is not universally applicable. I agree. But we should not overlook that non-liberal countries are usually those that mostly strive with extreme commodification of labour. So why should they, though being inegalitarian domestically, oppose a redistribution of wealth at the global level? In this regard, I perfectly agree with Allen Buchanan (2000, p. 710) when in response to Rawls's theory of international justice (Rawls 1999b) he maintained: 'egalitarian principles for determining the distribution of benefits and burdens among peoples are not inconsistent with inegalitarian distributions within peoples'. Moreover, the first participants in the MDL group might also have recourse to the principle of conditionality to encourage other economic partners to opt in. If the pressure for MDL became strong enough in some countries, the public opinion of these countries might press the respective governments to impose participation in MDL as a prerequisite for weaker economic partners to continue or to increase trade relations. As countries do usually have recourse to trade sanctions to 'punish' those members of the global community that violate shared norms, 'trade rewards' might be employed to sustain MDL.

As far as results are concerned, we come to the last big question regarding MDL funds. Once we have collected the money, or at least some of it, how do we spend it? Remember that the first tenet of cosmopolitan philosophy is individualism, meaning that 'the ultimate units of concern' are single individuals, and not families, local groups or states. Regarding MDL taxation, we could renounce the full implementation of the cosmopolitan tenet of generality – actually it would be the best strategy. In spending this money, instead, it is

---

[10]   Pogge (2008, p. 217) also gives the example of the moral mobilisation that in the nineteenth century led the British government to give up the slave trade.

extremely important to bypass states, because the risk of intermediate filters that would prevent MDL resources from reaching the poor is extremely real. Therefore, we need a mechanism that targets the poor directly and allows them to give concrete feedback. As far as I know, one idea that might yield both results is that of development vouchers, proposed some years ago by the American economist William Easterly (2006, pp. 330–33).

Development vouchers for a minimum de-commodification of labour would work like this. Firstly, we identify those agencies that should be in charge of distributing resources to the poor. We could rely on existing NGOs or aid agencies, but we would also probably need new ones. These agencies should have available vaccinations, drugs, seeds, food supplements, cooking stoves, and all those things that people might need. Secondly, the global fund for MDL would issue 'development vouchers' (it would probably be more appropriate to call them 'de-commodification vouchers' in this case) that would target directly the people experiencing extreme commodification. This process should be led by an impartial organisation that is in charge of the fund, in collaboration with states, UN agencies and NGOs.[11] Once the person receives the voucher she can go to whatever aid agency is operating in her territory and spend it on whatever she needs – it might be medicine, a utensil, some fertiliser, or even a medical examination, whatever is most important to her at the time.[12] The agency that receives the voucher in return for the performance can successively turn it in to the global fund for MDL and get the money back to cover the cost of the service.

In this way, the poor would be self-responsible for their own minimum de-commodification, choosing all the things they need. At the same time, they would also choose the aid agency from which they wish the service to be issued. Aid agencies have all the interest in meeting the requests coming from the poor because they would be like 'customers', who can give up the

---

[11]   Obviously, the biggest obstacle at this stage consists in selecting the people who actually fall below the minimum de-commodification threshold. I defined it, rather vaguely, as the situation in which a minimum livelihood in terms of food, housing, health, education and the capability to relate to others without feeling shame is not guaranteed, independently from market participation. This theoretical idea should probably be spelled out in numbers, specifying, for example, what the quantity of food and health is that corresponds to that 'minimum'. Much of the success of this operation consists in the capacity of states and agencies to correctly target those below the threshold. I am clearly aware that we would never have a perfect allocation of vouchers. Some persons who deserve it would be excluded while some others would get it undeservedly. Again, what really matters is making the redistributive mechanism as efficient as possible, given the difficult contingencies in which it would operate.

[12]   Aid agencies might collaborate with existing national structures to provide services to the needy.

'company' they are dissatisfied with and turn to another new one that provides better services.[13] Healthy competition would arise between agencies, because if they did not manage to get a sufficient amount of 'development customers', they would not get enough vouchers to turn into money from the global fund, their costs would be higher than proceeds, and the budget would go down.

We might have difficulties in areas where extremely commodified individuals need services that can only be offered by infrastructures that do not exist (e.g. health clinics). In these cases, the global fund might issue collective vouchers to be allocated to villages or local groups. The members of the community would vote on how to use these vouchers, so they could decide to invest the funds in professional training, in a hospital, in a veterinary clinic, and so on. Of course, there might be places where the democratic procedure would not function properly, or where it would be impossible to issue collective vouchers. This is true, but as I said before, we have to accept the difficulties, such as the fact that the process of the minimum de-commodification would never be perfect. The point is investing time and energy in making it always better.

The example of the 'development vouchers' is just an attempt to discuss how the money collected into the global fund for MDL might be concretely spent. But the issue is completely open, and I am sure that other people – also those same people that should be minimally de-commodified – might come up with more technical and convincing proposals for implementing the theory of MDL. There are several options for de-commodifying someone, even working on the restoration of public goods. Imagine, for example, a small village on the coast where former fishermen have been made poor and exploitable by huge fishing vessels from abroad that have destroyed the water fauna with their huge nets. In this case, these fishermen might be minimally de-commodified by simply reducing the activity of large fishing boats.

Lastly, it might be argued that still another method for spending money from the global fund for de-commodification could be to give cash only to those who fall below the MDL threshold, instead of the voucher. This would correspond to an unconditional unemployment subsidy,[14] to be paid to whoever experi-

---

[13]   In this regard, I agree with Easterly (2006, p. 332) when he says: 'Americans fought a revolution on the principle of "no taxation without representation". Could Americans and other parts of the West extend that principle to the rest: "no intervention without representation"? (And I hope I have made clear that non-representative tyrants from the Rest cannot provide such "representation"). Westerns: don't do things to or for other people without giving them a way to let you know – and hold you accountable for – what you have actually done to or for them.'

[14]   In Chapter 3, I explained why the unconditional basic income is normatively incompatible with MDL.

ences a state of extreme commodification, and whose allocation is independent from any commitment of the recipient to undertake positive actions to enter the labour market. Yet, money might be useless in a desert. Very often, people have serious difficulties in converting dollars into the services they need, especially in the contexts of humanitarian crises. Moreover, the main advantage of development vouchers over cash payments is that the former scheme could activate a virtuous scheme of competition among those agents entrusted with providing aid, hence yielding strong incentives for them to provide the poor with products and services that otherwise would be unavailable in their local contexts. Even more importantly, perhaps, it could be an incentive for both the public and the private sectors to invest in research projects aimed at ameliorating the lives of the world poor – be they drugs, nutritional products, utensils, and suchlike. For one thing, the problems that exist with investing in innovative goods targeted on the world's poor is that the latter usually have very limited purchasing power. The vouchers, backed by the global fund for MDL, are supposed to create a new market for these products,[15] because they would give the world's poor the chance to remunerate those agents that provide them with basic goods and services; hence, it is logical to expect that some people will try to conquer shares of this new market.

The last remark leads me to emphasise an important characteristic that development vouchers have in common with both universal basic income and unconditional unemployment subsidies, and which distinguishes them all from classic approaches to aid – consisting in giving direct assistance to the poor instead of the purchasing power for buying it. The former approaches are non- paternalistic. And from the prospective of commodification this is not a superfluous thing, because both cash and vouchers would give the poor the chance of deciding what they need to get minimally de-commodified. Again, this is not irrelevant, for were we simply interested in giving humanitarian assistance to persons in dire needs, we could identify a standard set of resources to be allocated regardless of individual requests. But since the aim of MDL is to allow people to secure a basic set of capabilities from the downturns of the market, I think that it is important to let people decide what they need for this objective to be accomplished. For example, two persons who experience exactly the same extreme level of labour commodification might prefer to receive different goods for getting minimally de-commodified. One person

---

[15]   Clearly, cash instead of vouchers would create also an incentive to investors to come up with new products for the world's poor. But I assume that the existence of an efficient system of distribution, such as we would have with the voucher scheme, can reassure investors that their goods will reach potential buyers also in the most difficult areas. Therefore, I believe that with vouchers the incentive for innovation would be even greater than with simple cash.

might simply want to receive food and medicines, whereas another person may prefer to be given agricultural tools instead of food, together with medicines. Or we can also imagine that a group of people would be willing to use their vouchers cumulatively to get a more costly service that would contribute to de-commodifying the whole community, for example the decontamination of a river where they used to fish. Moreover, with development vouchers, development agents would be somehow accountable to the world's poor and there would also be an incentive for inventing and providing solutions that otherwise would be unavailable.

On the other hand, we should also notice that the advantages of development vouchers, as originally proposed by Easterly and here re-elaborated to fit within the frame of MDL, would progressively decrease the more we move from developing to developed contexts. If we look at the situation of a person living in a condition of extreme commodification in a metropolitan city, for example, it would be unreasonable to hold that the means for her MDL are out of her reach. She can find whatever she fancies in her city, while what she really lacks is the purchasing power to get what she needs. Therefore, in this kind of context I imagine that it would be much more reasonable to let people use vouchers to gain access to existing services and retailers, instead of building up a brand-new scheme of assistance such as the one I described earlier for poor regions.

In conclusion, the best way to spend the money collected in the MDL fund would probably be, in my view, a mixed system of vouchers, with the reinforcement of existing aid agencies, and also the creation of new ones, in particularly poor contexts, where they would be organised in virtuous competitions, not forgetting the contribution of existing providers of goods and services in developed countries. Nonetheless, the project of MDL is open to very different forms of implementation. And I am sure that development economists and policy makers could devise proposals and schemes that are much more refined and precise than the one I have sketched above. I have dwelt on development vouchers because they seem to me a rational strategy that might be easily globalised. My aim was to try to reason on how to spend the proceeds of a global tax for MDL in a way that respects the basic tenets of moral cosmopolitanism. Moreover, the voucher scheme is based on a competitive model guided by market principles. In the previous chapters I have repeatedly criticised global capitalism for allowing domination to occur. Proposing the development vouchers as a solution to the negative effects of economic systemic domination, I also want to emphasise again that I am not against the market as such, but only against the shortcomings of an unregulated market, and that I recognise the market's capacity to yield results that are unachievable through other modes of production.

Bibliography

Abizadeh, A. (2007), 'Cooperation, pervasive impact, and coercion: on the scope of distributive justice', *Philosophy and Public Affairs*, **35** (4), 318–58.

Alstott, A.A. (2001), 'Good for women', in Joshua Cohen and Philippe Van Parijs (eds), *What's Wrong with a Free Lunch?*, Boston, MA: Beacon Press, pp. 75–9.

Arcarons J., D. Raventos Pañella and L. Torrens Mèlich (2014), 'Feasibility of financing a basic income', *Basic Income Studies*, **9** (1–2), 79–93.

Armstrong, C. (2012), *Global Distributive Justice*, Cambridge, Cambridge University Press.

Arneson, R.J. (1981), 'What's wrong with exploitation?', *Ethics*, **91** (2), 202–27.

Arnold, S. and J.R. Harris (2017), 'What is arbitrary power?', *Journal of Political Power*, **10** (1), 55–70.

Avi-Yonah, R.S. (2000), 'Globalization, tax competition, and the fiscal crisis of the welfare state', *Harvard Law Review*, **113** (7), 1573–676.

Avi-Yonah, R.S. (2019), 'Globalization, tax competition and the fiscal crisis of the welfare state: a twentieth anniversary retrospective', University of Michigan Law & Economics Research Paper No. 19-002, 1 May, available at: https://ssrn.com/abstract=3367340.

Axelsen, D.V. and L. Nielsen (2015), 'Sufficiency as freedom from duress', *Journal of Political Philosophy*, **23** (4), 406–26.

Baker, J. (2008), 'All things considered, should feminists embrace basic income?', *Basic Income Studies: An International Journal of Basic Income Research*, **3** (3), 1–8.

Baldwin, R. (2016), *The Great Convergence: Information Technology and the New Globalization*, Cambridge, MA: The Belknap Press of Harvard University Press.

Bales, K. (2012), *Disposable People: New Slavery in the Global Economy*, updated with a new preface, Berkeley: University of California Press.

Barry, B. (1973), 'The liberal theory of justice: a critical examination of the principal doctrines', in John Rawls, *A Theory of Justice*, Oxford: Clarendon Press.

Bauman, Z. (1999), *In Search of Public Space*, Cambridge: Polity Press.

Bauman, Z. (2003), *Wasted Lives: Modernity and Its Outcasts*, Cambridge: Polity Press.

Beck, U. (1999), *World Risk Society*, Cambridge: Polity Press.

Beck, U. (2009 [2007]), *World at Risk* (trans. Ciaran Cronin), Cambridge: Polity Press.

Beitz, C. (1999/1979), *Political Theory and International Relations*, revised edition, Princeton, NJ: Princeton University Press.

Benería, L. (2007), 'Paid and unpaid labor: meanings and debates', in Alison M. Jaggar (ed.), *Just Methods: An Interdisciplinary Feminist Reader*, Boulder, CO and London: Paradigm Publishers.

Blake, M. (2001), 'Distributive justice, state coercion, and autonomy', *Philosophy & Public Affairs*, **30** (3), 257–96.

Block, F. (2001), 'Introduction', in Karl Polanyi, *The Great Transformation*, Boston, MA: Beacon Press.

Block, F. (2003), 'Karl Polanyi and the writing of "The Great Transformation"', *Theory and Society*, **32** (3), 275–306.

Block, F. and M. Somers (2003), 'In the shadow of Speenhamland: social policy and the Old Poor Law', *Politics & Society*, **31** (2), 283–323.

Bohman, J. (2004), 'Republican cosmopolitanism', *Journal of Political Philosophy*, **12** (3), 336–52.

Bourdieu, P. (2000), 'Making the economic habitus: Algerian workers revisited', *Ethnography*, **1** (17), 17–41.

Brock, G. (2009), *Global Justice: A Cosmopolitan Account*, Oxford: Oxford University Press.

Buchanan, A. (2000), 'Rawls's Law of Peoples: rules for a vanished Westphalian world', *Ethics*, **110** (4), 697–721.

Buckinx, B., J. Trejo-Mathys and T. Waligore (2015), 'Domination across borders: an introduction', in Barbara Buckinx, Jonathan Trejo-Mathys and Timothy Waligore (eds), *Domination and Global Political Justice: Conceptual, Historical and Institutional Perspectives*, New York: Routledge, pp. 1–34.

Buğra, A. (2007), 'Polanyi's concept of double movement and politics in the contemporary market society', in Ayşe Buğra and K. Ağartan (eds), *Reading Karl Polanyi for the Twenty-First Century: Market Economy as a Political Project*, New York: Palgrave Macmillan, pp. 173–90.

Calder, T. (2010), 'Shared responsibility, global structural injustice, and restitution', *Social Theory and Practice*, **36** (2), 263–90.

Caney, S. (2001), 'Cosmopolitan justice and equalizing opportunities', *Metaphilosophy*, **32** (1–2), 113–34.

Caney, S. (2005), *Justice Beyond Borders: A Global Political Theory*, Oxford: Oxford University Press.

Capik, P. and M. Dej (eds) (2019), *Relocation of Economic Activity: Contemporary Theory and Practice in Local, Regional and Global Perspectives*, New York: Springer.

Carter, I. (2008), 'How are power and unfreedom related?', in Cécile Laborde and John Maynor (eds), *Republicanism and Political Theory*, Malden, MA: Blackwell Publishing, pp. 58–82.

Casal, P. (2007), 'Why sufficiency is not enough', *Ethics*, **117** (2), 296–326.

Cassee, A. (2019), 'International tax competition and justice: the case for global minimum tax rates', *Politics, Philosophy & Economics*, **18** (3), 242–63.

Christman, J. (1991), 'Self-ownership, equality, and the structure of property rights', *Political Theory*, **19** (1), 28–46.

Cicerchia, L. (2019), 'Structural domination in the labor market', *European Journal of Political Theory*, DOI: 10.1177/1474885119851094, 1–21.

Clifford, C. (2018), 'Elon Musk: free cash handouts "will be necessary" if robots take humans' jobs', *CNBC Make it*, 18 June, accessed 3 April 2020 at https://www.cnbc.com/2018/06/18/elon-musk-automated-jobs-could-make-ubi-cash-handouts-necessary.html.

Cohen, G.A. (1988), *History, Labour and Freedom: Themes from Marx*, Oxford: Clarendon Press.

Copp, D. (1992), 'The right to an adequate standard of living: justice, autonomy, and the basic needs', *Social Philosophy & Policy*, **9** (1), 231–61.

Corvino, F. (2015), 'Punishing atypical dirty hands: assessing the moral value of coordination failure, *International Journal of Applied Philosophy*, **29** (2), 281–97.

Corvino, F. (2019a), 'The moral implications of the global basic structure as a subject of justice', *Glocalism: Journal of Culture, Politics and Innovation*, **2019** (2), 1–36.

Corvino, F. (2019b), 'Utility, priorities, and quiescent sufficiency', *Etica & Politica/ Ethics & Politics*, **21** (3), 525–52.

Corvino, F. (2019c), 'La giustizia globale al tempo della globalizzazione convergente', *Notizie di Politeia*, **35** (136), 185–204.

Cotula, L., S. Vermeulen, R. Leonard and J. Keeley (2009), *Land grab or development opportunity? Agricultural investment and international land deals in Africa*, FAO, IIED and IFAD, available at http://www.fao.org/3/a-ak241e.pdf.

Crisp, Roger (2003), 'Equality, priority, and compassion', *Ethics*, **113** (4), 745–63.

Crisp, R. (2017), 'Well-being', in Edward N. Zalta (ed.), *The Stanford Encyclopedia of Philosophy*, https://plato.stanford.edu/archives/fall2017/entries/well-being/.

Crouch, C. (2013), *Making Capitalism Fit for Society*, Cambridge: Polity Press.

Crouch, C. and W. Streeck (1997), 'Introduction: the future of capitalist diversity', in Colin Crouch and Wolfgang Streeck (eds), *Political Economy of Modern Capitalism: Mapping Convergence and Diversity*, London: Sage Publications, pp, 1–18.

Cunliffe, J. and G. Erreygers (2004), *The Origins of Universal Grants: An Anthology of Historical Writings on Basic Capital and Basic Income*, New York: Palgrave Macmillan.

Dagger, R. (2006), 'Neo-republicanism and the civic economy', *Politics, Philosophy & Economics*, **5** (2), 151–73.

Dale, G. (2010), *Karl Polanyi: The Limits of the Market*, Cambridge: Polity Press.

Davis, M. (2006), *Planet of Slums*, London and New York: Verso.

De Angelis, M. (1999), 'Marx's Theory of Primitive Accumulation: a suggested reinterpretation', UEL, Department of Economics, Working Paper No. 29, May 2000.

De Masi, D. (2017), *Lavorare gratis, lavorare tutti: perché il futuro è dei disoccupati*, Milan: Rizzoli.

De Soto, H. (2000), *The Mystery of Capital: Why Capitalism Triumphs in the West and Fails Everywhere Else*, New York: Basic Books.

De Wispelaere, J. and L. Stirton (2011), 'The administrative efficiency of basic income', *Policy & Politics*, **39** (1), 115–32.

Douste-Blazy, P. and R. Filipp (2017), 'No pain, big gain: how micro-levies save lives', *Foreign Affairs*, 25 October, accessed 3 March 2020 at https://www.foreignaffairs.com/sponsored/no-pain-big-gain-how-micro-levies-save-lives.

Dworkin, R. (1981a), 'What is equality? Part 1: equality of welfare', *Philosophy and Public Affairs*, **10** (3), 185–246.

Dworkin, R. (1981b), 'What is equality? Part 2: equality of resources', *Philosophy and Public Affairs*, **10** (4), 283–345.

Easterly, W. (2006), *The White Man's Burden: Why the West's Efforts to Aid the Rest Have Done So Much Ill and So Little Good*, Oxford: Oxford University Press.

Emmons, D.C. (1973), 'Act vs. rule-utilitarianism', *Mind*, **82** (326), 226–33.

Esping-Andersen, Gøsta (1990), *The Three Worlds of Welfare Capitalism*, Cambridge: Polity Press.

Farago, J. (2019), 'A (grudging) defense of the $120,000 banana: Maurizio Cattelan is more than a prankster, and "comedian," his potassium-rich latest work, is more than an overpriced piece of fruit', *The New York Times*, 8 December, accessed 23 December 2019 at https://www.nytimes.com/2019/12/08/arts/design/a-critics-defense-of-cattelan-banana-.html.

Federici, S. (2004), *Caliban and the Witch: Women, the Body and Primitive Accumulation*, Brooklyn, NY: Autonomedia.

Flanigan, J. (2018), 'The feminist case for a universal basic income', *Slate*, 25 January, accessed 14 February 2020 at https://slate.com/human-interest/2018/01/the-feminist -case-for-universal-basic-income.html.

Florida, R. (2005), *Cities and the Creative Class*, New York and London: Routledge.

Ford, M. (2015), *Rise of the Robots: Technology and the Threat of a Jobless Future*, New York: Basic Books.

Ford, M. (2016), 'Economic growth isn't over, but it doesn't create jobs like it used to', *Harvard Business Review*, 14 March, accessed 22 March 2020 at https://hbr.org/ 2016/03/economic-growth-isnt-over-but-it-doesnt-create-jobs-like-it-used-to.

Forst, R. (2001), 'Towards a critical theory of transnational justice', *Metaphilosophy*, **32** (1–2), 160–79.

Frankfurt, H. (1987), 'Equality as a moral ideal', *Ethics*, **98** (1), 21–43.

Fraser, N. (2014), 'Can society be commodities all the way down? Post-Polanyian reflections on capitalist crisis', *Economy and Society*, **43** (4), 541–58.

Fraser, N. (2017), 'Why two Karls are better than one: integrating Polanyi and Marx in a critical theory of the current crisis', Working Paper der DFG-Kollegforscher_ innengruppe Postwachstumsgesellschaften, Nr. 1/2017, Jena 2017.

Frey, C.B. and M.A. Osborne (2013), 'The future of employment: how susceptible are jobs to computerization?', Working Paper published by The Oxford Martin Programme on the Impacts of Future Technology, 17 September, available at https:// www.oxfordmartin.ox.ac.uk/downloads/academic/future-of-employment.pdf.

Genshel, P. (2002), 'Globalization, tax competition, and the welfare state', *Politics & Society*, **30** (2), 245–75.

Gompertz, Will (2012), *What Are You Looking At? The Surprising, Shocking, and Sometimes Strange Story of 150 Years of Modern Art*. New York: Penguin Books.

Gourevitch, A. (2013), 'Labor republicanism and the transformation of work', *Political Theory* **41** (4): 591–617.

Gourevitch, A. (2015), *From Slavery to the Cooperative Commonwealth: Labor and Republican Liberty in the Nineteenth Century*, Cambridge: Cambridge University Press.

Graetz, G. and G. Michaels (2017), 'Is modern technology responsible for jobless recoveries?', *The American Economic Review*, **107** (5), 168–73.

Hale, T., D. Held and K. Young (2013), *Gridlock: Why Global Cooperation is Failing when We Need It Most*, Cambridge: Polity Press.

Hannah, S. (2019), 'The fight against climate change is a fight against capitalism', *open-Democracy*, 13 August, accessed 28 December 2019 at https://www.opendemocracy .net/en/oureconomy/fight-against-climate-change-fight-against-capitalism/.

Harvard Magazine (2014), 'Time to tax carbon: enhancing environmental quality and economic growth', September/October, available at http://harvardmag.com/pdf/ 2014/09-pdfs/0914-52.pdf.

Harvey, D. (2004), 'The "new" imperialism: accumulation by dispossession', *Socialist Register*, **40**, 63–87.

Harvey, D. (2010), *A Companion to Marx's Capital*, London and New York: Verso.

Heilinger, J.C. (2020), *Cosmopolitan Responsibility: Global Justice, Relational Equality, and Individual Agency*, Boston, MA/Berlin: de Gruyter.

Held, D. (2010), *Cosmopolitanism: Ideals and Reality*, Cambridge: Polity Press.

Henry, B. (2018), '"Ask the other questions": how to make a good use of intersectionality', *Iride: Filosofia e discussione pubblica*, **2**, 319–26.

Holtug, N. (2007), 'Prioritarianism', in Nils Holtug and Kasper Lippert Rasmussen (eds), *Egalitarianism: New Essays on the Nature and Value of Equality*, Oxford: Oxford University Press, pp. 125–56.

Holtug, N. (2015), 'Theories of value aggregation: utilitarianism, egalitarianism, prioritarianism', in Iwao Hirose and Jonas Olson (eds), *The Oxford Handbook of Value Theory*, Oxford: Oxford University Press, pp. 267–84.

Honneth, A. (2008), *Reification: A New Look at an Old Idea* (Tanner Lectures), Oxford: Oxford University Press.

Hudis, P. (2010), 'Accumulation, imperialism, and pre-capitalist formations: Luxemburg and Marx on the non-western world', *Socialist Studies/Études socialistes*, **6** (2), 75–91.

Huseby, R. (2010), 'Sufficiency: restated and defended', *Journal of Political Philosophy*, **18** (2), 178–97.

ILO (2017a), *Global estimates of modern slavery: forced labour and forced marriage*, available at https://www.ilo.org/wcmsp5/groups/public/---dgreports/---dcomm/documents/publication/wcms_575479.pdf.

ILO (2017b), *World Employment and Social Outlook: Trends 2017*, available at https://www.ilo.org/wcmsp5/groups/public/---dgreports/---dcomm/---publ/documents/publication/wcms_541211.pdf.

ILO (2020), *World Employment and Social Outlook: Trends 2020*, available at https://www.ilo.org/wcmsp5/groups/public/---dgreports/---dcomm/---publ/documents/publication/wcms_734455.pdf.

Jackson, W.A. (1999), 'Basic income and the right to work: a Keynesian approach', *Journal of Post Keynesian Economics*, **21** (4), 639–62.

Jaeggi, R. (2014), *Alienation* (ed. Frederick Neuhouser, trans. Frederick Neuhouser and Alan E. Smith), New York: Columbia University Press.

Jaeggi, R. (2015), 'Towards an immanent critique of forms of life', *Raisons politiques*, **57** (1), 13–29.

Jaeggi, R. (2016), 'What is wrong with capitalism? Dysfunctionality, exploitation and alienation: three approaches to the critique of capitalism', *Southern Journal of Philosophy*, **54** (S1), 44–65.

Jaeggi, R. (2018), *Critique of Forms of Life* (trans. Ciaran Cronin), Cambridge, MA: The Belknap Press of Harvard University Press.

James, A. (2005), 'Constructing justice for existing practice: Rawls and the status quo', Philosophy & Public Affairs, **33** (3), 281–316.

James, A. (2012), *Fairness in Practice: A Social Contract for a Global Economy*, Oxford: Oxford University Press.

Jhabvala, R. (2019), Basic income can transform women's lives, *openDemocracy*, 19 September, accessed 14 February 2020 at https://www.opendemocracy.net/en/beyond-trafficking-and-slavery/basic-income-can-transform-womens-lives/.

Keynes, J.M. (2008 [1930]), 'Economic possibilities for our grandchildren', in Lorenzo Pecchi and Gustavo Piga (eds), *Revisiting Keynes: Economic Possibilities for our Grandchildren*, Cambridge MA: The MIT Press, pp. 17–26.

Khanna, P. (2016), 'Rise of the Titans', *Foreign Policy*, March/April (217), 50–55.

Kimmelman, M. (2017), 'The Dutch have solutions to rising seas: the world is watching', *The New York Times*, 15 June, accessed 2 March 2020 at https://www.nytimes.com/interactive/2017/06/15/world/europe/climate-change-rotterdam.html.

Klein, N. (2019), *On Fire: The Burning Case for a Green New Deal*, New York: Simon & Schuster.

Kramer, M.H. (2008), 'Liberty and domination', in Cécile Laborde and John Maynor (eds), *Republicanism and Political Theory*, Malden, MA: Blackwell Publishing, pp. 31–57.

Laborde, C. (2010), 'Republicanism and global justice: a sketch', *European Journal of Political Theory*, **9** (1), 48–69.

Laborde, C. and M. Ronzoni (2016), 'What is a free state? Republican internationalism and globalisation', *Political Studies*, **64** (2), 279–96.

Lazonick, W. (1974), 'Karl Marx and enclosures in England', *Review of Radical Political Economics*, **6** (1), 1–59.

Lindblom, Charles E. (2001), *The Market System: What It Is, How It Works, and What To Make of It*, New Haven, CT and London: Yale University Press.

Lister, M. (2014), 'Climate change refugees', *Critical Review of International Social and Political Philosophy*, **17** (5), 618–34.

Locke, J. (2003 [1689]), 'Two treatises of government', in Ian Shapiro (ed.), *Two Treaties of Government and A Letter Concerning Toleration*, New Haven, CT and London: Yale University Press.

Loretoni, A. (2018), 'Un femminismo intersezionale e multidisciplinare', *Iride: Filosofia e discussione pubblica*, **2**, 307–18.

Lovett, F. (2010), *A General Theory of Domination and Justice*, Oxford and New York: Oxford University Press.

Lovett, F. (2012), 'What counts as arbitrary power?', *Journal of Political Power*, **5** (1): 137–52.

Luxemburg, Rosa (2003 [1913]), *The Accumulation of Capital* (trans. Agnes Schwarzschild), London and New York: Routledge.

Maddison, Angus (2005), *Growth and Interaction in the World Economy: The Roots of Modernity*, Washington, DC: The AEI Press.

Mandel, Ernest (1973), 'The causes of alienation', in Ernest Mandel and George Novack (eds), *The Marxist Theory of Alienation*, Atlanta, GA: Pathfinder Press, pp. 13–30.

Manyika, J., S. Lund, M. Chui, J. Bughin, J. Woetzel, P. Batra, R. Ko and S. Sanghvi (2017), *Jobs Lost, Jobs Gained: Workforce Transitions in a Time of Automation*, McKinsey Global Institute, available at https://www.mckinsey.com/~/media/McKinsey/Featured%20Insights/Future%20of%20Organizations/What%20the%20future%20of%20work%20will%20mean%20for%20jobs%20skills%20and%20wages/MGI-Jobs-Lost-Jobs-Gained-Report-December-6-2017.ashx.

Marx, K. (1975 [1844]), 'Excerpts from James Mill's *Elements of Political Economy*', in Lucio Colletti (ed.), *Early Writings* (trans. Rodney Livingstone and Gregor Benton), London: Penguin Books, pp. 259–78.

Marx, K. (1988 [1844]), 'Economic and philosophical manuscripts of 1844', in Karl Marx and Frederick Engels, *Economic and Philosophical Manuscripts of 1844 and the Communist Manifesto* (trans. Martin Milligan), New York: Prometheus Books, pp. 13–170.

Marx, K. (1994 [1864]), 'Chapter Six. Results of the direct production process', in Karl Marx and Frederick Engels, *Collected Works: Volume 34 – Marx:1861–1864* (trans. Ben Fowkes), London: Lawrence and Wishart, pp. 355–466.

Marx, K. (2013 [1867]), *Capital: A Critical Analysis of Capitalistic Production, Volume 1 and Volume 2*, Ware, UK: Wordsworth Editions.

Marx, K. and F. Engels (1988 [1848]), 'Manifesto of the Communist Party', in Karl Marx and Frederick Engels, *Economic and Philosophical Manuscripts of 1844 and the Communist Manifesto* (trans. Martin Milligan), New York: Prometheus Books, pp. 203–43.

Maxton, G. (2015), 'Economic growth doesn't create jobs, it destroys them', *The Guardian*, 21 April, accessed 25 March 2020 at https://www.theguardian.com/sustainable-business/2015/apr/21/jobs-economic-growth-inequality-environment-club-of-rome.

Maynor, J.W. (2003), *Republicanism in the Modern World*, Cambridge: Polity Press.

McAfee, A. and E. Brynjolfsson (2016), 'Human work in the robotic future: policy for the age of automation', *Foreign Affairs*, **95** (4), 19–150.

McCall, L. (2005), 'The complexity of intersectionality', *Signs*, **30** (3), 1771–800.

McDuff, P. (2019), 'Ending climate change requires the end of capitalism. Have we got the stomach for it?', *The Guardian*, 18 March, accessed 19 December 2019 at https://www.theguardian.com/commentisfree/2019/mar/18/ending-climate-change-end-capitalism#maincontent.

Meyer, L.H. (2003), Past and future: the case for a threshold notion of harm', in Lukas H. Meyer, Stanley Paulson and Thomas W. Pogge (eds), *Rights, Culture and the Law: Themes from the Legal and Political Philosophy of Joseph Raz*, Oxford: Oxford University Press, pp. 143–58.

Milanovic, B. (2016), *Global Inequality: A New Approach for the Age of Globalization*, Cambridge, MA: The Belknap Press of Harvard University Press.

Milanovic, B. (2019), *Capitalism, Alone: The Future of the System that Rules the World*, Cambridge, MA: The Belknap Press of Harvard University Press.

Miller, D. (2007), *Nationalism and Global Responsibility*, Oxford: Oxford University Press.

Miller, R. (2005), 'Cosmopolitan respect and patriotic principle', in Gillian Brock and Harry Brighouse (eds), *The Political Philosophy of Cosmopolitanism*, Cambridge: Cambridge University Press, pp. 148–63.

Miner, L. and J. Wilks (2020), 'Rising sea levels: how the Netherlands found ways of working with the environment', *Euronews*, 25 February, accessed 2 March 2020 at https://www.euronews.com/2019/10/14/rising-sea-levels-how-the-netherlands-found-ways-of-working-with-the-environment.

Moellendorf, D. (2002), *Cosmopolitan Justice*, Cambridge, MA: Westview Press.

Morrone, A., K. Scrivens, C. Smith and C. Balestra (2011), 'Measuring vulnerability and resilience in OECD countries', paper prepared for the *IARIW-OECD Conference on Economic Insecurity*, Paris, France, 22–3 November, accessed at http://www.iariw.org/papers/2011/morronepaper.pdf.

Mulgan, T. (2007), *Understanding Utilitarianism*, Stocksfield Hall, UK: Acumen.

Murphy, L. (1998), 'Institutions and the demands of justice', *Philosophy and Public Affairs*, **27** (4), 251–91.

Musto, M. (2010), 'Revisiting Marx's concept of alienation', *Socialism and Democracy*, **24** (3), 79–101.

Nagel, T. (2005), 'The problem of global justice', *Philosophy & Public Affairs*, **33** (2), 113–47.

Nester, W. (2010), *Globalization: A Short History of the Modern World*, New York: Palgrave Macmillan.

Nichols, R. (2015), 'Disaggregating primitive accumulation', *Radical Philosophy*, **194**, 18–28.

Nielsen, L. and David V. Axelsen (2017), 'Capabilitarian sufficiency: capabilities and social justice', *Journal of Human Development and Capabilities*, **18** (1), 46–59.

Nozick, R. (1974), *Anarchy, State, and Utopia*, Oxford: Blackwell Publishers.

Nussbaum, M. (1995), 'Aristotle on the human nature and the foundations of ethics', in J.E.J. Altham and Ross Harrison (eds), *World, Mind, and Ethics: Essays on the Ethical Philosophy of Bernard Williams*, Cambridge: Cambridge University Press, pp. 86–131.

Nussbaum, M. (2000), *Women and Human Development: The Capability Approach*, Cambridge: Cambridge University Press.

Nussbaum, M. (2006), *Frontiers of Justice: Disability, Nationality, Species Membership*, Cambridge, MA: The Belknap Press of Harvard University Press.

Nussbaum, M. (2011), *Creating Capabilities: The Human Development Approach*, Cambridge, MA: The Belknap Press of Harvard University Press.

Otsuka, M. (1998), 'Self-ownership and equality: a Lockean reconciliation', *Philosophy & Public Affairs*, **27** (1), 65–92.

Our World in Data (2019), 'World population living in extreme poverty, 1820–2015', accessed 12 January 2020 at https://ourworldindata.org/grapher/world-population-in -extreme-poverty-absolute.

Oxfam (2020), Time to care: unpaid and underpaid care work and the global inequality crisis, available at https://oxfamilibrary.openrepository.com/bitstream/handle/ 10546/620928/bp-time-to-care-inequality-200120-en.pdf.

Özel, H. (1997), 'Reclaiming humanity: the social theory of Karl Polanyi', PhD thesis, Department of Economics, University of Utah, August 1997, available at http:// content.lib.utah.edu/cdm/ref/collection/etd2/id/1928.

Pettit, P. (1996), 'Freedom as antipower', *Ethics*, **106** (3), 576–604.

Pettit, P. (1997), *Republicanism: A Theory of Freedom and Government*, Oxford: Oxford University Press.

Pettit, P. (2006), 'Freedom in the market', *Politics, Philosophy & Economics*, **5** (2), 131–49.

Pettit, P. (2007), 'A Republican right to basic income?', *Basic Income Studies*, **2** (2), 1–8.

Pettit, P. (2008), 'Republican freedom: three axioms, four theorems', in Cécile Laborde and John Maynor (eds), *Republicanism and Political Theory*, Malden, MA: Blackwell Publishing, pp. 102–30.

Pettit, P. (2012), *On the People's Terms: A Republican Theory and Model of Democracy*, Cambridge: Cambridge University Press.

Pirni, A. (2017), 'Connessioni di destino: cura, interdipendenza, convivialismo', *La società degli individui*, **58** (1), 56–70.

Pogge, T.W. (1989), *Realizing Rawls*, Ithaca, NY: Cornell University Press.

Pogge, T.W. (2007), 'Severe poverty as a human rights violation', in T.W. Pogge (ed.), *Freedom from Poverty as a Human Right: Who Owes What to the Very Poor?*, Oxford: Oxford University Press (co-published with UNESCO).

Pogge, T.W. (2008), *World Poverty and Human Rights*, second edition, Cambridge: Polity Press.

Pogge, T.W. (2010), 'Responses to the critics', in Alison M. Jaggar (ed.), *Thomas Pogge and His Critics*, Cambridge: Polity Press.

Polanyi, Karl (2001/1944), *The Great Transformation*, Boston, MA: Beacon Press.

Pulkka, V.-V. (2017), 'A free lunch with robots: can basic income stabilize the digital economy?', *Transfer*, **23** (3), 295–311.

Putnam, Robert D. (2000), *Bowling Alone: The Collapse and Revival of American Community*, New York: Simon & Schuster.

Raventós, D. (2007), *Basic Income: The Material Conditions of Freedom* (trans. Julie Wark), London and Ann Arbor, MI: Pluto Press.

Rawls, J. (1999a/1971), *A Theory of Justice*, revised edition, Cambridge: The Belknap Press of Harvard University Press.

Rawls, J. (1999b), *The Law of Peoples, with 'The Idea of Public Reason Revisited'*, Cambridge MA: Harvard University Press.

Rawls, J. (2001), *Justice as Fairness: A Restatement*, Cambridge MA: Harvard University Press.

Rawls, J. (2005/1993), *Political Liberalism*, expanded edition, New York: Columbia University Press.

Risse, M. (2005), 'Do we owe the global poor assistance or rectification?', *Ethics & International Affairs*, **19** (1), 9–18.

Risse, M. and M. Meyer (2019), 'Tax competition and global interdependence', *The Journal of Political Philosophy*, **27** (4), 480–98.

Roberts, W.C. (2017), 'What was primitive accumulation? Reconstructing the origin of a critical concept', *European Journal of Political Theory*, https://doi.org/10.1177/1474885117735961, 1–21.

Robertson, C.J., A. Lamin and G. Livanis (2010), 'Stakeholder perceptions of offshoring and outsourcing: the role of embedded issues', *Journal of Business Ethics*, **95** (2), 167–89.

Robeyns, I. (2016), 'Capabilitarianism', *Journal of Human Development and Capabilities*, **17** (3), 397–414.

Roemer, J.E. (1982), 'Property relations vs. surplus value in Marxian exploitation', *Philosophy & Public Affairs*, **11** (4), 281–313.

Roemer, J.E. (1985), 'Should Marxists be interested in exploitation?', *Philosophy & Public Affairs*, **14** (1), 30–65.

Roemer, J.E. (2017), 'Socialism revised', *Philosophy & Public Affairs*, **45** (3), 261–315.

Ronzoni, M. (2009), 'The global order: a case of background injustice? A practice-dependent account, *Philosophy & Public Affairs*, **37** (3), 229–56.

Roser, M. (2017), 'The global decline of extreme poverty – was it only China?', *Our World in Data*, 7 March, accessed 12 January 2020 at https://ourworldindata.org/the-global-decline-of-extreme-poverty-was-it-only-china.

Russell, B. (2004 [1935]), *In Praise of Idleness*, London: Routledge.

Sangiovanni, A. (2007), 'Global justice, reciprocity, and the state', *Philosophy & Public Affairs*, **35** (1), 3–39.

Sangiovanni, A. (2008), 'Justice and the priority of politics to morality', *The Journal of Political Philosophy*, **16** (2), 137–64.

Sangiovanni, A. (2016), 'How practices matter', *The Journal of Political Philosophy*, **24** (1), 3–23.

Sangiovanni, A. (2018), 'Structural injustice and individual responsibility', *Journal of Social Philosophy*, **49** (3), 461–83.

Sassen, Saskia (2014), *Expulsions: Brutality and Complexity in the Global Economy*, Cambridge, MA: The Belknap Press of Harvard University Press.

Sayers, S. (2011), *Marx and Alienation: Essays on Hegelian Themes*, London: Palgrave Macmillan.

Scanlon, T. (1973), 'Rawls' theory of justice', *University of Pennsylvania Law Review*, **121** (5), 1020–69.

Scheffler, S. (2001), *Boundaries and Allegiances: Problems of Justice and Responsibility in Liberal Thought*, Oxford: Oxford University Press.

Sen, A. (1992), *Inequality Reexamined*, Cambridge, MA: Harvard University Press.

Sen, A. (1999), *Development as Freedom*, Oxford: Oxford University Press.

Shields, L. (2012), 'The prospects for sufficientarianism', *Utilitas*, **24** (1), 101–17.

Shields, L. (2016), *Just Enough: Sufficiency as a Demand of Justice*, Edinburgh: Edinburgh University Press.

Shue, H. (1996), *Basic Rights: Subsistence, Affluence, and U.S. Foreign Policy*, Princeton, NJ: Princeton University Press.

Singer, P. (1972), 'Famine, affluence, and morality', *Philosophy and Public Affairs*, **1** (3), 229–43.

Singer, P. (2009), *The Life You Can Save: How to Play Your Part in Ending World Poverty*, London: Picador.

Skinner, Q. (1997), *Liberty before Liberalism*, Cambridge: Cambridge University Press.

Skinner, Q. (2008), 'Freedom as the absence of arbitrary power', in Cécile Laborde and John Maynor (eds), *Republicanism and Political Theory*, Malden, MA: Blackwell Publishing, pp. 83–101.

Standing, G. (2007), 'Labor recommodification in the global transformation', in Ayşe Buğra and K. Ağartan (eds), *Reading Karl Polanyi for the Twenty-First Century: Market Economy as a Political Project*, New York: Palgrave Macmillan, pp. 67–94.

Standing, G. (2017), *Basic Income: And How We Can Make It Happen*, London: Pelican Books.

Standing, G. (2019), 'Basic income as common dividends: piloting a transformative policy. A report for the Shadow Chancellor of the Exchequer', *Progressive Economy Forum*, 7 May, available at https://www.progressiveeconomyforum.com/wp-content/uploads/2019/05/PEF_Piloting_Basic_Income_Guy_Standing.pdf.

Steiner, H. (1994), *An Essay On Rights*, Oxford: Blackwell Publishers.

Steiner, H. (2002), 'Silver spoons and golden genes: talent differentials and distributive justice', in D. Archard and C.M. Macleod (eds), *The Moral and Political Status of Children*, Oxford: Oxford University Press, pp. 183–94.

Steiner, H. (2009), 'Left libertarianism and the ownership of natural resources', *Public Reason*, **1** (1), 1–8.

Stiglitz. J.E. (2001), 'Foreword', in Karl Polanyi, *The Great Transformation*, Boston, MA: Beacon Press.

Stiglitz, J.E. (2017), *Globalisation and its Discontents Revisited: Anti-Globalization in the Era of Trump*, London: Penguin Books.

Swiss Federal Office for the Environment (2007), 'Global solidarity in financing adaptation, a Swiss proposal for a funding scheme', paper for further discussion, Berne, available at http://www.news.admin.ch/NSBSubscriber/message/attachments/10526.pdf.

Tanzi, V. (2016), 'Lakes, oceans, and taxes: why the world needs a world tax authority', in Thomas Pogge and Krishen Mehta (eds), *Global Tax Fairness*, Oxford: Oxford University Press, pp. 251–64.

Taylor, R. (2017), *Exit Left: Markets and Mobility in Republican Thought*, Oxford: Oxford University Press.

The Workhouse (n.d.), 'The Old Poor Law', accessed 8 October 2019 at http://www.workhouses.org.uk/poorlaws/oldpoorlaw.shtml.

Thompson, B. (2019), 'Climate change and displacement: how conflict and climate change form a toxic combination that drives people from their homes', 15 October, accessed 14 January 2020 at https://www.unhcr.org/news/stories/2019/10/5da5e18c4/climate-change-and-displacement.html.

Tobin, J. (1974), 'A proposal for international monetary reform', *Eastern Economic Journal*, **4** (3–4), 153–9.

Turner, A. (2019), 'Capitalism in the last chance saloon', *Project Syndicate*, accessed 20 December 2019 at https://www.project-syndicate.org/commentary/can-capitalism -combat-climate-change-by-adair-turner-2019-08?barrier=accesspaylog.

Turner, M. (1990), 'Enclosures in Britain 1750–1830', in L.A. Clarkson, *The Industrial Revolution: A Compendium*, London: Palgrave Macmillan, pp. 211–95.

UNCTAD (2019), *State of Commodity Dependence*, available at https://unctad.org/en/ PublicationsLibrary/ditccom2019d1_en.pdf.

UNDP (1990), *Human Development Report 1990*, available at http://hdr.undp.org/sites/ default/files/reports/219/hdr_1990_en_complete_nostats.pdf.

UNDP (1994), *Human Development Report 1994*, available at http://hdr.undp.org/sites/ default/files/reports/255/hdr_1994_en_complete_nostats.pdf.

UNDP (2014), *Human Development Report 2014: Sustaining Human Progress: Reducing Vulnerabilities and Building Resilience*, available at http://hdr.undp.org/ sites/default/files/hdr14-report-en-1.pdf.

Unger, P. (1996), *Living High and Letting Die: Our Illusion of Innocence*, New York and Oxford: Oxford University Press.

UNICEF (2019), *The State of Food Security and Nutrition in the World 2019: Safeguarding against Economic Slowdowns and Downturns – in Brief*, available at https://www.unicef.org/media/55926/file/SOFI-2019-in-brief.pdf.

Valentini, L. (2011), 'Coercion and justice', *American Political Science Review*, **105** (1), 205–20.

Vallentyne, P. (2000), 'Introduction: left-libertarianism – a primer', in Peter Vallentyne and Hillel Steiner (eds), *Left-Libertarianism and Its Critics*, New York: Palgrave, pp. 1–20.

Vallentyne, P. and H. Steiner (eds) (2000), *The Origins of Left-Libertarianism: An Anthology of Historical Writings*, New York: Palgrave.

van der Gaag, N. (2014), *Feminism and Men*, London: Zed Books.

Van Parijs, P. (1984), 'What (if anything) is intrinsically wrong with capitalism?', *Philosophica*, **34** (2), 85–102.

Van Parijs, P. (1992), 'Basic income capitalism', *Ethics*, **102** (3), 465–84.

Vrousalis, N. (2013), 'Exploitation, vulnerability, and social domination', *Philosophy & Public Affairs*, **41** (2), 131–57.

Vrousalis, N. (2014), 'G. A. Cohen on exploitation', *Politics, Philosophy & Economics*, **13** (2), 151–64.

Vrousalis N. (2020), 'The capitalist cage: structural domination and collective agency in the market', *Journal of Applied Philosophy*, https://doi.org/10.1111/japp.12414.

Wahl, P. (2016), 'More than just another tax: the thrilling battle over the financial trans-action tax: background, progress, and challenges', in Thomas Pogge and Krishen Mehta (eds), *Global Tax Fairness*, Oxford: Oxford University Press, pp. 204–20.

Waldron, J. (1992), 'Superseding historic injustice', *Ethics*, **103** (1), 4–28.

West, J. (2016), 'A fair deal in extractives: the company profit-related contract', in Thomas Pogge and Krishen Mehta (eds), *Global Tax Fairness*, Oxford: Oxford University Press, pp. 298–315.

White, B., S.M. Borras Jr., R. Hall , I. Scoones and W. Wolford (2012), 'The new enclosures: critical perspectives on corporate land deals', *The Journal of Peasant Studies*, **39** (3–4), 619–47.

Widerquist, K. (2013), *Independence, Propertylessness, and Basic Income: A Theory of Freedom as the Power to Say No*, New York: Palgrave Macmillan.

Wily, Alden Lizzy (2012), 'The global land grab: the new enclosures', in David Bollier and Silke Helfrich (eds), *The Wealth of the Commons: A World Beyond Market*, Amherst, MA: Levellers Press, pp. 132–40.

Wolff, Jonathan (2002), *Why Read Marx Today?*, Oxford: Oxford University Press.

World Bank (2011), *Rising Global Interest in Farmland: Can It Yield Sustainable and Equitable Benefits?*, available at http://documents.worldbank.org/curated/en/998581468184149953/pdf/594630PUB0ID1810Box358282B01PUBLIC1.pdf.

World Economic Forum (2019), *The Global Risks Report 2019, 14th Edition*, available at http://www3.weforum.org/docs/WEF_Global_Risks_Report_2019.pdf.

Young, I.M. (2011), *Responsibility for Justice*, Oxford: Oxford University Press.

Ypi, L. (2012), *Global Justice and Avant-Garde Political Agency*, Oxford: Oxford University Press.

Zwolinski, M. (2019), 'Hayek, republican freedom, and the universal basic income', *The Niskanen Center*, 6 November, accessed 19 November 2019 at https://www.niskanencenter.org/hayek-republican-freedom-and-the-universal-basic-income/.

Zwolinski, M. and A. Wertheimer (2017), 'Exploitation', in Edward N. Zalta (ed.), *The Stanford Encyclopedia of Philosophy*, https://plato.stanford.edu/archives/sum2017/entries/exploitation/.

Index